SIKH PRAYERS

Other titles on Sikhism by the same author :

1. Dictionary of Guru Granth Sahib
2. Conceptual Dictionary of Guru Granth Sahib
3. Dictionary of Mythological References in Guru Granth Sahib
4. Sikhism and Major World Religions
5. Guru Granth Sahib : An Analytical Study
6. Yoga of the Sikhs
7. The Sikh Philosophy
8. Outlines of Sikh Thought
9. Sikh Ethics
10. Life and Ideals of Guru Gobind Singh
11. Travels of Guru Nanak
12. Philosophy of Guru Nanak
13. Sikhism and Guru Granth Sahib
14. The Sikh and Sikhism

SIKH PRAYERS

JAPU, RAHRĀSI
AND
KĪRTAN SOHILĀ

WHICH FORM PART OF
GURU GRANTH SAHIB

SURINDAR SINGH KOHLI

SINGH BROS.
AMRITSAR

ISBN 81-7205-156-5

First Edition July 1995

Reprints :

November 1996

June 2001

Price : Rs. 80-00

Published by :

SINGH BROTHERS

•

Bazar Mai Sewan, Amritsar - 143 006

•

S.C.O. 98, City Centre, Amritsar - 143 001

E-mail : singhbro@vsnl.com

Website : www.singhbrothers.com

Printers :

PRINTWELL, 146, INDUSTRIAL FOCAL POINT, AMRITSAR.

CONTENTS

INTRODUCTION

A Prayer is a personal communication addressed to a deity in the form of supplication, adoration, praise, contrition or thanks-giving. But in Sikhism all other deities except God have been rejected. All other gods, goddesses, angels and the spirits are prone to death. Why should one serve or remember him, who takes birth and then dies down (Var Gujri M-3, p. 509). Even Brahmas, Vishnus and Shivas pass away after the lapse of their fixed period of life. (10 Swayyas Dasam Granth). Only one Lord will be there in all the ages. Who has not died and who will not die ? (Maru M-1, p. 1022). Death is a certainty and the souls because of their actions undergo transmigration, the human being wears the garments of both pleasure and pain, happiness and sorrow, (Var Majh M-1, p. 149), which he receives from the Lord, according to his worth. But the suffering mostly pervades in our lives. The so-called pleasures of the world also bring pain. As many are the pleasures of the body, so many are the sufferings (Var Malar M. 1, p. 1287). The sensuous pleasures result in sufferings and maladies (Basant M-1, p. 1189). Guru Nanak Dev has said, "There is suffering in birth and suffering in death and suffering in all the dealings of the world" (Var Sarang M-4, Shalok M-1, p. 1240). "There is suffering in separation, there is suffering in hunger; there is suffering of the mighty Yama. There is also suffering caused by physical ailment" (Malar M-1, p. 1256). Guru Nanak Dev has also conclusively said, "Though the Jivas move towards their destruction by the fire of suffering, still the suffering itself is the remedy (Var Sarang M-4, Shalok M-1, p. 1240). And this peace-giving remedy is the Prayer, gushing out from the core of the heart.

The formal prayer is like a ritual. Everyday the prayer is offered in Sikh temples in the morning as well as in the evening. The real prayer is neither ritualistic nor it can be captured in the vesture of language, by the human beings without devotion, faith and love. The prayer creates a bridge between the soul and the Lord. It wells up in the mind of the man of God. The prayers are offered not only by the men of God but also by the men of the world. The men of the world may express worldly demands in their formal prayers. They may also pray from their hearts if they need something for themselves very badly. They may also request for a grave danger to be averted from someone whom they love. The men of God may express worldly requirements which can help in their spiritual quest. They may also pray for strength to be granted to them for the welfare and service of humanity, in which they visualise the All-Pervasive Lord. Even the formal prayer of the Sikhs ends with the following words :

"Nānak Nām Chaṛdī Kalā,
Tere Bhāṇe Sarbat Dā Bhalā."

(The Name of the Lord emanating from the Guru (Guru Nanak) may bring high spirits and the welfare of all in his will).

Most of the hymns of *Guru Granth Sahib* written by the Sikh Gurus and radical saints are the prayers offered to the Lord or the Guru. A Sikh offers his prayers in the presence of *Guru Granth Sahib*, the Sikh scripture, if he can. But if he is out of his home or in journey, he can offer his prayers anytime at any place. The prayers fixed for daily observance are recorded in the beginning of *Guru Granth Sahib*. There are some later additions in *Rahrasi*. They are meant for three times during the day viz.

1. *Japu* a longer bānī of Guru Nanak Dev—in the morning.
2. *So-Daru* or *Rahras* consisting of nine hymns of the Gurus and a few additional hymns of the third, fifth and tenth Gurus alongwith the *Ardaas* (traditional prayer)—in the evening.
3. *Sohila* or *Aarti* or *Kirtan Sohila* consisting of five hymns of the Gurus—at bed time.

Bhai Gurdas, the Sikh theologian has made a mention of these prayers in the first Var.

Besides the above daily observances, a Sikh offers his prayers based on the hymns of the scripture at any time convenient to him. At the beginning of his prayer he says, "I pray with folded hands; If Thou likest, Thou may set it right. With Thy Grace, engage me in Thy devotion; This person Nanak may always remember the Lord." (Suhi M-5, pp.736-37). The prayer can be offered before the Lord with utmost humility (Var Asa M-1, p. 474). The Sikh says, "Am I worthy of offering Prayer—my sins and virtues are both evident before Thee" (Asa M-1, p. 30). "The Prayer of the man of God does not go in vain." (Bilawal M-5, p. 819). He begins his prayer like this :

"I pray before Thee, the soul and body are Thine. Nanak says all the glory is Thine, none knows my name." (Asa M-5, p. 383) "All are Thine and Thou art for all. Thou art the capital for all. All in their prayers beg from Thee." (Var Sri Rag M-4, p. 81). When in a congregation, the Sikh sings in a chorus :

Thou art the Lord and I offer my Prayer to Thee
The soul and body are Thy Commodities. Thou art the mother and father and we are Thy children. There are many comforts in Thy Grace. None knows Thy limits, O Highest of the High Lord. All the world works under Thy direction. All Thy creation is obedient to Thee. Thou knowest Thyself alone Thy work and bounds. Nanak Thy servant, is a sacrifice to Thee.

(Gauri Sukhmani M-5, p. 268)

The prayers of the man of God can be rendered in the following words :

Keep me, O Lord, under Thy shelter by Thy Grace
I do not know how to serve Thee, I the lowly and foolish,
O, my dearest Lord, I am proud of Thee.
We the sinners always err and Thou art the Forgiver.
We fall into innumerable vices and Thou art
the Donor of virtues to virtueless,
Our actions consist in forsaking the Lord and
enjoying the company of His maid-servant maya.
Thou givest everything in Thy mercy and we are ungrateful.
We are absorbed in Thy gift and not Thee, O Lord.
Nothing is outside Thee, O the Remover of fear of
birth and death.
Says Nanak, O Gracious Guru, I am in Thy shelter,
Emancipate this fool.

(Bilawal M-5, p.809)

Never forget, O Lord, Thy servant.
Pervade in my heart, O my Lord God, Think of our
affection from the very beginning.
Purifier of sinners is Thy reputation; do not think of our
vices in Thy heart.
Thou art the breath of my life, my wealth and comfort,
burn away the curtain of ego graciously.
How can the fish live without water, how can the infant
live without milk ?
Nanak, Thy devotee is thirsty of Thy Lotus-feet, the essence
of comfort lies in having their sight, O Lord.

(Bilawal M-5, p. 829)

The devotee in his prayers can talk of nothing else except the suffering of separation, the profound love and the eternal union with the Lord. But the necessities of worldly life which help in the spiritual development may also form part of the prayer. We give below an instance of such a prayer :

The man of God is in profound love with the Lord,
O my sweetheart, Thou art my friend, everything is in Thy house,
I ask for honour and strength, bestow on me the wealth and offspring.
O Supreme Bliss and supreme treasure full of spiritual and worldly resources.
Nanak is happily absorbed in Thy devotion with love and fear and is for ever a sacrifice to Thee.

(Kanra M-5, p. 1238)

This booklet on Sikh Prayers will be useful for all the Sikhs, men, women and children, throughout the world. It will enable them to understand them not only in original, but also in English rendering. For their convenience the original text alongwith transliteration, glossary. translation and comments have been provided.

29-5-92 ***Surindar Singh Kohli***

JAPU

THE MORNING PRAYER

ਮੂਲ ਮੰਤਰ

(THE PRIMARY SACRED FORMULA)

Text :

ੴ ਸਤਿ ਨਾਮੁ ਕਰਤਾ ਪੁਰਖੁ ਨਿਰਭਉ ਨਿਰਵੈਰੁ ਅਕਾਲ ਮੂਰਤਿ
ਅਜੂਨੀ ਸੈਭੰ ਗੁਰ ਪ੍ਰਸਾਦਿ ॥

Transliteration :

Ik Aumkār Sati Nāmu Kartā Purakhu Nirbhau Nirvairu
Akāl Mūrati Ajūnī Saibhaṁ Gur Prasādi.

Glossary :

੧—The One ; ੴ—The manifested as well as unmanifested Brahman ; ਸਤਿ—truth ; ਨਾਮੁ—name (of the Lord) ; ਕਰਤਾ—creator ; ਪੁਰਖੁ—Purusha, soul of the universe ; ਨਿਰਭਉ (ਨਿਰ+ਭਉ)—without fear ; ਨਿਰਵੈਰੁ (ਨਿਰ+ਵੈਰੁ)—without enmity ; ਅਕਾਲ (ਅ+ਕਾਲ)—deathless, immortal ; ਮੂਰਤਿ—form, image, idol, being ; ਅਜੂਨੀ (ਅ+ਜੂਨੀ)—unborn , ਸੈਭੰ (ਸ੍ਵੈ+ਭੂ)—self-existent ; ਗੁਰ—Guru, Preceptor, Teacher, Guide ; ਪ੍ਰਸਾਦਿ—grace.

Translation :

There is only One God, who is both Manifested as well as Unmanifested. His Name is 'Truth'. He is the creator-soul of the universe. He is without fear. He is without enmity. He is Immortal Being. He does not take birth. He is Self-Existent. (He can be realised through) the grace of the Guru.

Comments :

The above primary sacred formula (mūl mantra) of Sikhism is the very first composition of *Guru Granth Sahib*, and placed in the very beginning of *Japu*. It has been repeated hundreds of times in the Sikh scripture both in the original and abbreviated forms. It is epigrammatic and contains in a pithy and terse style, the Nature of Brahman (God). *IK-AUṀKĀRA* signifies the two aspects of Brahman i.e. the Transcendent (*nirguna*) and the Immanent (*saguna*). Since Brahman is one without a second, He is Fearless and Devoid of Enmity. He is Truth i.e. Ever-existent, Immortal Lord. He is the Creator of the whole cosmos including the gods and goddesses. He Himself does not take birth. This fact rejects the Incarnation Theory. He can only be realised through the guidance of the Guru.

This basic formula is the shortest sacred prayer of Sikhism and is meant to be recited or muttered in a low tone under the instructions of the preceptor in order to realise the Lord (God).

ਜਪੁ

JAPU

ਜਪੁ : to utter in a low voice, repeat internally, mutter.

Comments :

This word can be linked either with the sacred formula preceding it or the composition which follows it. In the former case it is an instruction to repeat internally or in a low voice the *mūl mantra* and in the latter case it is the name of the composition that follows it.

The composition that follows contains two *shlokas*, one in the beginning and the other at the end. The first may be called the prologue and the other the epilogue. Within these two *shlokas*, there are thirty-eight *pauṛīs* or stanzas.

THE SHLOKA IN THE BEGINNING

Text :

ਆਦਿ ਸਚੁ ਜੁਗਾਦਿ ਸਚੁ ॥
ਹੈ ਭੀ ਸਚੁ ਨਾਨਕ ਹੋਸੀ ਭੀ ਸਚੁ ॥੧॥

Transliteration :

Ādi sacu, jugādi sacu,
Hai bhī sacu, Nānak hosī bhī sacu.1.

Glossary :

ਆਦਿ—beginning ; ਸਚੁ—Truth (God), Ever-Existent ; ਜੁਗਾਦਿ (ਜੁਗ+ਆਦਿ)—from the beginning of the *Yugas* (ages) ; ਹੈ ਭੀ—is also at the present ; ਨਾਨਕ—Name of the Poet, the first Guru of the Sikhs—the founder of Sikhism ; ਹੋਸੀ ਭੀ—will also be.

Translation :

The Truth i.e. God was in the beginning, He was in the beginning of the ages, He is also Truth in the present and shall also be Truth in future according to Nanak.

Comments :

This shloka makes it clear that God is Ever-Existent. He was there in the past. He is there in the present. He will be there in the future. This fact of the Everlasting Existence of God has been identified with Eternal Truth.

FIRST STANZA

Text :

ਸੋਚੈ ਸੋਚਿ ਨ ਹੋਵਈ ਜੇ ਸੋਚੀ ਲਖ ਵਾਰ ॥
ਚੁਪੈ ਚੁਪ ਨ ਹੋਵਈ ਜੇ ਲਾਇ ਰਹਾ ਲਿਵਤਾਰ ॥
ਭੁਖਿਆ ਭੁਖ ਨ ਉਤਰੀ ਜੇ ਬੰਨਾ ਪੁਰੀਆ ਭਾਰ ॥
ਸਹਸ ਸਿਆਣਪਾ ਲਖ ਹੋਹਿ ਤ ਇਕ ਨ ਚਲੈ ਨਾਲਿ ॥
ਕਿਵ ਸਚਿਆਰਾ ਹੋਈਐ ਕਿਵ ਕੂੜੈ ਤੁਟੈ ਪਾਲਿ ॥
ਹੁਕਮਿ ਰਜਾਈ ਚਲਣਾ ਨਾਨਕ ਲਿਖਿਆ ਨਾਲਿ ॥੧॥

Transliteration :

Socai soci na hovaī je socī lakh vār.
Cupai cup na hovaī je lāi rahā livtār.
Bhukhiā bhukh na utarī je bamnā puriā bhār.
Sahas siāṇapā lakh hohi ta ik na calai nāli.
Kiv saciārā hoīai kiv kūṛai tuṭai pāli.
Hukami rajāī calaṇā Nānak likhiā nāli.1.

Glossary :

ਸੋਚੈ—by thinking ; ਸੋਚਿ—think, thought ; ਨ—not ; ਹੋਵਈ—become ; ਜੇ—if ; ਸੋਚੀ—ponder, think, thinking ; ਲਖ—lakh ; ਵਾਰ—times ; ਚੁਪੈ—by keeping silent ; ਚੁਪਿ—silence ; ਲਾਇ ਰਹਾ—be absorbed ; ਲਿਵਤਾਰ—be in tune with ; ਭੁਖਿਆ—hungry ; ਭੁਖ—hunger ; ਉਤਰੀ—satiated ; ਬੰਨਾ—gather together ; ਪੁਰੀਆ—worlds ; ਭਾਰ—loads ; ਸਹਸ—thousands; ਸਿਆਣਪਾ—wisdoms ; ਹੋਹਿ—be ; ਤ—but, then ; ਇਕ—one ; ਚਲੈ—goes ; ਨਾਲਿ—with ; ਕਿਵ—how ; ਸਚਿਆਰਾ—truthful ; ਹੋਈਐ—become ; ਕੂੜੈ—falsehood ; ਤੁਟੈ—break, demolished ; ਪਾਲਿ—wall ; ਹੁਕਮਿ—by the order; ਰਜਾਈ—Lord's Will ; ਚਲਣਾ—obeying ; ਲਿਖਿਆ—written, ordained.

Translation :

By thinking, one cannot become clear in thought (about God), even if one ponders over it lakhs of times. By keeping silent, one cannot be really silent, even if he tries to remain absorbed and makes effort to be in tune with Ultimate Reality. The hunger of the hungry cannot be satiated even if the loads of the wealth of worlds are gathered together. Thousands and lakhs of wisdoms are of no avail and none of them leads towards the Court of the Lord. How can, then, one become Truthful and the wall of falsehood can be demolished? Nanak the poet also records with the above question that (in order to become truthful) the Order and Will of the Lord must be obeyed.

Comments :

In the very first stanza, Guru Nanak Dev has posed the basic question : How to be Truthful? since Truth is God Himself, as we have seen in the preceding *shloka.* The remaining stanzas of the poem are, in fact, an answer to this question. Unless and until the attributes of God are imbibed in life, one cannot comprehend the ultimate Reality. No achievement can be made by constant thinking or remaining silent or amassing loads of wealth or through worldly wisdom. The achievement can be made only by submitting our will to the Will of the Lord.

SECOND STANZA

Text :

ਹੁਕਮੀ ਹੋਵਨਿ ਆਕਾਰ ਹੁਕਮੁ ਨ ਕਹਿਆ ਜਾਈ ॥
ਹੁਕਮੀ ਹੋਵਨਿ ਜੀਅ ਹੁਕਮਿ ਮਿਲੈ ਵਡਿਆਈ ॥
ਹੁਕਮੀ ਉਤਮੁ ਨੀਚੁ ਹੁਕਮਿ ਲਿਖਿ ਦੁਖ ਸੁਖ ਪਾਈਅਹਿ ॥

ਇਕਨਾ ਹੁਕਮੀ ਬਖਸੀਸ ਇਕਿ ਹੁਕਮੀ ਸਦਾ ਭਵਾਈਅਹਿ ॥
ਹੁਕਮੈ ਅੰਦਰਿ ਸਭੁ ਕੋ ਬਾਹਰਿ ਹੁਕਮ ਨ ਕੋਇ ॥
ਨਾਨਕ ਹੁਕਮੈ ਜੇ ਬੁਝੈ ਤ ਹਉਮੈ ਕਹੈ ਨ ਕੋਇ ॥੨॥

Transliteration :

Hukamī hovani ākār hukamu na kahiā jāī.
Hukamī hovani jīa hukami milai vaḍiāī.
Hukamī utamu nīcu hukami likhi dukh sukh pāīahi.
Ikanā hukamī bakhsīs iki hukamī sadā bhavāīahi.
Hukamai aṁdari sabhu ko bāhari hukam na koi.
Nānak hukamai je bujhai ta haumai kahai na koi.2.

Glossary :

ਹੁਕਮੀ—by order, by command ; ਹੋਵਨਿ—become, come into being ; ਆਕਾਰ—form, body ; ਹੁਕਮੁ—order, command ; ਨ—not ; ਕਹਿਆ ਜਾਈ—said, described ; ਜੀਅ—jiva, embodied soul ; ਹੁਕਮਿ—by order ; ਮਿਲੈ—achieved, obtained ; ਵਡਿਆਈ—greatness ; ਉਤਮੁ—superior ; ਨੀਚੁ—inferior ; ਲਿਖਿ—put in writing ; ਦੁਖ—sorrow ; ਸੁਖ—comfort ; ਪਾਈਅਹਿ—obtain ; ਇਕਨਾ—some ; ਬਖਸੀਸ—under grace ; ਇਕਿ—some ; ਸਦਾ—always ; ਭਵਾਈਅਹਿ—made to wander ; ਹੁਕਮੈ—under command ; ਅੰਦਰਿ—within ; ਸਭੁ ਕੋ—everybody, all ; ਬਾਹਰਿ—outside ; ਨ ਕੋਇ—none ; ਜੇ—if ; ਬੁਝੈ—comprehend, understand; ਤ—then ; ਹਉਮੈ—ego ; ਕਹੈ—speak, talk.

Translation :

The forms come into being under the command of the Lord ; this command cannot be described. Under this command the jivas come into being and under this command honours are obtained. Under this command they are superior and inferior and under this command the sorrows and comforts are obtained according to the Writ (of the Lord). Some come under His grace and some are made to wander forever. Everybody is under this command and none is outside it. The poet says : if this command (of the Lord) is comprehended, then no one talks in ego.

Comments :

In order to become truthful, the command of the Lord must at first be comprehended. Under the Will of the Lord, the whole creation has come into being. Every created being has a writ on his forehead and passes his life according to this writ. Those who comprehend God's command, become ego-less. They are under the Grace of the Lord.

Third Stanza

Text :

ਗਾਵੈ ਕੋ ਤਾਣੁ ਹੋਵੈ ਕਿਸੈ ਤਾਣੁ ॥
ਗਾਵੈ ਕੋ ਦਾਤਿ ਜਾਣੈ ਨੀਸਾਣੁ ॥
ਗਾਵੈ ਕੋ ਗੁਣ ਵਡਿਆਈਆ ਚਾਰ ॥
ਗਾਵੈ ਕੋ ਵਿਦਿਆ ਵਿਖਮੁ ਵੀਚਾਰੁ ॥
ਗਾਵੈ ਕੋ ਸਾਜਿ ਕਰੇ ਤਨੁ ਖੇਹ ॥
ਗਾਵੈ ਕੋ ਜੀਅ ਲੈ ਫਿਰਿ ਦੇਹ ॥
ਗਾਵੈ ਕੋ ਜਾਪੈ ਦਿਸੈ ਦੂਰਿ ॥
ਗਾਵੈ ਕੋ ਵੇਖੈ ਹਾਦਰਾ ਹਦੂਰਿ ॥
ਕਥਨਾ ਕਥੀ ਨ ਆਵੈ ਤੋਟਿ ॥
ਕਥਿ ਕਥਿ ਕਥੀ ਕੋਟੀ ਕੋਟਿ ਕੋਟਿ ॥
ਦੇਦਾ ਦੇ ਲੈਦੇ ਥਕਿ ਪਾਹਿ ॥
ਜੁਗਾ ਜੁਗੰਤਰਿ ਖਾਹੀ ਖਾਹਿ ॥
ਹੁਕਮੀ ਹੁਕਮੁ ਚਲਾਏ ਰਾਹੁ ॥
ਨਾਨਕ ਵਿਗਸੈ ਵੇਪਰਵਾਹੁ ॥੩॥

Transliteration :

Gāvai ko tāṇu hovai kisai tāṇu.
Gāvai ko dāti jāṇai nīsāṇu.
Gāvai ko guṇ vaḍiāīā cār.
Gāvai ko vidiā vikhamu vicāru.
Gāvai ko sāji kare tanu kheh.
Gāvai ko jīa lai phiri deh.
Gāvai ko jāpai disai dūri.
Gāvai ko vekhai hādarā hadūri.
Kathanā kathī na āvai toṭi.
Kathi kathi kathī koṭī koṭi koṭi.
Dedā de laide thaki pāhi.
Jugā jugaṁtari khāhī khāhi.
Hukamī hukamu calāe rāhu.
Nānak vigasai veparavāhu.3.

Glossary :

ਗਾਵੈ—sings ; ਕੋ—someone ; ਤਾਣੁ—might, power ; ਹੋਵੈ—has ; ਦਾਤਿ—bounty, gift ; ਜਾਣੈ—knows ; ਨੀਸਾਣੁ—token, sign ; ਗੁਣ—quality ; ਵਡਿਆਈ—greatness, excellence ; ਆਚਾਰ—bearing, demeanour ; ਵਿਦਿਆ—knowledge ; ਵਿਖਮੁ—difficult ; ਵੀਚਾਰੁ—idea ; ਸਾਜਿ—create ; ਤਨੁ—body ; ਕਰੇ ਖੇਹ—reduce to dust ; ਜੀਅ—life, soul ; ਲੈ—takes ; ਫਿਰਿ—again ; ਦੇਹ—gives ; ਜਾਪੈ—seems ; ਦਿਸੈ—appears, is seen ; ਦੂਰਿ—far away ; ਵੇਖੈ—sees ; ਹਾਦਰਾ ਹਦੂਰਿ—present everywhere ; ਕਥਨਾ ਕਥੀ—bring under description ; ਨ—not ; ਆਵੈ—comes ; ਤੋਟਿ—dearth ; ਕਥਿ—describe ; ਕੋਟੀ ਕੋਟਿ—millions ; ਦੇਦਾ—giver ; ਦੇ—gives ; ਲੈਦੇ—receivers ; ਥਕਿ ਪਾਹਿ—grow tired ; ਜੁਗਾ—ages ; ਜੁਗੰਤਰਿ—in the ages ; ਖਾਹੀ—consumers ; ਖਾਹਿ—consume, eat ; ਚਲਾਏ—to make walk ; ਰਾਹੁ—path ; ਵਿਗਸੈ—remain in bliss ; ਵੇਪਰਵਾਹੁ—carefree.

Translation :

Only that person can sing the Praises of the Might of the Lord who has been blessed with that power. Someone sings about His Gifts, considering them His Token of Grace. Someone sings about His Attributes, His Excellences and His Demeanour. Someone sings about the knowledge about Him, whose study is arduous. Someone sings about His Faculties of creating the body and then reducing it to dust. Someone sings about His power of taking away life and then restoring it. Someone sings about His seeming remoteness. Someone sings about His displayed closeness. There is no end to the discourses about Him. Millions are busy in describing Him. He as Giver continues to Give, but the recipients may grow weary. They use His Gifts throughout the Ages. He as commander steers His creation through His command and as carefree Lord, He is always in Bliss.

Comments :

The Lord is All-Powerful, considering Him Omnipotent the beings sing His Praises. He is Beneficent, the Giver, the Embodiment of all qualities, the Central Theme of all Sciences and Arts, the Creator, Preserver and Destroyer, the Nearest and seemingly Farthest, Unintelligible and Inexpressible, the Blissful, the Commander and carefree Lord. All these Attributes are being sung by the Beings. The Giver continues to give, but the receiver may get tired.

FOURTH STANZA

Text :

ਸਾਚਾ ਸਾਹਿਬੁ ਸਾਚੁ ਨਾਇ ਭਾਖਿਆ ਭਾਉ ਅਪਾਰੁ ॥
ਆਖਹਿ ਮੰਗਹਿ ਦੇਹਿ ਦੇਹਿ ਦਾਤਿ ਕਰੇ ਦਾਤਾਰੁ ॥
ਫੇਰਿ ਕਿ ਅਗੈ ਰਖੀਐ ਜਿਤੁ ਦਿਸੈ ਦਰਬਾਰੁ ॥
ਮੁਹੌ ਕਿ ਬੋਲਣੁ ਬੋਲੀਐ ਜਿਤੁ ਸੁਣਿ ਧਰੇ ਪਿਆਰੁ ॥
ਅੰਮ੍ਰਿਤ ਵੇਲਾ ਸਚੁ ਨਾਉ ਵਡਿਆਈ ਵੀਚਾਰੁ ॥
ਕਰਮੀ ਆਵੈ ਕਪੜਾ ਨਦਰੀ ਮੋਖ ਦੁਆਰੁ ॥
ਨਾਨਕ ਏਵੈ ਜਾਣੀਐ ਸਭੁ ਆਪੇ ਸਚਿਆਰੁ ॥੪॥

Transliteration :

Sācā sāhibu sācu nāi bhākhiā bhāu apāru.
Ākhahi maṁgahi dehi dehi dāti kare dātāru.
Pheri ki agai rakhīai jitu disai darbāru.
Muhau ki bolaṇu bolīai jitu suṇi dhare piāru.
Aṁmrit velā sacu nāu vaḍiāī vīcāru.
Karmī āvai kapaṛā nadarī mokh duāru.
Nānak evai jāṇīai sabhu āpe saciāru.4.

Glossary :

ਸਾਚਾ—True ; ਸਾਹਿਬੁ—Lord ; ਸਾਚੁ—true ; ਨਾਇ—Name ; ਭਾਖਿਆ—
describe ; ਭਾਉ—love ; ਅਪਾਰੁ—infinite ; ਆਖਹਿ—say, speak ; ਮੰਗਹਿ—beg ;
ਦੇਹਿ ਦੇਹਿ—give, please give ; ਦਾਤਿ—bounty, gift ; ਦਾਤਿ ਕਰੇ—bestows
the gift ; ਦਾਤਾਰੁ—The Beneficent Lord ; ਫੇਰਿ—in return ; ਕਿ—what ;
ਅਗੈ—before ; ਰਖੀਐ—place, put ; ਜਿਤੁ—by which, whereby ; ਦਿਸੈ—be
seen ; ਦਰਬਾਰੁ—court (of the Lord) ; ਮੁਹੌ—with mouth ; ਬੋਲਣੁ—words ;
ਬੋਲੀਐ—uttered ; ਸੁਣਿ—hear ; ਧਰੇ ਪਿਆਰੁ—make love ; ਅੰਮ੍ਰਿਤ—Ambrosia ;
ਅੰਮ੍ਰਿਤ ਵੇਲਾ—ambrosial time ; ਸਚੁ—truth, true ; ਨਾਉ—Name (of the
Lord) ; ਵਡਿਆਈ—greatness ; ਵੀਚਾਰੁ—reflection ; ਕਰਮੀ—(through)
actions ; ਆਵੈ—comes ; ਕਪੜਾ—(physical) garb, body ; ਨਦਰੀ—
(through) grace ; ਮੋਖ—salvation ; ਦੁਆਰੁ—door, gate ; ਏਵੈ—in this
way, thus ; ਜਾਣੀਐ—know ; ਸਭੁ—all ; ਆਪੇ—Himself ; ਸਚਿਆਰੁ—The
True Lord.

Translation :

The Lord is True and His Name is True and True are those
people who utter the Name with boundless love. The people pray

to the Lord and beg from Him saying "Give, Give O Lord" and the Beneficent Lord gives. But, what can be placed before the Lord in return, so that His court may be seen ? Which words may be uttered from the mouth, so that on listening to it the Lord may bear love for us ? The True Name of the Lord be uttered in the early hours of the morning and His Greatness be reflected upon. By (good) actions this human body is obtained, but the gate of salvation is reached by His Grace. It may be known this way, says Nanak, that the True Lord Himself is all in all.

Comments :

After knowing that the Beneficent Lord Almighty is all in all, that He is ever-existent and His Name is eternal, it is the primary duty of the being to remember Him by repeating His Name with utmost love. The Lord is the only Giver and all the gifts are to be begged from Him. The Lord is Graceful and He listens to the Prayers and gives all the gifts to the seekers. But what the human being can give in return or utter from his mouth, so that he becomes worthy of the love of the Lord and get near Him in His court ? The Guru himself has answered this question. Our previous good actions are responsible for the attainment of human birth, but the salvation can only be achieved through the Grace of the Lord. For the achievement of the Grace, the man should utter the Name of the Lord in the early hours of the morning and reflect upon His Greatness.

FIFTH STANZA

Text :

ਥਾਪਿਆ ਨ ਜਾਇ ਕੀਤਾ ਨ ਹੋਇ ॥
ਆਪੇ ਆਪਿ ਨਿਰੰਜਨੁ ਸੋਇ ॥
ਜਿਨਿ ਸੇਵਿਆ ਤਿਨਿ ਪਾਇਆ ਮਾਨੁ ॥
ਨਾਨਕ ਗਾਵੀਐ ਗੁਣੀ ਨਿਧਾਨੁ ॥
ਗਾਵੀਐ ਸੁਣੀਐ ਮਨਿ ਰਖੀਐ ਭਾਉ ॥
ਦੁਖੁ ਪਰਹਰਿ ਸੁਖੁ ਘਰਿ ਲੈ ਜਾਇ ॥
ਗੁਰਮੁਖਿ ਨਾਦੰ ਗੁਰਮੁਖਿ ਵੇਦੰ ਗੁਰਮੁਖਿ ਰਹਿਆ ਸਮਾਈ ॥
ਗੁਰੁ ਈਸਰੁ ਗੁਰੁ ਗੋਰਖੁ ਬਰਮਾ ਗੁਰੁ ਪਾਰਬਤੀ ਮਾਈ ॥
ਜੇ ਹਉ ਜਾਣਾ ਆਖਾ ਨਾਹੀ ਕਹਣਾ ਕਥਨੁ ਨ ਜਾਈ ॥

ਗੁਰਾ ਇਕ ਦੇਹਿ ਬੁਝਾਈ ॥
ਸਭਨਾ ਜੀਆ ਕਾ ਇਕੁ ਦਾਤਾ ਸੋ ਮੈ ਵਿਸਰਿ ਨ ਜਾਈ ॥੫॥

Transliteration :

Thāpiā na jāi kītā na hoi.
Āpe āpi niraṁjanu soi.
Jini seviā tini pāiā mānu.
Nānak gāvīai guṇī nidhānu.
Gāvīai suṇīai mani rakhīai bhāu.
Dukhu parahari sukhu ghari lai jāi.
Gurmukhi nādaṁ gurmukhi vedaṁ gurmukhi rahiā samāī.
Guru Īsaru Guru Gorakhu Baramā Guru Pārbatī māī.
Je hau jāṇā ākhā nāhī kahaṇā kathanu na jāī.
Gurā ik dehi bujhāī.
Sabhanā jīā kā iku dātā so mai visari na jāī.5.

Glossary :

ਥਾਪਿਆ—established ; ਨ ਜਾਇ—cannot be ; ਕੀਤਾ—created ; ਨ ਹੋਇ—cannot be ; ਆਪੇ ਆਪਿ—Himself ; ਨਿਰੰਜਨੁ—The Pure Lord, who is not affected by maya ; ਸੋਇ—He ; ਜਿਨਿ—those who ; ਸੇਵਿਆ—serve ; ਤਿਨਿ—they ; ਪਾਇਆ—obtained ; ਮਾਨੁ—honour ; ਗਾਵੀਐ—sing ; ਸੁਣੀਐ—hear ; ਮਨਿ—mind ; ਰਖੀਐ—keep ; ਭਾਉ—love ; ਦੁਖੁ—sorrow ; ਪਰਹਰਿ—shed ; ਸੁਖੁ—happiness ; ਘਰਿ—home ; ਲੈ ਜਾਇ—take ; ਗੁਰਮੁਖਿ—Guruward, the enlightened person ; ਨਾਦੰ—sound, word ; ਵੇਦੰ—knowledge ; ਰਹਿਆ ਸਮਾਈ—be absorbed, merged ; ਈਸਰੁ—Shiva ; ਗੋਰਖੁ—the sustainer i.e. Vishnu ; ਬਰਮਾ—Brahmā ; ਗੁਰੁ—Guru ; ਪਾਰਬਤੀ—the wife of Shiva ; ਮਾਈ—(ਮਾ) Lakshmi + (ਈ) Saraswati ; ਜੇ—if ; ਹਉ—I ; ਜਾਣਾ—know ; ਆਖਾ—describe ; ਨਾਹੀ—not ; ਕਹਣਾ—say, speak ; ਕਥਨੁ—describe ; ਨ ਜਾਈ—cannot be ; ਗੁਰਾ—The Guru, O Guru ; ਇਕ—The one (Lord) ; ਦੇਹਿ—given ; ਬੁਝਾਈ—understand ; ਸਭਨਾ—all ; ਜੀਆ—jivas ; ਕਾ—of ; ਦਾਤਾ—the Beneficent (Lord) ; ਸੋ—He ; ਮੈ—I, me ; ਵਿਸਰਿ—forget.

Translation :

The Lord can neither be created nor installed. He, the Pure one is all in all Himself. Those, who have served Him, are honoured by Him, therefore, O Nanak, the Praises of the Treasure of Qualities, be sung. They should be sung and heard, keeping the mind absorbed in His Love. In this way the sorrows willl be shed and the entrance will be obtained in the abode of happiness. The Word and the knowledge are in the mouth of the Guru, where the Lord Permeates. The Guru is Shiva, Vishnu, Brahma and mother-goddess (for me). Even if I cognise the Lord, I dare not describe Him because He is Indescribable. O Guru, give me the comprehension of the One Lord, who is the only Bestower for all beings. I may never forget Him.

Comments :

In this stanza, Guru Nanak Dev has brought forward two important ideas :

1. That the Lord-God cannot be installed as an idol. No idol can represent Him. His service consists in the contemplation on his name and singing His Praises. He is the Treasure-house of qualities. Our miseries can end if we keep ourselves in tune with Him.

2. That the Lord can only be realised through the Grace of the Guru, who is the real God or Divinity for humanity. He can only give cognisance of the Indescribable Lord. Therefore the Guru is beseeched for help, so that the Bestower of all beings, is never forgotten.

Sixth Stanza

Text :

ਤੀਰਥਿ ਨਾਵਾ ਜੇ ਤਿਸੁ ਭਾਵਾ ਵਿਣੁ ਭਾਣੇ ਕਿ ਨਾਇ ਕਰੀ ॥
ਜੇਤੀ ਸਿਰਠਿ ਉਪਾਈ ਵੇਖਾ ਵਿਣੁ ਕਰਮਾ ਕਿ ਮਿਲੈ ਲਈ ॥
ਮਤਿ ਵਿਚਿ ਰਤਨ ਜਵਾਹਰ ਮਾਣਿਕ ਜੇ ਇਕ ਗੁਰ ਕੀ ਸਿਖ ਸੁਣੀ ॥
ਗੁਰਾ ਇਕ ਦੇਹਿ ਬੁਝਾਈ ॥
ਸਭਨਾ ਜੀਆ ਕਾ ਇਕੁ ਦਾਤਾ ਸੋ ਮੈ ਵਿਸਰਿ ਨ ਜਾਈ ॥੬॥

Transliteration :

Tīrathi nāvā je tisu bhāvā viṇu bhāṇe ki nāi karī.
Jetī siraṭhi upāī vekhā viṇu karmā ki milai laī.
Mati vici ratan jawāhar māṇik je ik gur kī sikh suṇī.
Gurā ik dehi bujhāī.
Sabhanā jīā kā iku dātā so mai visari na jāī.6.

Glossary :

ਤੀਰਥਿ—pilgrim station ; ਨਾਵਾ—bathe ; ਜੇ—if ; ਤਿਸੁ—Him ; ਭਾਵਾ—please, like ; ਵਿਣੁ—without ; ਭਾਣੇ—pleasing ; ਕਿ—what ; ਨਾਇ

ਕਰੀ—bathe ; ਜੇਤੀ—all ; ਸਿਰਠਿ—world ; ਉਪਾਈ—created ; ਵੇਖਾ—see ; ਕਰਮਾ—actions ; ਮਿਲੈ—obtain ; ਲਈ—take ; ਮਤਿ—intellect ; ਵਿਚਿ—in ; ਰਤਨ ਜਵਾਹਰ ਮਾਣਿਕ—precious stones ; ਇਕ—one ; ਗੁਰ—Guru ; ਕੀ—of ; ਸਿਖ—instruction ; ਸੁਣੀ—hear.

Translation :

If I become pleasing to the Lord, I shall consider it as bath at the pilgrim stations. Why should I take a bath (at the pilgrim stations), if I do not become pleasing to Him ? All the created world that I see, what does it take and obtain without good actions ? If we hearken to the advice of the Guru, our intellect contains gems, jewels and rubies. O Guru, give me the understanding of the One Lord, Who is the Bestower for all beings. I may never forget Him.

Comments :

In this stanza, the Grace of the Lord is considered supreme, which comes by following the discipline of the Guru. The human intellect becomes highly refined and invaluable. It leads to good and great actions. Without the Grace of the Lord, the rituals are meaningless and worthless.

Seventh Stanza

Text :

ਜੇ ਜੁਗ ਚਾਰੇ ਆਰਜਾ ਹੋਰ ਦਸੂਣੀ ਹੋਇ॥
ਨਵਾ ਖੰਡਾ ਵਿਚਿ ਜਾਣੀਐ ਨਾਲਿ ਚਲੈ ਸਭੁ ਕੋਇ॥
ਚੰਗਾ ਨਾਉ ਰਖਾਇ ਕੈ ਜਸੁ ਕੀਰਤਿ ਜਗਿ ਲੇਇ॥
ਜੇ ਤਿਸੁ ਨਦਰਿ ਨ ਆਵਈ ਤ ਵਾਤ ਨ ਪੁਛੈ ਕੇ॥
ਕੀਟਾ ਅੰਦਰਿ ਕੀਟੁ ਕਰਿ ਦੋਸੀ ਦੋਸੁ ਧਰੇ॥
ਨਾਨਕ ਨਿਰਗੁਣਿ ਗੁਣੁ ਕਰੇ ਗੁਣਵੰਤਿਆ ਗੁਣੁ ਦੇ॥
ਤੇਹਾ ਕੋਇ ਨ ਸੁਝਈ ਜਿ ਤਿਸੁ ਗੁਣੁ ਕੋਇ ਕਰੇ॥੭॥

Transliteration :

Je jug cāre ārjā hor dasūṇī hoi.
Navā khaṁḍā vici jāṇīai nāli calai sabhu koi.
Caṁgā nāu rakhāi kai jasu kīrati jagi lei.
Je tisu nadari na āvaī ta vāt na puchai ke.
Kīṭā aṁdari kīṭu kari dosī dosu dhare.

Nānak nirguṇi guṇu kare guṇvaṁtiā guṇu de.
Tehā koi na sujhaī ji tisu guṇu koi kare.7.

Glossary :

ਜੇ—if ; ਜੁਗ—ages ; ਚਾਰੇ—the four ; ਆਰਜਾ—age ; ਹੋਰ—more ; ਦਸੂਣੀ—ten times ; ਹੋਇ—become ; ਨਵਾ—nine ; ਖੰਡਾ—regions ; ਵਿਚਿ—in ; ਜਾਣੀਐ—known ; ਨਾਲਿ—with ; ਚਲੈ—go ; ਸਭੁ ਕੋਇ—all, everyone ; ਚੰਗਾ—good ; ਨਾਉ—name ; ਰਖਾਇ ਕੈ—assume ; ਜਸੁ—praise ; ਕੀਰਤਿ—praise ; ਜਗਿ—world ; ਲੇਇ—obtain ; ਤਿਸੁ—Him ; ਨਦਰਿ—grace ; ਨ—not ; ਆਵਈ—come ; ਤ—then ; ਵਾਤ ਨ ਪੁਛੈ ਕੇ—none would care ; ਕੀਟਾ—worms ; ਅੰਦਰਿ—amongst ; ਕੀਟੁ ਕਰਿ—be considered a worm ; ਦੋਸੀ—sinner ; ਦੋਸੁ ਧਰੇ—be accused ; ਨਿਰਗੁਣਿ—without qualities ; ਗੁਣੁ—quality ; ਕਰੇ—give, grant ; ਗੁਣਵੰਤਿਆ—virtuous ; ਗੁਣੁ ਦੇ—bestow quality ; ਤੇਹਾ—such ; ਕੋਇ—any ; ਨ ਸੁਝਈ—does not think ; ਜਿ—who ; ਤਿਸੁ—Him ; ਕੋਇ ਕਰੇ—give any.

Translation :

If the span of human life is extended to the four ages, which may still be further extended ten times ; if one becomes renowned in all the nine regions and the whole world follows him ; if he becomes the centre of applause of the whole world and earns a good name ; even then if the Gracious glance of the Lord does not fall upon him, none would care for him and he would be considered a worm among worms and a sinner among sinners. The Gracious Lord grants qualities to those who are without them and also qualities to those who are already pious. But I cannot think of anyone who can give any quality to Him.

Comments :

Long life and great renown have no worth without the Grace of the Lord. It is He who bestows qualities and virtues on human beings who have nothing to give back to Him (except love and total surrender).

EIGHTH STANZA

Text :

ਸੁਣਿਐ ਸਿਧ ਪੀਰ ਸੁਰਿ ਨਾਥ ॥
ਸੁਣਿਐ ਧਰਤਿ ਧਵਲ ਆਕਾਸ ॥

ਸੁਣਿਐ ਦੀਪ ਲੋਅ ਪਾਤਾਲ ॥
ਸੁਣਿਐ ਪੋਹਿ ਨ ਸਕੈ ਕਾਲੁ ॥
ਨਾਨਕ ਭਗਤਾ ਸਦਾ ਵਿਗਾਸੁ ॥
ਸੁਣਿਐ ਦੂਖ ਪਾਪ ਕਾ ਨਾਸੁ ॥੮॥

Transliteration :

Suṇiai sidh pīr suri nāth.
Suṇiai dharati dhaval ākās.
Suṇiai dīp loa pātāl.
Suṇiai pohi na sakai kālu.
Nānak bhagatā sadā vigāsu.
Suṇiai dūkh pāp kā nāsu.8.

Glossary :

ਸੁਣਿਐ—By hearing ; ਸਿਧ—adept ; ਪੀਰ—Guru, preceptor ; ਸੁਰਿ—god ; ਨਾਥ—yogi ; ਧਰਤਿ—earth ; ਧਵਲ—bull supporting the earth in the nether region ; ਆਕਾਸ—sky, heaven ; ਦੀਪ—continent ; ਲੋਅ—world ; ਪਾਤਾਲ—nether region ; ਪੋਹਿ ਨ ਸਕੈ—does not affect ; ਕਾਲੁ—death ; ਭਗਤਾ—devotees ; ਸਦਾ—ever, always ; ਵਿਗਾਸੁ—bliss, happiness ; ਦੂਖ—sorrow ; ਪਾਪ—sin ; ਕਾ—of ਨਾਸੁ—destruction.

Translation :

By hearing the Name of the Lord, one attains the status of an adept, preceptor, god and a great yogi. By hearing the Name of the Lord one gets the knowledge about the earth, its supporting bull and heaven. By hearing the Name of the Lord one gets the knowledge of continents, worlds and nether regions. By hearing the Name of the Lord, the death cannot have any dreadful effect on the mortal. The devotees (who hear the Name of the Lord) are always in bliss and on hearing the Name, their sorrows and sins are destroyed.

Comments :

This stanza mentions the great attainments achieved by hearing the Name of the Lord, *Shravan* is the first step towards God-realisation.

NINTH STANZA

Text :

ਸੁਣਿਐ ਈਸਰੁ ਬਰਮਾ ਇੰਦੁ ॥
ਸੁਣਿਐ ਮੁਖਿ ਸਾਲਾਹਣ ਮੰਦੁ ॥
ਸੁਣਿਐ ਜੋਗ ਜੁਗਤਿ ਤਨਿ ਭੇਦ ॥
ਸੁਣਿਐ ਸਾਸਤ ਸਿੰਮ੍ਰਿਤਿ ਵੇਦ ॥
ਨਾਨਕ ਭਗਤਾ ਸਦਾ ਵਿਗਾਸੁ ॥
ਸੁਣਿਐ ਦੂਖ ਪਾਪ ਕਾ ਨਾਸੁ ॥੯॥

Transliteration :

Suṇiai Īsaru Baramā Iṁdu.
Suṇiai mukhi sālāhaṇ maṁdu
Suṇiai jog jugati tani bhed.
Suṇiai Sāsat Siṁmriti Veda.
Nānak bhagatā sadā vigāsu.
Suṇiai dūkh pāp kā nāsu.9.

Glossary :

ਸੁਣਿਐ—by hearing ; ਈਸਰੁ—Shiva ; ਬਰਮਾ—Brahma ; ਇੰਦੁ—Indra ; ਮੁਖਿ—mouth ; ਸਾਲਾਹਣ—praise ; ਮੰਦੁ—the bad ones, evil persons ; ਜੋਗ—yoga ; ਜੁਗਤਿ—method ; ਤਨਿ—body ; ਭੇਦ—secret ; ਸਾਸਤ—Shastras, the six philosophic systems ; ਸਿੰਮ੍ਰਿਤਿ—Simritis, ceremonial treatises ; ਵੇਦ—Vedas.

Translation :

By hearing the Name of the Lord, the status of Shiva, Brahma and Indra is achieved ; by hearing the Name of the Lord the evil-minded persons sing the praise of the Lord with their mouths ; by hearing the Name of the Lord one comprehends the method of yoga (union with the Lord) and the secrets of the body ; by hearing the Name of the Lord one gets the knowledge of Shastras, Simritis and Vedas. The devotees (who hear the Name of the Lord) are always in bliss and on hearing the Name, their sorrows and sins are destroyed.

Comments :

Like the previous stanza, this stanza also mentions the great attainments achieved by hearing the Name of the Lord.

TENTH STANZA

Text :

ਸੁਣਿਐ ਸਤੁ ਸੰਤੋਖੁ ਗਿਆਨੁ ॥
ਸੁਣਿਐ ਅਠਸਠਿ ਕਾ ਇਸਨਾਨੁ ॥
ਸੁਣਿਐ ਪੜਿ ਪੜਿ ਪਾਵਹਿ ਮਾਨੁ ॥
ਸੁਣਿਐ ਲਾਗੈ ਸਹਜਿ ਧਿਆਨੁ ॥
ਨਾਨਕ ਭਗਤਾ ਸਦਾ ਵਿਗਾਸੁ ॥
ਸੁਣਿਐ ਦੂਖ ਪਾਪ ਕਾ ਨਾਸੁ ॥੧੦॥

Transliteration :

Suṇiai satu saṁtokhu giānu.
Suṇiai aṭhsaṭhi kā isanānu.
Suṇiai paṛi paṛi pāvahi mānu.
Suṇiai lāgai sahaji dhiānu.
Nānak bhagatā sadā vigāsu.
Suṇiai dūkh pāp kā nāsu.10.

Glossary :

ਸਤੁ—truth ; ਸੰਤੋਖੁ—contentment ; ਗਿਆਨੁ—knowledge ; ਅਠਸਠਿ—sixty-eight (holy shrines) ; ਕਾ—of ; ਇਸਨਾਨੁ—bath ; ਪੜਿ ਪੜਿ—reading constantly ; ਪਾਵਹਿ—receive ; ਮਾਨੁ—honour ; ਲਾਗੈ—gets ; ਸਹਜਿ—with ease, the highest spiritual state ; ਧਿਆਨੁ—meditation.

Translation :

By hearing the Name of the Lord, truth, contentment and knowledge are obtained ; by hearing the Name of the Lord the merit of the bath at sixty-eight pilgrim stations is attained; by hearing the Name of the Lord, one receives honours which are ordinarily received on the attainment of great learning ; by hearing the Name of the Lord, one is spontaneously absorbed in meditation. The devotees (who hear the Name of the Lord) are always in bliss and on hearing the Name, their sorrows and sins are destroyed.

Comments :

Like the previous two stanzas, this stanza also mentions the great attainments achieved by hearing the Name of the Lord.

Eleventh Stanza

Text :

ਸੁਣਿਐ ਸਰਾ ਗੁਣਾ ਕੇ ਗਾਹ ॥
ਸੁਣਿਐ ਸੇਖ ਪੀਰ ਪਾਤਿਸਾਹ ॥
ਸੁਣਿਐ ਅੰਧੇ ਪਾਵਹਿ ਰਾਹੁ ॥
ਸੁਣਿਐ ਹਾਥ ਹੋਵੈ ਅਸਗਾਹੁ ॥
ਨਾਨਕ ਭਗਤਾ ਸਦਾ ਵਿਗਾਸੁ ॥
ਸੁਣਿਐ ਦੂਖ ਪਾਪ ਕਾ ਨਾਸੁ ॥੧੧॥

Transliteration :

Suṇiai sarā guṇā ke gāh.
Suṇiai sekh pīr pātisāh.
Suṇiai aṁdhe pāvahi rāhu.
Suṇiai hāth hovai asagāhu.
Nānak bhagatā sadā vigāsu.
Suṇiai dūkh pāp kā nāsu.11.

Glossary :

ਸੁਣਿਐ—by hearing ; ਸਰਾ—oceans ; ਗੁਣਾ ਕੇ—of qualities ; ਗਾਹ—tread ; ਸੇਖ—saint, scholar ; ਪੀਰ—guru, religious guide ; ਪਾਤਿਸਾਹ—king ; ਅੰਧੇ—blind ; ਪਾਵਹਿ—get ; ਰਾਹੁ—path ; ਹਾਥ ਹੋਵੈ—become fathomable ; ਅਸਗਾਹੁ—unfathomable.

Translation :

By hearing the Name of the Lord one fathoms the oceans of virtues ; by hearing the Name of the Lord, one achieves the status of a Sheikh (a man of authority), a Pīr (religious leader) and a king ; by hearing the Name of the Lord the blind find out the path ; by hearing the Name of the Lord, the unfathomable Lord is fathomed. The devotees (who hear the Name of the Lord) are always in bliss and on hearing the Name, their sorrows and sins are destroyed.

Comments :

Like the previous three stanzas, this stanza also mentions the great attainments achieved by hearing the Name of the Lord.

TWELFTH STANZA

Text :

ਮੰਨੇ ਕੀ ਗਤਿ ਕਹੀ ਨ ਜਾਇ ॥
ਜੇ ਕੋ ਕਹੈ ਪਿਛੈ ਪਛੁਤਾਇ ॥
ਕਾਗਦਿ ਕਲਮ ਨ ਲਿਖਣਹਾਰੁ ॥
ਮੰਨੇ ਕਾ ਬਹਿ ਕਰਨਿ ਵੀਚਾਰੁ ॥
ਐਸਾ ਨਾਮੁ ਨਿਰੰਜਨੁ ਹੋਇ ॥
ਜੇ ਕੋ ਮੰਨਿ ਜਾਣੈ ਮਨਿ ਕੋਇ ॥੧੨॥

Transliteration :

Maṁne kī gati kahī na jāi.
Je ko kahai pichai pachutāi.
Kāgadi kalam na likhaṇhāru.
Maṁne kā bahi karani vīcāru.
Aisā namū niraṁjanu hoi.
Je ko maṁni jāṇai mani koi.12.

Glossary :

ਮੰਨੇ—by believing, by thinking constantly ; ਕੀ—of ; ਗਤਿ—condition, state ; ਕਹੀ ਨ ਜਾਇ—cannot be described ; ਜੇ—if ; ਕੋ—any ; ਕਹੈ—says ; ਪਿਛੈ—afterwards ; ਪਛੁਤਾਇ—repents ; ਕਾਗਦਿ—paper ; ਕਲਮ—pen ; ਨ—not ; ਲਿਖਣਹਾਰੁ—scribe ; ਕਾ—of ; ਬਹਿ—sit ; ਕਰਨਿ ਵੀਚਾਰੁ—reflect ; ਐਸਾ—such ; ਨਾਮੁ—Name (of the Lord) ; ਨਿਰੰਜਨੁ—Pure Lord, Immaculate Lord ; ਹੋਇ—is ; ਮੰਨਿ—believe ; ਜਾਣੈ—understand ਮਨਿ—mind ; ਕੋਇ—any.

Translation :

The state of the person thinking constantly about the Name of the Lord, cannot be described. If anyone tries to express it, he repents afterwards. If some persons reflect upon the state of constant thinking on the Name of the Lord, it cannot be described with pen on paper. Such is the Name of the Immaculate Lord, if one may think constantly about it in his mind.

Comments :

After the state of hearing the Name of the Lord, there comes the state of thinking constantly on the Name. The merit of both these states is inexpressible.

Thirteenth Stanza

Text :

ਮੰਨੈ ਸੁਰਤਿ ਹੋਵੈ ਮਨਿ ਬੁਧਿ ॥
ਮੰਨੈ ਸਗਲ ਭਵਣ ਕੀ ਸੁਧਿ ॥
ਮੰਨੈ ਮੁਹਿ ਚੋਟਾ ਨਾ ਖਾਇ ॥
ਮੰਨੈ ਜਮ ਕੈ ਸਾਥਿ ਨ ਜਾਇ ॥
ਐਸਾ ਨਾਮੁ ਨਿਰੰਜਨੁ ਹੋਇ ॥
ਜੇ ਕੋ ਮੰਨਿ ਜਾਣੈ ਮਨਿ ਕੋਇ ॥੧੩॥

Transliteration :

Maṁnai surati hovai mani budhi.
Maṁnai sagal bhavaṇ kī sudhi.
Maṁnai muhi coṭā nā khāi.
Maṁnai jam kai sāthi na jāi.
Aisā nāmu niraṁjanu hoi.
Je ko maṁni jāṇai mani koi.13.

Glossary :

ਮੰਨੈ—by believing ; ਸੁਰਤਿ ਹੋਵੈ—receive comprehension, procure understanding ; ਮਨਿ—mind ; ਬੁਧਿ—intellect ; ਸਗਲ—all ; ਭਵਣ—spheres ; ਕੀ—of ; ਸੁਧਿ—awakening ; ਮੁਹਿ—mouth, face ; ਚੋਟਾ—blows ; ਨ ਖਾਇ—not suffer ; ਜਮ—Yama, angel of death ; ਸਾਥਿ—with ; ਨ ਜਾਇ—not go.

Translation :

By believing in the Name of the Lord, the mind and intellect receive divine comprehension ; by believing in the Name of the Lord, the awareness of all the spheres is obtained ; by believing in the Name of the Lord, one does not suffer blows on his face ; by believing in the Name of the Lord, one does not go with the messenger of death. Such is the Name of the Immaculate Lord, if one may think constantly about it in his mind.

Comments :

In this stanza, like the previous one, the merit of believing in the Name of the Lord, has been mentioned.

FOURTEENTH STANZA

Text :

ਮੰਨੈ ਮਾਰਗਿ ਠਾਕ ਨ ਪਾਇ ॥
ਮੰਨੈ ਪਤਿ ਸਿਉ ਪਰਗਟੁ ਜਾਇ ॥
ਮੰਨੈ ਮਗੁ ਨ ਚਲੈ ਪੰਥੁ ॥
ਮੰਨੈ ਧਰਮ ਸੇਤੀ ਸਨਬੰਧੁ ॥
ਐਸਾ ਨਾਮੁ ਨਿਰੰਜਨੁ ਹੋਇ ॥
ਜੇ ਕੋ ਮੰਨਿ ਜਾਣੈ ਮਨਿ ਕੋਇ ॥੧੪॥

Transliteration :

Maṁnai māragi ṭhāk na pāi.
Maṁnai pati siu pargaṭu jāi.
Maṁnai magu na calai paṁthu.
Maṁnai dharam setī sanbaṁdhu.
Aisā nāmu niraṁjanu hoi.
Je ko maṁni jāṇai mani koi.14.

Glossary :

ਮੰਨੈ—By believing ; ਮਾਰਗਿ—path ; ਠਾਕ—obstructed ; ਨ ਪਾਇ—not get ; ਪਤਿ—honour ; ਸਿਉ—with ; ਪਰਗਟੁ ਜਾਇ—depart ; ਮਗੁ—(worldly) ways ; ਨ ਚਲੈ—does not walk ; ਪੰਥੁ—other (ritualistic) paths ; ਧਰਮ—piety, righteousness ; ਸੇਤੀ—with ; ਸਨਬੰਧੁ—relation.

Translation :

By believing in the Name of the Lord, no obstruction comes in the path of the devotee ; by believing in the Name of the Lord, the devotee goes away with honour and renown ; by believing in the Name of the Lord, the devotee does not move on diverse ways and paths ; by believing in the Name of the Lord, the devotee is associated only with righteousness. Such is the Name of the Immaculate Lord, if one may think constantly about it in his mind.

Comments :

In this stanza, like the previous two stanzas, the merit of believing in the Name of the Lord has been mentioned.

Fifteenth Stanza

Text :

ਮੰਨੈ ਪਾਵਹਿ ਮੋਖੁ ਦੁਆਰੁ ॥
ਮੰਨੈ ਪਰਵਾਰੈ ਸਾਧਾਰੁ ॥
ਮੰਨੈ ਤਰੈ ਤਾਰੇ ਗੁਰੁ ਸਿਖ ॥
ਮੰਨੈ ਨਾਨਕ ਭਵਹਿ ਨ ਭਿਖ ॥
ਐਸਾ ਨਾਮੁ ਨਿਰੰਜਨੁ ਹੋਇ ॥
ਜੇ ਕੋ ਮੰਨਿ ਜਾਣੈ ਮਨਿ ਕੋਇ ॥੧੫॥

Transliteration :

Maṁnai pāvahi mokhu duāru.
Maṁnai paravārai sādhāru.
Maṁnai tarai tārai guru sikh.
Maṁnai Nānak bhavahi na bhikh.
Aisā nāmu niraṁjanu hoi.
Je ko maṁni jāṇai mani koi.15.

Glossary :

ਮੰਨੈ—By believing ; ਪਾਵਹਿ—achieve, obtain ; ਮੋਖ—salvation ; ਦੁਆਰੁ—door, gate ; ਪਰਵਾਰੈ—of family ; ਸਾਧਾਰੁ—redeem, reform ; ਤਰੈ—swims ; ਤਾਰੇ—causes others to swim ; ਗੁਰੁ ਸਿਖ—the disciples of the Guru ; ਭਵਹਿ—wander ; ਭਿਖ—begging.

Translation :

By believing in the Name of the Lord, the devotee attains the door of emancipation ; by believing in the Name of the Lord, the devotee redeems all his family ; by believing in the Name of the Lord, the disciple of the Guru swims himself and also causes others to swim (the ocean of *Saṁsāra*) ; by believing in the Name of the Lord, says Nanak, the devotee does not go abegging. Such is the Name of the Immaculate Lord, if one may think constantly about it in his mind.

Comments :

In this as well as in the previous three stanzas, the merit of believing in the Name of the Lord, has been mentioned.

Sixteenth Stanza

Text :

ਪੰਚ ਪਰਵਾਣ ਪੰਚ ਪਰਧਾਨੁ ॥
ਪੰਚੇ ਪਾਵਹਿ ਦਰਗਹਿ ਮਾਨੁ ॥
ਪੰਚੇ ਸੋਹਹਿ ਦਰਿ ਰਾਜਾਨੁ ॥
ਪੰਚਾ ਕਾ ਗੁਰੁ ਏਕੁ ਧਿਆਨੁ ॥
ਜੇ ਕੋ ਕਹੈ ਕਰੈ ਵੀਚਾਰੁ ॥
ਕਰਤੇ ਕੈ ਕਰਣੈ ਨਾਹੀ ਸੁਮਾਰੁ ॥
ਧੌਲੁ ਧਰਮੁ ਦਇਆ ਕਾ ਪੂਤੁ ॥
ਸੰਤੋਖੁ ਥਾਪਿ ਰਖਿਆ ਜਿਨਿ ਸੂਤਿ ॥
ਜੇ ਕੋ ਬੁਝੈ ਹੋਵੈ ਸਚਿਆਰੁ ॥
ਧਵਲੈ ਉਪਰਿ ਕੇਤਾ ਭਾਰੁ ॥
ਧਰਤੀ ਹੋਰੁ ਪਰੈ ਹੋਰੁ ਹੋਰੁ ॥
ਤਿਸ ਤੇ ਭਾਰੁ ਤਲੈ ਕਵਣੁ ਜੋਰੁ ॥
ਜੀਅ ਜਾਤਿ ਰੰਗਾ ਕੇ ਨਾਵ ॥
ਸਭਨਾ ਲਿਖਿਆ ਵੁੜੀ ਕਲਾਮ ॥
ਏਹੁ ਲੇਖਾ ਲਿਖਿ ਜਾਣੈ ਕੋਇ ॥
ਲੇਖਾ ਲਿਖਿਆ ਕੇਤਾ ਹੋਇ ॥
ਕੇਤਾ ਤਾਣੁ ਸੁਆਲਿਹੁ ਰੂਪੁ ॥
ਕੇਤੀ ਦਾਤਿ ਜਾਣੈ ਕੌਣੁ ਕੂਤੁ ॥
ਕੀਤਾ ਪਸਾਉ ਏਕੋ ਕਵਾਉ ॥
ਤਿਸ ਤੇ ਹੋਏ ਲਖ ਦਰੀਆਉ ॥
ਕੁਦਰਤਿ ਕਵਣ ਕਹਾ ਵੀਚਾਰੁ ॥
ਵਾਰਿਆ ਨ ਜਾਵਾ ਏਕ ਵਾਰ ॥
ਜੋ ਤੁਧੁ ਭਾਵੈ ਸਾਈ ਭਲੀ ਕਾਰ ॥
ਤੂ ਸਦਾ ਸਲਾਮਤਿ ਨਿਰੰਕਾਰ ॥੧੬॥

Transliteration :

Pamc paravāṇ pamc pardhānu.
Pamce pāvahi daragahi mānu.
Pamce sohahi dari rājānu.
Pamcā kā guru eku dhiānu.
Je ko kahai karai vīcāru.
Karte kai karaṇai nāhī sumāru.
Dhaulu dharamu diā kā pūtu.

Saṁtokhu thāpi rakhiā jini sūti.
Je ko bujhai hovai saciāru.
Dhavalai upari ketā bhāru.
Dharatī horu parai horu horu.
Tis te bhāru talai kavaṇu joru.
Jīa jāti raṁgā ke nāv.
Sabhanā likhiā vuṛī kalām.
Ehu lekhā likhi jāṇai koi.
Lekhā likhiā ketā hoi.
Ketā tāṇu suālihu rūpu.
Ketī dāti jāṇai kauṇu kūtu.
Kītā pasāu eko kavāu.
Tis te hoe lakha darīāu.
Qudarati kavaṇ kahā vīcāru.
Vāriā na jāvā ek vāra.
Jo tudhu bhāvai sāī bhalī kār.
Tū sadā salāmati niraṁkār.16.

Glossary :

ਪੰਚ—the elect, the select one ; ਪਰਵਾਣ—acceptable ; ਪਰਧਾਨੁ—chief, supreme ; ਪੰਚੇ—the select ; ਪਾਵਹਿ—receive ; ਦਰਗਹਿ—court (of the Lord) ; ਮਾਨੁ—honour ; ਸੋਹਹਿ—are graceful ; ਦਰਿ—(in the) doors, in the courts ; ਰਾਜਾਨੁ—kings ; ਪੰਚਾ ਕਾ—of the selected ones ; ਗੁਰੁ—Guru ; ਏਕੁ—one ; ਧਿਆਨੁ—attention ; ਜੇ—if ; ਕੋ—any ; ਕਹੈ—describe ; ਕਰੈ ਵੀਚਾਰੁ—reflect ; ਕਰਤੇ—creator ; ਕੇ—of; ਕਰਣੈ—creation doing ; ਕਾ—of ; ਨਾਹੀ—not ; ਸੁਮਾਰੁ—enumeration, calculation ; ਧੌਲੁ—the mythical bull ; ਧਰਮੁ—piety, righteousness ; ਦਇਆ—compassion, mercy ; ਪੂਤੁ—son ; ਸੰਤੋਖੁ—contentment ; ਥਾਪਿ ਰਖਿਆ—established ; ਜਿਨਿ—who ; ਸੂਤਿ—in order, systematize ; ਬੁਝੈ—understand ; ਹੋਵੈ—becomes ; ਸਚਿਆਰੁ—truthful ; ਧਵਲੈ—bull ; ਉਪਰਿ—on ; ਕੇਤਾ—how much ; ਭਾਰੁ—load ; ਧਰਤੀ—earth ; ਹੋਰੁ—more ; ਪਰੈ—beyond ; ਤਿਸ ਤੇ—which ; ਤਲੈ—below, underneath ; ਕਵਣੁ—what ; ਜੋਰੁ—power ; ਜੀਅ—jiva ; ਜਾਤਿ—kind ; ਰੰਗਾ—colours ; ਕੇ—and ; ਨਾਵ—names ; ਸਭਨਾ—all ; ਲਿਖਿਆ—written ; ਵੁੜੀ—flowed ; ਕਲਾਮ—pen ; ਏਹੁ—this ; ਲੇਖਾ—account ; ਲਿਖਿ—write ; ਜਾਣੈ—knows ; ਕੋਇ—any, few ; ਲਿਖਿਆ—written, scribed ; ਕੇਤਾ—much ; ਹੋਇ—will be ; ਤਾਣੁ—might ; ਸੁਆਲਿਹੁ—fascinating ; ਰੂਪੁ—beauty ; ਕੇਤੀ—much ; ਦਾਤਿ—gift, bounty ; ਜਾਣੈ—knows ; ਕੌਣੁ—who ; ਕੂਤੁ—valuation ; ਕੀਤਾ—did ; ਪਸਾਉ—

expansion ; ਏਕੋ—one ; ਕਵਾਉ—word ; ਲਖ—lakhs ; ਦਰੀਆਉ—rivers ; ਕੁਦਰਤਿ—nature ; ਕਵਣ—what ; ਕਹਾ—describe ; ਵੀਚਾਰੁ—thoughts ; ਵਾਰਿਆ ਨ ਜਾਵਾ—cannot be a sacrifice ; ਏਕ ਵਾਰ—once ; ਜੋ—whatever ; ਤੁਧੁ ਭਾਵੈ—pleases you ; ਸਾਈ—the same ; ਭਲੀ—good ; ਕਾਰ—deed ; ਤੂ—You, Thou ; ਸਦਾ—ever, always ; ਸਲਾਮਤਿ—safe ; ਨਿਰੰਕਾਰ—The Transcendent Lord.

Translation :

The distinguished disciples, called *Panch* (Elect or Alderno) are approved (by the Lord) and supreme. They receive honours in the court of the Lord and bedeck the hall of the Sovereign. They concentrate only on their Guru. If anyone says and reflects, the doing (work) of the Creator is beyond enumeration. The mythical bull of Dharma (righteousness) is the son of compassion, which has established (the earth) in order with contentment. If anyone understands this, he becomes truthful. He comprehends the immensity of load on the bull. There are more and more worlds beyond this earth. What power is supporting their weight from below ? There are jivas (beings) of many kinds, colours and names. The writ from the pen of the Lord is inscribed on all beings. If anyone knows (the method) of writing such an account, the written account will become enormous. What power and fascinating beauty (is yours, O Lord) ? How great are Thy bounties (gifts) ? Who can assess their extent ? With one utterance Thou has created the expanses, whereby lakhs of the rivers (of life) began to flow. How can I reflect and describe Thy Nature, O Lord, I cannot be a sacrifice to Thee even once. Whatever pleases Thee, is right. Thou art ever safe, O Formless Lord.

Comments :

In this stanza three vital issues have been brought forth. Firstly, those devotees who hear and believe constantly the Name of the Lord, have been designated as *Panchs,* those who are the distinguished devotees and are honoured in both the worlds, this world in the life and the next world after death. They are attuned in mind, speech and deed with their preceptor. Secondly, all the beings of this world of immense expanse with diverse kinds, colours and names, having unaccountable writs of God on their foreheads, and with great power and fascinating beauty and endowed with various gifts given by the Beneficent Lord, abide with the support of Dharma (righteousness) who is not merely a mythological Bull, but established and set in order by Divine compassion and forbearance. Thirdly, this wide expanse has been created by a single utterance of the Transcendent Lord, when lakhs of the rivers of life began to flow.

Seventeenth Stanza

Text :

ਅਸੰਖ ਜਪ ਅਸੰਖ ਭਾਉ ॥
ਅਸੰਖ ਪੂਜਾ ਅਸੰਖ ਤਪਤਾਉ ॥
ਅਸੰਖ ਗਰੰਥ ਮੁਖਿ ਵੇਦ ਪਾਠ ॥
ਅਸੰਖ ਜੋਗ ਮਨਿ ਰਹਹਿ ਉਦਾਸ ॥
ਅਸੰਖ ਭਗਤ ਗੁਣ ਗਿਆਨ ਵੀਚਾਰ ॥
ਅਸੰਖ ਸਤੀ ਅਸੰਖ ਦਾਤਾਰ ॥
ਅਸੰਖ ਸੂਰ ਮੁਹ ਭਖ ਸਾਰ ॥
ਅਸੰਖ ਮੋਨਿ ਲਿਵ ਲਾਇ ਤਾਰ ॥
ਕੁਦਰਤਿ ਕਵਣ ਕਹਾ ਵੀਚਾਰੁ ॥
ਵਾਰਿਆ ਨ ਜਾਵਾ ਏਕ ਵਾਰ ॥
ਜੋ ਤੁਧੁ ਭਾਵੈ ਸਾਈ ਭਲੀ ਕਾਰ ॥
ਤੂ ਸਦਾ ਸਲਾਮਤਿ ਨਿਰੰਕਾਰ ॥੧੭॥

Transliteration :

Asaṁkh jap asaṁkh bhāu.
Asaṁkh pūjā asaṁkh tapatāu.
Asaṁkh graṁth mukhi ved pāṭh.
Asaṁkh jog mani rahahi udās.
Asaṁkh bhagat guṇ giān vīcār.
Asaṁkh satī asaṁkh dātār.
Asaṁkh sūr muh bhakh sār.
Asaṁkh moni liv lāi tār.
Qudrati kavaṇ kahā vīcāru.
Vāriā na jāvā ek vār.
Jo tudhu bhāvai sāī bhalī kār.
Tū sadā salāmati niraṁkār.17.

Glossary :

ਅਸੰਖ—numberless, innumerable ; ਜਪ—meditation ; ਭਾਉ—love ;

ਪੂਜਾ—worship ; ਤਪਤਾਉ—practising austerities ; ਗਰੰਥ—The Book, The Scripture ; ਮੁਖਿ—mouth ; ਵੇਦ—Veda ; ਪਾਠ—recitation ; ਜੋਗ—yoga ; ਮਨਿ—mind ; ਰਹਹਿ—remain ; ਉਦਾਸ—detached ; ਭਗਤ—devotee ; ਗੁਣ—virtue ; ਗਿਆਨ—knowledge ; ਵੀਚਾਰ—reflection ; ਸਤੀ—truthful, ਦਾਤਾਰ—Benefactor ; ਸੂਰ—warrior ; ਮੁਹ—mouth, face ; ਭਖ—eat ; ਸਾਰ—steel ; ਮੋਨਿ—silence, an ascetic observing silence ; ਲਿਵ—love ; ਲਾਇ ਤਾਰ—to be in tune with.

Translation :

There are innumerable beings busy in meditation and devotion with love. There are innumerable persons busy in worship and countless are those who practise austerities. There are innumerable persons who study scriptures and recite the Vedas orally. There are innumerable persons who practise yoga and in mind remain detached (from the world). There are innumerable devotees who reflect over the attributes and cognition about the Lord. There are innumerable men of piety as well as men of bounty. There are innumerable warriors who bear the blows of steel on their faces. There are innumerable men observing silence who remain in tune with the Lord. How can I reflect and describe Thy Nature, O Lord, I cannot be a sacrifice to Thee even once. Whatever pleases Thee, is right. Thou are ever safe, O Formless Lord.

Comments :

Continuing his concept of creation from the last stanza, Guru Nanak Dev focusses our attention on those created beings who are engaged in right type of pursuits. They are countless in number and are the creation of the same Lord.

EIGHTEENTH STANZA

Text :

ਅਸੰਖ ਮੂਰਖ ਅੰਧ ਘੋਰ ॥
ਅਸੰਖ ਚੋਰ ਹਰਾਮਖੋਰ ॥
ਅਸੰਖ ਅਮਰ ਕਰਿ ਜਾਹਿ ਜੋਰ ॥
ਅਸੰਖ ਗਲਵਢ ਹਤਿਆ ਕਮਾਹਿ ॥
ਅਸੰਖ ਪਾਪੀ ਪਾਪੁ ਕਰਿ ਜਾਹਿ ॥
ਅਸੰਖ ਕੂੜਿਆਰ ਕੂੜੇ ਫਿਰਾਹਿ ॥

ਅਸੰਖ ਮਲੇਛ ਮਲੁ ਭਖਿ ਖਾਹਿ ॥
ਅਸੰਖ ਨਿੰਦਕ ਸਿਰਿ ਕਰਹਿ ਭਾਰੁ ॥
ਨਾਨਕੁ ਨੀਚੁ ਕਹੈ ਵੀਚਾਰੁ ॥
ਵਾਰਿਆ ਨ ਜਾਵਾ ਏਕ ਵਾਰ ॥
ਜੋ ਤੁਧੁ ਭਾਵੈ ਸਾਈ ਭਲੀ ਕਾਰ ॥
ਤੂ ਸਦਾ ਸਲਾਮਤਿ ਨਿਰੰਕਾਰ ॥੧੮॥

Transliteration :

Asaṁkh murakh aṁdh ghor.
Asaṁkh cor harām khor.
Asaṁkh amar kari jāhi jor.
Asaṁkh galvaḍh hatiā kamāhi.
Asaṁkh pāpī pāpu kari jāhi.
Asaṁkh kūṛiār kūṛe phirāhi.
Asaṁkh malech malu bhakhi khāhi.
Asaṁkh niṁdak siri karahi bhāru.
Nānaku nīcu kahai vīcāru.
Vāriā na jāvā ek vār.
Jo tudhu bhāvai sāī bhalī kār.
Tū sadā salāmati niraṁkār.

Glossary :

ਅਸੰਖ—numberless, innumerable ; ਮੂਰਖ—fools ; ਅੰਧ ਘੋਰ—highly blind, appallingly blind ; ਚੋਰ—thieves ; ਹਰਾਮਖੋਰ—the devourer of forbidden thing, a corrupt person ; ਅਮਰ—rule, command ; ਕਰਿ ਜਾਹਿ—do ; ਜੋਰ—by force ; ਗਲਵਢ—cut-throats ; ਹਤਿਆ—murder ; ਕਮਾਹਿ—commit ; ਪਾਪੀ—sinner ; ਪਾਪੁ—sin ; ਕਰਿ ਜਾਹਿ—do, commit ; ਕੂੜਿਆਰ—liars ; ਕੂੜੇ—in falsehood ; ਫਿਰਾਹਿ—wander ; ਮਲੇਛ—an outcast, barbarian ; ਮਲੁ—dirt, filth ; ਭਖਿ ਖਾਹਿ—eat ; ਨਿੰਦਕ—slanderers ; ਸਿਰਿ—head ; ਕਰਹਿ ਭਾਰੁ—carry load ; ਨੀਚੁ—lowly ; ਕਹੈ—says, speaks ; ਵੀਚਾਰੁ—reflection, consideration.

Translation :

There are innumerable foolish persons groping blindly in pitch darkness. There are innumerable thieves and countless persons busy in unlawful indulgence. There are innumerable persons who pass away after ruling with force. There are innumerable cut-throats who commit murders. There are innumerable sinners who lead vicious lives. There are innumerable liars, who roam in the arena of falsehood. There are innumerable *malechas* (barbarians) who eat unlawful dirty material. There are innumerable slanderers, who carry loads of calumny on their heads. Nanak, the lowly, says after consideration : How can I reflect and describe Thy Nature, O Lord ; I cannot be a sacrifice to Thee even once. Whatever pleases Thee, is right. Thou art ever safe, O Formless Lord.

Comments :

Continuing his concept of creation from the last two stanzas, Guru Nanak Dev focusses our attention on those created beings, who are engaged in evil pursuits. They are countless in number and are creation of the same Lord. In Zoroastrianism, two ultimate powers have been mentioned. One is *Ahur Mazda,* the power of Goodness and Light and the other is *Ahriman,* the power of badness and darkness. Guru Nanak Dev has rejected such a concept, bringing out clearly that the Good and Bad creations are the work of the same Lord.

Nineteenth Stanza

Text :

ਅਸੰਖ ਨਾਵ ਅਸੰਖ ਥਾਵ ॥
ਅਗੰਮ ਅਗੰਮ ਅਸੰਖ ਲੋਅ ॥
ਅਸੰਖ ਕਹਹਿ ਸਿਰਿ ਭਾਰੁ ਹੋਇ ॥
ਅਖਰੀ ਨਾਮੁ ਅਖਰੀ ਸਾਲਾਹ ॥
ਅਖਰੀ ਗਿਆਨੁ ਗੀਤ ਗੁਣ ਗਾਹ ॥
ਅਖਰੀ ਲਿਖਣੁ ਬੋਲਣੁ ਬਾਣਿ ॥
ਅਖਰਾ ਸਿਰਿ ਸੰਜੋਗੁ ਵਖਾਣਿ ॥
ਜਿਨਿ ਏਹਿ ਲਿਖੇ ਤਿਸੁ ਸਿਰਿ ਨਾਹਿ ॥
ਜਿਵ ਫੁਰਮਾਏ ਤਿਵ ਤਿਵ ਪਾਹਿ ॥
ਜੇਤਾ ਕੀਤਾ ਤੇਤਾ ਨਾਉ ॥
ਵਿਣੁ ਨਾਵੈ ਨਾਹੀ ਕੋ ਥਾਉ ॥
ਕੁਦਰਤਿ ਕਵਣ ਕਹਾ ਵੀਚਾਰੁ ॥
ਵਾਰਿਆ ਨ ਜਾਵਾ ਏਕ ਵਾਰ ॥
ਜੋ ਤੁਧੁ ਭਾਵੈ ਸਾਈ ਭਲੀ ਕਾਰ ॥
ਤੂ ਸਦਾ ਸਲਾਮਤਿ ਨਿਰੰਕਾਰ ॥੧੯॥

Transliteration :

Asaṁkh nāv asaṁkh thāv.
Agaṁm agaṁm asaṁkh loa.
Asaṁkh kahahi siri bhāru hoi.
Akharī Nāmu akharī sālāh.
Akharī giānu gīt guṇ gāh.
Akharī likhaṇu bolaṇu bāṇi.
Akharā siri saṁjogu vakhāṇi.
Jini ehi likhe tisu siri nāhi.
Jiv phurmāe tiv tiv pāhi.
Jetā kītā tetā nāu.
Viṇu nāvai nāhī ko thāu.
Qudarati kavaṇ kahā vīcāru.
Vāriā na jāvā ek vār.
Jo tudhu bhāvai sāī bhalī kār.
Tū sadā salāmati niraṁkār.19.

Glossary :

ਅਸੰਖ—numberless, innumerable ; ਨਾਵ—names ; ਥਾਵ—places ; ਅਗੰਮ—unapproachable ; ਲੋਅ—worlds ; ਕਹਹਿ—say, speak ; ਸਿਰਿ—head ; ਭਾਰੁ ਹੋਇ—are loaded ; ਅਖਰੀ—letters, words ; ਨਾਮੁ—The Name ; ਸਾਲਾਹ—praise ; ਗਿਆਨੁ—knowledge ; ਗੀਤ—song ; ਗੁਣ—quality, attribute ; ਗਾਹ—sing ; ਲਿਖਣੁ—writing ; ਬੋਲਣੁ—speaking ; ਬਾਣਿ—hymns, sacred verses ; ਸਿਰਿ— head ; ਸੰਜੋਗੁ—meeting, destiny ; ਸਿਰਿ ਸੰਜੋਗੁ—writ on the head ; ਵਖਾਣਿ—describe ; ਜਿਨਿ—who ; ਏਹਿ—these ; ਲਿਖੇ—wrote ; ਤਿਸੁ—Him ; ਨਾਹਿ—not ; ਜਿਵ—as ; ਫੁਰਮਾਏ—ordains ; ਤਿਵ—so ; ਪਾਹਿ—obtain ; ਜੇਤਾ—as much ; ਕੀਤਾ—created ; ਤੇਤਾ—so much ; ਨਾਉ—name ; ਵਿਣੁ—without ; ਨਾਵੈ—The Name (of the Lord) ; ਨਾਹੀ—no ; ਕੋ—any ; ਥਾਉ—place.

Translation :

There are innumerable names and places. There are innumerable inaccessible worlds. Even the utterance of the word 'innumerable' makes our head burdensome. The name is constituted by syllables and the syllables in unison constitute the praise. The syllables in unison constitute the chanted songs of knowledge and attributes. The syllables in unison constitute the written and uttered hymns. The syllables in unison describe the destiny on the head. He who has scribed the writ does not have (any writ) on His head. The beings receive the writ as ordained (by Him). Whatever has been created has a name. There is no place without the Name. How can I reflect and describe Thy Nature. O Lord, ; I cannot be a sacrifice to Thee even once. Whatever pleases Thee, is right. Thou art ever safe, O Formless Lord !

Comments :

Continuing his concept of creation from the last three stanzas, Guru Nanak Dev focusses our attention on the inaccessible universe of innumerable names and places. The names are constituted by syllables which are of great significance as through them the hymns are prepared and the songs of knowledge and attributes of the Lord are chanted. The writ of destiny on the head of every being is written with syllables. The Lord who scribes this writ is Himself without any writ. Whatever has been created has a name. There is no place without the name. The Guru, in a way, reminds us about the Name of the Lord, which has also been constituted through syllables.

TWENTIETH STANZA

Text :

ਭਰੀਐ ਹਥੁ ਪੈਰੁ ਤਨੁ ਦੇਹ ॥
ਪਾਣੀ ਧੋਤੈ ਉਤਰਸੁ ਖੇਹ ॥
ਮੂਤ ਪਲੀਤੀ ਕਪੜੁ ਹੋਇ ॥
ਦੇ ਸਾਬੂਣੁ ਲਈਐ ਓਹੁ ਧੋਇ ॥
ਭਰੀਐ ਮਤਿ ਪਾਪਾ ਕੈ ਸੰਗਿ ॥
ਓਹੁ ਧੋਪੈ ਨਾਵੈ ਕੈ ਰੰਗਿ ॥
ਪੁੰਨੀ ਪਾਪੀ ਆਖਣੁ ਨਾਹਿ ॥
ਕਰਿ ਕਰਿ ਕਰਣਾ ਲਿਖਿ ਲੈ ਜਾਹੁ ॥
ਆਪੇ ਬੀਜਿ ਆਪੇ ਹੀ ਖਾਹੁ ॥
ਨਾਨਕ ਹੁਕਮੀ ਆਵਹੁ ਜਾਹ ॥੨੦॥

Transliteration :

Bhariai hathu pairu tanu deh.
Pāṇī dhotai utarasu kheh.
Mūt palītī kaparu hoi.
De sābūṇu laīai ohu dhoi.
Bhariai mati pāpā kai saṁgi.

Ohu dhopai nāvai kai ramgi.
Pumnī pāpī ākhaṇu nāhi.
Kari kari karaṇā likhi lai jāhu.
Āpe bīji āpe hī khāhu.
Nānak hukamī āvahu jāhu.20.

Glossary :

ਭਰੀਐ—besmeared, soiled ; ਹਥੁ—hands ; ਪੈਰੁ—feet ; ਤਨੁ—body ; ਦੇਹ—body ; ਪਾਣੀ—water ; ਧੋਤੈ—washed ; ਉਤਰਸੁ—drops ; ਖੇਹ—dust, dirt ; ਮੂਤ—urine ; ਪਲੀਤੀ—polluted ; ਕਪੜੁ—cloth ; ਹੋਇ—becomes ; ਦੇ—give, apply ; ਸਾਬੂਣੁ—soap ; ਲਈਐ ਧੋਇ—washed ; ਓਹੁ—that ; ਮਤਿ—intellect ; ਪਾਪਾ—sins ; ਕੈ ਸੰਗਿ—with ; ਧੋਪੈ—washed ; ਨਾਵੈ—Name (of the Lord) ; ਕੈ—of ; ਰੰਗਿ—love ; ਪੁੰਨੀ—virtuous ; ਪਾਪੀ—sinner ; ਆਖਣੁ—by speech ; ਨਾਹਿ—not ; ਕਰਿ ਕਰਿ ਕਰਣਾ—repeated actions ; ਲਿਖਿ ਲੈ ਜਾਹੁ—are written ; ਆਪੇ—himself ; ਬੀਜਿ—sow ; ਹੀ—also ; ਖਾਹੁ—eat ; ਹੁਕਮੀ— by order ; ਆਵਹੁ—come ; ਜਾਹੁ—go.

Translation :

If the hands, feet and other parts of the body are besmeared, the dust is removed by washing them. If the garment gets polluted with urine, it is washed clean by the application of soap. Do not defile yourself with sins, they will be washed away with the love of the Name of the Lord. One does not become virtuous or vicious by mere words. The repeated actions shall scribe him thus. One sows himself and reaps himself. Under the Lord's Will, says Nanak, one may come and go.

Comments :

Just as the dust on the body is washed away with water and the soiled clothes with soap, the sins are washed away by the love of the Name of the Lord. One has to be up and doing and lead a virtuous life. None can become virtuous by mere talk, he has to sow the seed of the Name of the Lord in the field of his body.

TWENTY-FIRST STANZA

Text :

ਤੀਰਥੁ ਤਪੁ ਦਇਆ ਦਤੁ ਦਾਨੁ ॥
ਜੇ ਕੋ ਪਾਵੈ ਤਿਲ ਕਾ ਮਾਨੁ ॥

ਸੁਣਿਆ ਮੰਨਿਆ ਮਨਿ ਕੀਤਾ ਭਾਉ ॥

ਅੰਤਰਗਤਿ ਤੀਰਥਿ ਮਲਿ ਨਾਉ ॥

ਸਭਿ ਗੁਣ ਤੇਰੇ ਮੈ ਨਾਹੀ ਕੋਇ ॥

ਵਿਣੁ ਗੁਣ ਕੀਤੇ ਭਗਤਿ ਨ ਹੋਇ ॥

ਸੁਅਸਤਿ ਆਥਿ ਬਾਣੀ ਬਰਮਾਉ ॥

ਸਤਿ ਸੁਹਾਣੁ ਸਦਾ ਮਨਿ ਚਾਉ ॥

ਕਵਣੁ ਸੁ ਵੇਲਾ ਵਖਤੁ ਕਵਣੁ ਕਵਣ ਥਿਤਿ ਕਵਣੁ ਵਾਰੁ ॥

ਕਵਣ ਸਿ ਰੁਤੀ ਮਾਹੁ ਕਵਣੁ ਜਿਤੁ ਹੋਆ ਆਕਾਰੁ ॥

ਵੇਲ ਨ ਪਾਈਆ ਪੰਡਤੀ ਜਿ ਹੋਵੈ ਲੇਖੁ ਪੁਰਾਣੁ ॥

ਵਖਤੁ ਨ ਪਾਇਓ ਕਾਦੀਆ ਜਿ ਲਿਖਨਿ ਲੇਖੁ ਕੁਰਾਣੁ ॥

ਥਿਤਿ ਵਾਰੁ ਨਾ ਜੋਗੀ ਜਾਣੈ ਰੁਤਿ ਮਾਹੁ ਨਾ ਕੋਈ ॥

ਜਾ ਕਰਤਾ ਸਿਰਠੀ ਕਉ ਸਾਜੇ ਆਪੇ ਜਾਣੈ ਸੋਈ ॥

ਕਿਵ ਕਰਿ ਆਖਾ ਕਿਵ ਸਾਲਾਹੀ ਕਿਉ ਵਰਨੀ ਕਿਵ ਜਾਣਾ ॥

ਨਾਨਕ ਆਖਣਿ ਸਭੁ ਕੋ ਆਖੈ ਇਕ ਦੂ ਇਕੁ ਸਿਆਣਾ ॥

ਵਡਾ ਸਾਹਿਬੁ ਵਡੀ ਨਾਈ ਕੀਤਾ ਜਾ ਕਾ ਹੋਵੈ ॥

ਨਾਨਕ ਜੇ ਕੋ ਆਪੌ ਜਾਣੈ ਅਗੈ ਗਇਆ ਨ ਸੋਹੈ ॥੨੧॥

Transliteration :

Tīrathu tapu diā datu dānu.

Je ko pāvai til kā mānu.

Suṇiā maṁniā mani kītā bhāu.

Aṁtaragati tīrathi mali nāu.

Sabhi guṇ tere mai nāhī koi.

Viṇu guṇ kīte bhagati na hoi.

Suasti āthi bāṇī baramāu.

Sati suhāṇu sadā mani cāu.

Kavaṇu su velā vakhatu kavaṇu kavaṇ thiti kavaṇu vāru.

Kavaṇ si rutī māhu kavaṇu jitu hoā ākāru.

Vel na pāīā paṁḍatī ji hovai lekhu Purāṇu.

Vakhatu na pāio Qādīā ji likhani lekhu Qurāṇu.

Thiti vāru na jogī jāṇai ruti māhu nā koī.

Jā kartā sirṭhī kau sāje āpe jāṇai soī.

Kiv kari ākhā kiv sālāhī kio varnī kiv jāṇā.

Nānak ākhaṇi sabhu ko ākhai ikdū iku siāṇā.

Vaḍā sāhibu vaḍī nāī kītā jā kā hovai.

Nānak je ko āpau jāṇai agai giā na sohai.21.

Glossary :

ਦਤੁ—give : ਦਾਨੁ—charity, alms ; ਜੇ—if ; ਕੋ—any ; ਪਾਵੈ—obtains ;

ਤਿਲ ਕਾ—like sesame, very small ; ਮਾਨੁ—honour ; ਸੁਣਿਆ—heard ; ਮੰਨਿਆ—believed ; ਮਨਿ—mind ; ਕੀਤਾ ਭਾਉ—loved ; ਅੰਤਰ—inner ; ਗਤਿ—salvation ; ਮਲਿ ਨਾਉ—bathe by thoroughly rubbing the body ; ਸਭਿ—all ; ਗੁਣ—qualities ; ਤੇਰੇ—Thine ; ਮੈ—mine ; ਨਾਹੀ—not ; ਵਿਣੁ—without ; ਗੁਣ ਕੀਤੇ—acquiring qualities ; ਭਗਤਿ—devotion ; ਨ ਹੋਇ—cannot be; ਸੁਅਸਤਿ—salutation, obeisance ; ਆਥਿ—maya, worldly riches ; ਬਾਣੀ—sacred speech ; ਬਰਮਾਉ—emanating from Brahman ; ਸਤਿ—Truth ; ਸੁਹਾਣੁ—beauty ; ਸਦਾ—always ; ਮਨਿ—mind ; ਚਾਉ—enthusiasm ; ਕਵਣੁ—what ; ਸੁ— that ; ਵੇਲਾ—time ; ਵਖਤੁ—time ; ਥਿਤਿ—lunar date ; ਵਾਰੁ—week day ; ਸਿ—that ; ਰੁਤੀ—season ; ਮਾਹੁ— month ; ਜਿਤੁ—when ; ਹੋਆ—to come into being ; ਆਕਾਰੁ—form, creation ; ਵੇਲ ਨ ਪਾਈਆ—did not know the time ; ਪੰਡਤੀ—Pundits ; ਜਿ—so that ; ਹੋਵੈ—be ; ਲੇਖੁ—writing ; ਪੁਰਾਣੁ—Purana ; ਵਖਤੁ ਨ ਪਾਇਓ—did not know the time ; ਕਾਦੀਆ—the Qadis, the Muslim Judges ; ਲਿਖਨਿ—scribe ; ਲੇਖੁ—writing ; ਕੁਰਾਣੁ—Quran ; ਜੋਗੀ—Yogi ; ਕੋਈ— anyone ; ਜਾ—That ; ਕਰਤਾ—creator ; ਸਿਰਠੀ—world ; ਕਉ ਸਾਜੇ—creates ; ਆਪੇ—Himself ; ਸੋਈ—the same ; ਕਿਵ ਕਰਿ—how ; ਆਖਾ—describe, express ; ਸਾਲਾਹੀ—praise ; ਕਿਉ—how ; ਵਰਨੀ—describe ; ਆਖਣਿ— speech, discourse ; ਸਭੁ ਕੋ—everyone ; ਆਖੈ—speak, say ; ਇਕ ਦੂ—from one ; ਇਕੁ—one ; ਸਿਆਣਾ—wise ; ਵਡਾ—great ; ਸਾਹਿਬੁ—Lord ; ਵਡੀ— great ; ਨਾਈ—Name ; ਕੀਤਾ—done ; ਜਾ ਕਾ—whose ; ਹੋਵੈ—comes to pass ; ਜੇ ਕੋ—if any ; ਆਪੌ—himself ; ਅਗੈ—hereafter ; ਗਇਆ—gone ; ਸੋਹੈ—be good looking.

Translation :

One attains only an iota of honour by the observance of rituals like pilgrimage, austerity, compassion and charity. He who hears, thinks constantly about the Name of the Lord with devotion in his mind, he attains salvation by bathing thoroughly in the shrine within himself. O Lord ! all the virtues are Thine, while I have none. Without practising virtues, there can be no devotion. I bow to the Lord who pervades both material and spiritual domains i.e. maya and Name. He is Truth, Beautiful and always Ecstatic in His mind. What was the time, the lunar date, the week day, the season and the month when the Creation came into being? The Pundit did not know the time, so that there could have been its written evidence in the Puranas. The Qadis did not know the time, so that they could have written about it in the Quran. The Yogi did not know the lunar date and the week day and none else could know the season and the month. The Lord who creates the world Himself only knows it. How should I express myself, how should I Praise the Lord, how should I describe and know. Everyone delivers the discourse, exhibiting himself wiser than the other. The Lord is Great, His Name is Great and whatever He does, comes to pass. If anyone considers himself able to do anything, having gone to the world hereafter he will not appear good-looking.

Comments :

Guru Nanak Dev has mentioned the following important points in this stanza :

(1) The observance of rituals cannot lead us to final emancipation. Only the Name of the Lord helps us in this direction.

(2) There can be no devotion without the practice of virtues.

(3) The Lord who is all-pervading is True, Beautiful and Blissful. He is *Satyam, Shivam* and *Sundaram.*

(4) Only the Lord Himself knows the time when He created the world. All the speculations regarding the creation of the world are mere guesses.

TWENTY-SECOND STANZA

Text :

ਪਾਤਾਲਾ ਪਾਤਾਲ ਲਖ ਆਗਾਸਾ ਆਗਾਸ ॥
ਓੜਕ ਓੜਕ ਭਾਲਿ ਥਕੇ ਵੇਦ ਕਹਨਿ ਇਕ ਵਾਤ ॥
ਸਹਸ ਅਠਾਰਹ ਕਹਨਿ ਕਤੇਬਾ ਅਸੁਲੂ ਇਕੁ ਧਾਤੁ ॥
ਲੇਖਾ ਹੋਇ ਤ ਲਿਖੀਐ ਲੇਖੈ ਹੋਇ ਵਿਣਾਸੁ ॥
ਨਾਨਕ ਵਡਾ ਆਖੀਐ ਆਪੇ ਜਾਣੈ ਆਪੁ ॥੨੨॥

Transliteration :

Pātālā pātāl lakh āgāsā āgās.
Oṛak oṛak bhāli thake ved kahani ik vāt.
Sahas aṭhārah kahani katebā asulū iku dhātu.
Lekhā hoi ta likhīai lekhai hoi viṇāsu.
Nānak vaḍā ākhīai āpe jāṇai āpu.22.

Glossary :

ਪਾਤਾਲਾ—nether worlds ; ਆਗਾਸਾ—skies, heavens ; ਓੜਕ—the final limit ; ਭਾਲਿ—seek ; ਥਕੇ—tired ; ਵੇਦ—Veda ; ਕਹਨਿ—speak ; ਇਕ

ਵਾਤ—with one voice ; ਸਹਸ—thousand ; ਅਠਾਰਹ—eighteen ; ਕਤੇਬਾ—Katebs, semitic scriptures ; ਅਸੁਲੁ—in reality ; ਇਕੁ—one ; ਧਾਤੁ—essence ; ਲੇਖਾ—account ; ਹੋਇ—be ; ਤ—then ; ਲਿਖੀਐ—write ; ਲੇਖੈ—describing the account ; ਵਿਣਾਸੁ—destruction ; ਵਡਾ—great ; ਆਖੀਐ—say, speak, call ; ਆਪੇ—Himself ; ਆਪੁ—self.

Translation :

There are lakhs of nether worlds and lakhs of skies. The Vedas (scriptures) say with one voice that those seeking the final limits (of the expanse) have grown weary and tired. Eighteen thousand Shlokas of Bhāgavat Purana and also the Semitic texts say that in reality, the essence is one. If there can be any account (of the Lord) then it can be written, but those who have been writing the account were themselves finished but not the account. The Lord be called Great, says Nanak. He himself knows His own-self.

Comments :

In this stanza, the Guru rejects the traditional idea of the seven skies and seven nether-worlds. According to him, the Great Lord is unaccountable. He knows alone the expanse of His own Creation. The scriptures also speak about One essence and point out towards the boundless creation.

Twenty-third Stanza

Text :

ਸਾਲਾਹੀ ਸਾਲਾਹਿ ਏਤੀ ਸੁਰਤਿ ਨ ਪਾਈਆ ॥
ਨਦੀਆ ਅਤੈ ਵਾਹ ਪਵਹਿ ਸਮੁੰਦਿ ਨ ਜਾਣੀਅਹਿ ॥
ਸਮੁੰਦ ਸਾਹ ਸੁਲਤਾਨ ਗਿਰਹਾ ਸੇਤੀ ਮਾਲੁ ਧਨੁ ॥
ਕੀੜੀ ਤੁਲਿ ਨ ਹੋਵਨੀ ਜੇ ਤਿਸੁ ਮਨਹੁ ਨ ਵੀਸਰਹਿ ॥੨੩॥

Transliteration :

Sālāhī sālāhi etī surati na pāīā.
Nadīā atai vāh pavahi samuṁdi na jāṇīahi.
Samuṁd sāh sultān girahā setī mālu dhanu.
Kīrī tuli na hovanī je tisu manahu na vīsarahi.23.

Glossary :

ਸਾਲਾਹੀ—eulogist, one who praises ; ਸਾਲਾਹਿ—praise ; ਏਤੀ—this

much ; ਸੁਰਤਿ—understanding ; ਨ—not ; ਪਾਈਆ—obtain ; ਨਦੀਆ—streams ; ਅਤੈ—and ; ਵਾਹ—rivulet ; ਪਵਹਿ—fall into ; ਸਮੁੰਦਿ—ocean ; ਜਾਣੀਅਹਿ—know, understand ; ਸਾਹ—king ; ਸੁਲਤਾਨ—king ; ਗਿਰਹਾ—mountain ; ਸੇਤੀ—of, with ; ਮਾਲੁ—property ; ਧਨੁ—wealth ; ਕੀੜੀ—ant ; ਤੁਲਿ—equal ; ਹੋਵਨੀ—become ; ਜੇ—if ; ਤਿਸੁ—her ; ਮਨਹੁ—in mind ; ਵੀਸਰਹਿ—forget.

Translation :

The Praisers praise (the Lord), but they have not obtained this much understanding, that the streams and rivulets fall into the ocean without knowing (its extent). The ocean like a king has property and wealth of the magnitude of a mountain, which cannot equal an ant, if she does not forget the Lord from her mind.

Comments :

In this stanza, the Guru has laid emphasis on this point that any being however big and wealthy cannot equal a being, very small and lowly, who has always in his mind the praises of the Great Lord.

TWENTY-FOURTH STANZA

Text :

ਅੰਤੁ ਨ ਸਿਫਤੀ ਕਹਣਿ ਨ ਅੰਤੁ ॥
ਅੰਤੁ ਨ ਕਰਣੈ ਦੇਣਿ ਨ ਅੰਤੁ ॥
ਅੰਤੁ ਨ ਵੇਖਣਿ ਸੁਣਣਿ ਨ ਅੰਤੁ ॥
ਅੰਤੁ ਨ ਜਾਪੈ ਕਿਆ ਮਨਿ ਮੰਤੁ ॥
ਅੰਤੁ ਨ ਜਾਪੈ ਕੀਤਾ ਆਕਾਰੁ ॥
ਅੰਤੁ ਨ ਜਾਪੈ ਪਾਰਾਵਾਰੁ ॥
ਅੰਤ ਕਾਰਣਿ ਕੇਤੇ ਬਿਲਲਾਹਿ ॥
ਤਾ ਕੇ ਅੰਤ ਨ ਪਾਏ ਜਾਹਿ ॥
ਏਹੁ ਅੰਤੁ ਨ ਜਾਣੈ ਕੋਇ ॥
ਬਹੁਤਾ ਕਹੀਐ ਬਹੁਤਾ ਹੋਇ ॥
ਵਡਾ ਸਾਹਿਬੁ ਊਚਾ ਥਾਉ ॥
ਊਚੇ ਉਪਰਿ ਊਚਾ ਨਾਉ ॥
ਏਵਡੁ ਊਚਾ ਹੋਵੈ ਕੋਇ ॥
ਤਿਸੁ ਊਚੇ ਕਉ ਜਾਣੈ ਸੋਇ ॥
ਜੇਵਡੁ ਆਪਿ ਜਾਣੈ ਆਪਿ ਆਪਿ ॥
ਨਾਨਕ ਨਦਰੀ ਕਰਮੀ ਦਾਤਿ ॥੨੪॥

Transliteration :

Aṁtu na siftī kahaṇi na aṁtu.
Aṁtu na karṇai deṇi na aṁtu.
Aṁtu na vekhaṇi suṇaṇi na aṁtu.
Aṁtu na jāpai kiā mani maṁtu.
Aṁtu na jāpai kītā ākāru.
Aṁtu na jāpai pārāvāru.
Aṁt kāraṇi kete bilalāhi.
Tā ke aṁt na pāe jāhi.
Ehu aṁtu na jāṇai koi.
Bahutā kahīai bahutā hoi.
Vaḍā sāhibu ūcā thāu.
Ūce upari ūca nāu.
Evaḍu ūcā hovai koi.
Tisu ūce kau jāṇai soi.
Jevaḍu āpi jāṇai āpi āpi.
Nānak nadarī karamī dāti.24.

Glossary :

ਅੰਤੁ—end, limit ; ਨ—not ; ਸਿਫਤੀ—praise ; ਕਹਣਿ—speak, utter ; ਕਰਣੈ—doing, working ; ਦੇਣਿ—giving ; ਵੇਖਣਿ—seeing ; ਸੁਣਣਿ—hearing ; ਜਾਪੈ—known ; ਕਿਆ—what ; ਮਨਿ—mind ; ਮੰਤੁ— motive ; ਕੀਤਾ—created ; ਆਕਾਰੁ—creation ; ਪਾਰਾਵਾਰੁ—limits of opposite sides ; ਕਾਰਣਿ—for ; ਕੇਤੇ—many ; ਬਿਲਲਾਹਿ—bewail ; ਤਾ ਕੇ—His ; ਪਾਏ ਜਾਹਿ—obtained, found ; ਏਹੁ—this ; ਜਾਣੈ—know ; ਕੋਇ—any ; ਬਹੁਤਾ—the more ; ਕਹੀਐ—describe ; ਹੋਇ—becomes ; ਵਡਾ—great ; ਸਾਹਿਬੁ—Sahib : The Lord ; ਊਚਾ—high ; ਥਾਉ—place, seat ; ਊਚੇ—high ; ਉਪਰਿ—higher ; ਨਾਉ—The Name (of the Lord) ; ਏਵਡੁ—as great ; ਹੋਵੈ—becomes ; ਕੋਇ—any ; ਤਿਸੁ—Him ; ਕਉ—to ; ਜਾਣੈ—knows ; ਸੋਇ—He ; ਜੇਵਡੁ—how great, as great ; ਆਪਿ—Himself ; ਨਦਰੀ—Graceful Lord ; ਕਰਮੀ—with grace ; ਦਾਤਿ—gift.

Translation :

There is no end to the Praises of the Lord and no end to their utterance. There is no end to the doing (creation) of the Lord and no end to His giving (gifts). There is no end to His seeing and hearing. The limit is not known about the motive of the Lord's mind. The limit of the Lord's created world is not known. The limit of God's entirety is not known. Many lament for knowing His limits, but His limits are never found. Nobody can know this limit. The more it is described, the more baffling it becomes. The Lord is Great, His seat is High. His Name is still higher. If anyone becomes as great and high, he alone then can know that Supernal Being. How much Great He is, He knows Himself. The Graceful Lord, with His Grace, bestows gifts, says Nanak.

Comments :

According to Guru Nanak Dev, the Lord is Infinite. He is Endless, Limitless and Boundless. There is no end to all His doings. None can know His Limits which are known only to the Lord Himself. None can describe His Greatness and Loftness. He is Graceful and Beneficent.

Twenty-fifth Stanza

Text :

ਬਹੁਤਾ ਕਰਮੁ ਲਿਖਿਆ ਨਾ ਜਾਇ ॥
ਵਡਾ ਦਾਤਾ ਤਿਲੁ ਨ ਤਮਾਇ ॥
ਕੇਤੇ ਮੰਗਹਿ ਜੋਧ ਅਪਾਰ ॥
ਕੇਤਿਆ ਗਣਤ ਨਹੀ ਵੀਚਾਰੁ ॥
ਕੇਤੇ ਖਪਿ ਤੁਟਹਿ ਵੇਕਾਰ ॥
ਕੇਤੇ ਲੈ ਲੈ ਮੁਕਰਿ ਪਾਹਿ ॥
ਕੇਤੇ ਮੂਰਖ ਖਾਹੀ ਖਾਹਿ ॥
ਕੇਤਿਆ ਦੂਖ ਭੂਖ ਸਦ ਮਾਰ ॥
ਏਹਿ ਭਿ ਦਾਤਿ ਤੇਰੀ ਦਾਤਾਰ ॥
ਬੰਦਿ ਖਲਾਸੀ ਭਾਣੈ ਹੋਇ ॥
ਹੋਰੁ ਆਖਿ ਨ ਸਕੈ ਕੋਇ ॥
ਜੇ ਕੋ ਖਾਇਕੁ ਆਖਣਿ ਪਾਇ ॥
ਓਹੁ ਜਾਣੈ ਜੇਤੀਆ ਮੁਹਿ ਖਾਇ ॥
ਆਪੇ ਜਾਣੈ ਆਪੇ ਦੇਇ ॥
ਆਖਹਿ ਸਿ ਭਿ ਕੇਈ ਕੇਇ ॥
ਜਿਸ ਨੋ ਬਖਸੇ ਸਿਫਤਿ ਸਾਲਾਹ ॥
ਨਾਨਕ ਪਾਤਿਸਾਹੀ ਪਾਤਿਸਾਹੁ ॥੨੫॥

Transliteration :

Bahutā karamu likhiā nā jāi.
Vadā dātā tilu na tamāi.

Kete maṁgahi jodh apār.
Ketiā gaṇat nahī vīcāru.
Kete khapi tuṭahi vekār.
Kete lai lai mukari pāhi.
Kete mūrakh khāhī khāhi.
Ketiā dūkh bhūkh sad mār.
Ehi bhi dāti terī dātār.
Baṁdi khalāsī bhāṇai hoi.
Horu ākhi na sakai koi.
Je ko khāiku ākhaṇi pāi.
Ohu jāṇai jetiā muhi khāi.
Āpe jāṇai āpe dei.
Ākhahi si bhi keī kei.
Jis no bakhse siphati sālāh.
Nānak pātisāhī pātisāhu.25.

Glossary :

ਬਹੁਤਾ—much, too much ; ਕਰਮੁ—Grace ; ਲਿਖਿਆ ਨ ਜਾਇ—cannot be written ; ਵਡਾ—great ; ਦਾਤਾ—Giver, Donor ; ਤਿਲੁ—sesame seed, very small quantity ; ਤਮਾਇ—greed ; ਕੇਤੇ—many ; ਮੰਗਹਿ—beg ; ਜੋਧ—warrior ; ਅਪਾਰ—very great, Infinite Lord ; ਕੇਤਿਆ—many ; ਗਣਤ—reckoning, accounting ; ਨਹੀ—not ; ਵੀਚਾਰੁ—think, ponder ; ਖਪਿ—to pine, to worry ; ਤੁਟਹਿ—break; ਵੇਕਾਰ—vice ; ਲੈ ਲੈ—take ; ਮੁਕਰਿ ਪਾਹਿ—deny ; ਮੂਰਖ—fools ; ਖਾਹੀ ਖਾਹਿ—continue eating ; ਦੂਖ—sorrow ; ਭੂਖ—hunger ; ਸਦ—perpetual ; ਮਾਰ—chastisement ; ਏਹਿ—this ; ਭਿ—also ; ਦਾਤਿ—gift ; ਤੇਰੀ—Yours, Thine ; ਦਾਤਾਰ—Giver, Bestower ; ਬੰਦਿ—bondage ; ਖਲਾਸੀ—freedom ; ਭਾਣੈ—Will ; ਹੋਇ—happens ; ਹੋਰੁ—other, else ; ਆਖਿ ਨ ਸਕੈ—cannot describe ; ਕੋਇ—anything ; ਕੋ—any ; ਖਾਇਕੁ—Boaster, prattler ; ਆਖਣਿ ਪਾਇ—makes bold to speak ; ਓਹੁ—he ; ਜੇਤੀਆ—how many ; ਮੁਹਿ ਖਾਇ—receives on the face ; ਆਪੇ—Himself ; ਦੇਇ—gives ; ਆਖਹਿ—describe, acknowledge ; ਸਿ—they ; ਭਿ—also ; ਕੇਈ ਕੇਇ—several ; ਜਿਸਨੋ—to whom ; ਬਖਸੇ—grants ; ਸਿਫਤਿ ਸਾਲਾਹ—praises ; ਪਾਤਿਸਾਹੀ—of kings ; ਪਾਤਿਸਾਹੁ—kings.

Translation :

His Graces are so many that they cannot be written. He is a Great Benefactor and has not even an iota of greed. Many a great warriors beg from Him. Those many are beyond reckoning and thinking. Many of them deplete themselves in vices. Many of them taking everything, also deny having taken. There are many fools who continue eating. There are many who undergo sorrow, hunger and perpetual chastisement, but O Beneficent Lord, this is also Thy gift. The bondage and freedom both happen under Thy Will. Nothing else can be described. If any prattler makes bold to speak, he only knows how many blows he receives on his face. The Lord Himself knows and Himself gives. Several people acknowledge His Munificence. He to whom the Lord grants His Praises, he is verily the king of kings.

Comments :

In this stanza, Guru Nanak Dev, lays emphasis on the bounties of the Gracious and Generous Lord. He is the Greatest Donor and Giver. Every one begs from Him. He continues to give, but there are many who even deny having received anything from Him. The sorrow, hunger and chastisement are also His Gifts because they are blessings in disguise. Everything occurs according to His Will. His Munificence is inexpressible. That person is really great, who sings the Praises of the Almighty.

Twenty-sixth Stanza

Text :

ਅਮੁਲ ਗੁਣ ਅਮੁਲ ਵਾਪਾਰ ॥
ਅਮੁਲ ਵਾਪਾਰੀਏ ਅਮੁਲ ਭੰਡਾਰ ॥
ਅਮੁਲ ਆਵਹਿ ਅਮੁਲ ਲੈ ਜਾਹਿ ॥
ਅਮੁਲ ਭਾਇ ਅਮੁਲਾ ਸਮਾਹਿ ॥
ਅਮੁਲੁ ਧਰਮੁ ਅਮੁਲੁ ਦੀਬਾਣੁ ॥
ਅਮੁਲੁ ਤੁਲੁ ਅਮੁਲੁ ਪਰਵਾਣੁ ॥
ਅਮੁਲੁ ਬਖਸੀਸ ਅਮੁਲੁ ਨੀਸਾਣੁ ॥
ਅਮੁਲੁ ਕਰਮੁ ਅਮੁਲੁ ਫੁਰਮਾਣੁ ॥
ਅਮੁਲੋ ਅਮੁਲੁ ਆਖਿਆ ਨ ਜਾਇ ॥
ਆਖਿ ਆਖਿ ਰਹੇ ਲਿਵ ਲਾਇ ॥
ਆਖਹਿ ਵੇਦ ਪਾਠ ਪੁਰਾਣ ॥
ਆਖਹਿ ਪੜੇ ਕਰਹਿ ਵਖਿਆਣ ॥
ਆਖਹਿ ਬਰਮੇ ਆਖਹਿ ਇੰਦ ॥
ਆਖਹਿ ਗੋਪੀ ਤੈ ਗੋਵਿੰਦ ॥
ਆਖਹਿ ਈਸਰ ਆਖਹਿ ਸਿਧ ॥

ਆਖਹਿ ਕੇਤੇ ਕੀਤੇ ਬੁਧ ॥
ਆਖਹਿ ਦਾਨਵ ਆਖਹਿ ਦੇਵ ॥
ਆਖਹਿ ਸੁਰਿ ਨਰ ਮੁਨਿ ਜਨ ਸੇਵ ॥
ਕੇਤੇ ਆਖਹਿ ਆਖਣਿ ਪਾਹਿ ॥
ਕੇਤੇ ਕਹਿ ਕਹਿ ਉਠਿ ਉਠਿ ਜਾਹਿ ॥
ਏਤੇ ਕੀਤੇ ਹੋਰਿ ਕਰੇਹਿ ॥
ਤਾ ਆਖਿ ਨ ਸਕਹਿ ਕੇਈ ਕੇਇ ॥
ਜੇਵਡੁ ਭਾਵੈ ਤੇਵਡੁ ਹੋਇ ॥
ਨਾਨਕ ਜਾਣੈ ਸਾਚਾ ਸੋਇ ॥
ਜੇ ਕੋ ਆਖੈ ਬੋਲੁ ਵਿਗਾੜੁ ॥
ਤਾ ਲਿਖੀਐ ਸਿਰਿ ਗਾਵਾਰਾ ਗਾਵਾਰੁ ॥੨੬॥

Transliteration :

Amul guṇ amul vāpār.
Amul vāparie amul bhaṁḍār.
Amul āvaḥi amul lai jāhi.
Amul bhāi amulā samāhi.
Amulu dharamu amulu dībāṇu.
Amulu tulu amulu parvāṇu.
Amul bakhsīs amulu nīsāṇu.
Amulu karamu amulu phurmāṇu.
Amulo amulu ākhiā na jāi.
Ākhi ākhi rahe liv lāi.
Ākhahi ved pāṭh Purāṇ.
Ākhahi paṛe karahi vakhiāṇ.
Ākhahi Barme ākhahi Iṁd.
Ākhahi gopī tai Goviṁd.
Ākhahi Īsar ākhahi sidh.
Ākhahi kete kīte budh.
Ākhahi dānav ākhahi dev.
Ākhahi suri nar muni jan sev.
Kete ākhahi ākhaṇi pāhi.
Kete kahi kahi uṭhi uṭhi jāhi.
Ete kīte hori karehi.
Tā ākhi na sakahi keī kei.
Jevaḍu bhāvai tevaḍu hoi.
Nānak jāṇai sācā soi.

Je ko ākhai bolu vigāṛu.
Tā likhīai siri gāvārā gāvāru.26.

Glossary :

ਅਮੁਲ—priceless, invaluable ; ਗੁਣ—quality, merit ; ਵਾਪਾਰ—trade ; ਵਾਪਾਰੀਏ—traders ; ਭੰਡਾਰ—stores ; ਆਵਹਿ—come ; ਲੈ ਜਾਹਿ—take away ; ਭਾਇ—love ; ਸਮਾਹਿ—absorption ; ਧਰਮੁ—Piety ; ਦੀਬਾਣੁ—court ; ਤੁਲੁ—scales ; ਪਰਵਾਣੁ—weights ; ਬਖਸੀਸ—Grace ; ਨੀਸਾਣੁ—sign, mark ; ਕਰਮੁ—action ; ਫੁਰਮਾਣੁ—command ; ਆਖਿਆ ਨ ਜਾਇ—cannot be expressed ; ਆਖਿ ਆਖਿ—to speak continually ; ਰਹੇ ਲਿਵ ਲਾਇ—remain absorbed ; ਆਖਹਿ—say, speak ; ਵੇਦ—Veda ; ਪਾਠ—recitation ; ਪੁਰਾਣ—Purana ; ਪੜੇ—literate, educated ; ਕਰਹਿ ਵਖਿਆਣ—deliver discourse ; ਬਰਮੇ—Brahmas ; ਇੰਦ—Indras ; ਗੋਪੀ—Gopis, milk-maids ; ਗੋਵਿੰਦ—Krishna ; ਈਸਰ—Shiva ; ਸਿਧ—adept ; ਕੇਤੇ—many ; ਕੀਤੇ—created ; ਬੁਧ—Buddhas ; ਦਾਨਵ—demons ; ਦੇਵ—gods ; ਸੁਰਿ—gods, demi-gods ; ਨਰ—men ; ਮੁਨਿ—munis, silent ones ; ਜਨ—persons ; ਸੇਵ—servant, service ; ਆਖਣਿ ਪਾਹਿ—make effort to describe ; ਕਹਿ ਕਹਿ—repeatedly speak ; ਉਠਿ ਉਠਿ ਜਾਹਿ—arise and depart ; ਏਤੇ—as many ; ਹੋਰ ਕਰੇਹਿ—create many more ; ਤਾ—then ; ਆਖਿ ਨ ਸਕਹਿ—cannot describe ; ਕੇਈ ਕੇਇ—some of (Thy Attributes) ; ਜੇਵਡੁ—as great ; ਭਾਵੈ—pleases ; ਤੇਵਡੁ—so great ; ਹੋਇ—becomes ; ਸਾਚਾ—True Lord ; ਸੋਇ—That ; ਆਖੈ—says, speaks ; ਬੋਲੁ—speech ; ਵਿਗਾੜੁ—impaired ; ਲਿਖੀਐ—described ; ਸਿਰਿ—(at the) head of ; ਗਾਵਾਰਾ ਗਾਵਾਰੁ—foolish of the foolish, most foolish.

Translation :

The qualities of the Lord are Invaluable. Those who trade in these qualities, they are also invaluable. Such traders and stores are invaluable. Those who come and take away the commodities of such stores are invaluable. Those who love and are absorbed in such works are invaluable. Their piety and their court are invaluable. Their scales and weights are invaluable. Their Grace and sign are invaluable. Their action and command are invaluable. Everything about them is invaluable and also inexpressible. Those who speak continually also remain absorbed. The Vedas and Puranas also talk about the Lord through their recitation. The educated also talk by delivering discourses. The Brahmas, Indras, Gopis and Krishnas also talk. The Shivas, adepts and many created Buddhas also talk. The demons, gods, demi-gods, men and munis (sages) talk while serving Him (the

Lord). Many people talk and many make effort to talk. Many repeatedly talk, arise and depart. If many more are created, even then they canot describe God's Attributes. Howsoever Great in size He wishes to become, He becomes. Only that True Lord knows this Himself. If anyone makes an impaired speech about the Lord, then he may be described as most foolish.

Comments :

This stanza describes the pricelessness and the Greatness of the Attributes of God. Those who trade in these godly qualities are also great. Many people talk about these qualities, but they are inexpressible. The Lord is much greater and beyond description. He can become as Great as He likes. It is foolish to talk ill of Him.

TWENTY-SEVENTH STANZA

Text :

ਸੋ ਦਰੁ ਕੇਹਾ ਸੋ ਘਰੁ ਕੇਹਾ ਜਿਤੁ ਬਹਿ ਸਰਬ ਸਮਾਲੇ ॥
ਵਾਜੇ ਨਾਦ ਅਨੇਕ ਅਸੰਖਾ ਕੇਤੇ ਵਾਵਣਹਾਰੇ ॥
ਕੇਤੇ ਰਾਗ ਪਰੀ ਸਿਉ ਕਹੀਅਨਿ ਕੇਤੇ ਗਾਵਣਹਾਰੇ ॥
ਗਾਵਹਿ ਤੁਹਨੋ ਪਉਣੁ ਪਾਣੀ ਬੈਸੰਤਰੁ ਗਾਵੈ ਰਾਜਾ ਧਰਮੁ ਦੁਆਰੇ ॥
ਗਾਵਹਿ ਚਿਤੁ ਗੁਪਤੁ ਲਿਖਿ ਜਾਣਹਿ ਲਿਖਿ ਲਿਖਿ ਧਰਮੁ ਵੀਚਾਰੇ ॥
ਗਾਵਹਿ ਈਸਰੁ ਬਰਮਾ ਦੇਵੀ ਸੋਹਨਿ ਸਦਾ ਸਵਾਰੇ ॥
ਗਾਵਹਿ ਇੰਦ ਇਦਾਸਣਿ ਬੈਠੇ ਦੇਵਤਿਆ ਦਰਿ ਨਾਲੇ ॥
ਗਾਵਹਿ ਸਿਧ ਸਮਾਧੀ ਅੰਦਰਿ ਗਾਵਨਿ ਸਾਧ ਵਿਚਾਰੇ ॥
ਗਾਵਨਿ ਜਤੀ ਸਤੀ ਸੰਤੋਖੀ ਗਾਵਹਿ ਵੀਰ ਕਰਾਰੇ ॥
ਗਾਵਨਿ ਪੰਡਿਤ ਪੜਨਿ ਰਖੀਸਰ ਜੁਗੁ ਜੁਗੁ ਵੇਦਾ ਨਾਲੇ ॥
ਗਾਵਹਿ ਮੋਹਣੀਆ ਮਨੁ ਮੋਹਨਿ ਸੁਰਗਾ ਮਛ ਪਇਆਲੇ ॥
ਗਾਵਨਿ ਰਤਨ ਉਪਾਏ ਤੇਰੇ ਅਠਸਠਿ ਤੀਰਥ ਨਾਲੇ ॥
ਗਾਵਹਿ ਜੋਧ ਮਹਾ ਬਲ ਸੂਰਾ ਗਾਵਹਿ ਖਾਣੀ ਚਾਰੇ ॥
ਗਾਵਹਿ ਖੰਡ ਮੰਡਲ ਵਰਭੰਡਾ ਕਰਿ ਕਰਿ ਰਖੇ ਧਾਰੇ ॥
ਸੇਈ ਤੁਧਨੋ ਗਾਵਹਿ ਜੋ ਤੁਧੁ ਭਾਵਨਿ ਰਤੇ ਤੇਰੇ ਭਗਤ ਰਸਾਲੇ ॥
ਹੋਰਿ ਕੇਤੇ ਗਾਵਨਿ ਸੇ ਮੈ ਚਿਤਿ ਨ ਆਵਨਿ ਨਾਨਕੁ ਕਿਆ ਵੀਚਾਰੇ ॥
ਸੋਈ ਸੋਈ ਸਦਾ ਸਚੁ ਸਾਹਿਬੁ ਸਾਚਾ ਸਾਚੀ ਨਾਈ ॥
ਹੈ ਭੀ ਹੋਸੀ ਜਾਇ ਨ ਜਾਸੀ ਰਚਨਾ ਜਿਨਿ ਰਚਾਈ ॥
ਰੰਗੀ ਰੰਗੀ ਭਾਤੀ ਕਰਿ ਕਰਿ ਜਿਨਸੀ ਮਾਇਆ ਜਿਨਿ ਉਪਾਈ ॥

ਕਰਿ ਕਰਿ ਵੇਖੈ ਕੀਤਾ ਆਪਣਾ ਜਿਵ ਤਿਸ ਦੀ ਵਡਿਆਈ ॥
ਜੋ ਤਿਸੁ ਭਾਵੈ ਸੋਈ ਕਰਸੀ ਹੁਕਮੁ ਨ ਕਰਣਾ ਜਾਈ ॥
ਸੋ ਪਾਤਿਸਾਹੁ ਸਾਹਾ ਪਾਤਿਸਾਹਿਬੁ ਨਾਨਕ ਰਹਣੁ ਰਜਾਈ ॥੨੭॥

Transliteration :

So daru kehā so gharu kehā jitu bahi sarab samāle.
Vāje nād anek asaṁkhā kete vāvaṇhāre.
Kete rāg parī siu kahīani kete gāvaṇhāre.
Gāvahi tuhano pauṇu pāṇī baisaṁtaru gāvai rājā dharamu duāre.
Gāvahi citu gupatu likhi jāṇahi likhi likhi dharamu vīcāre.
Gāvahi Īsaru Baramā Devī sohani sadā sawāre.
Gāvahi Iṁd Iṁdāsaṇi baiṭhe devtiā dari nāle.
Gāvahi Sidh samādhī aṁdari gāvani sādh vicāre.
Gāvani jatī satī saṁtokhī gāvahi vīr karāre.
Gāvani Paṁḍit paṛani rakhīsar jugu jugu vedā nāle.
Gāvahi mohaṇīā manu mohani surgā mach piāle.
Gāvani ratan upāe tere aṭhsaṭhi tīrath nāle.
Gāvahi jodh mahā bal sūrā gāvahi khāṇī cāre.
Gāvahi khaṁḍ maṁḍal varabhaṁḍā kari kari rakhe dhāre.
Seī tudhno gāvahi jo tudu bhāvani rate tere bhagat rasāle.
Hori kete gāvani se mai citi na āvani Nānaku kiā vīcāre.
Soī soī sadā sacu sāhibu sācā sācī nāī.
Hai bhī hosī jāi na jāsī racnā jini racāī.
Raṁgī raṁgī bhātī kari kari jinsī māiā jini upāī.
Kari kari vekhai kītā āpaṇā jiv tis dī vaḍiāī.
Jo tisu bhāvai soī karasī hukamu na karaṇā jāī.
So pātisāhu sāhā pātisāhibu Nānak rahaṇu rajāī.27.

Glossary :

ਸੋ—That ; ਦਰੁ—gate ; ਕੇਹਾ—which, what ; ਘਰੁ—house ; ਜਿਤੁ—wherein ; ਬਹਿ—sit ; ਸਰਬ—all ; ਸਮਾਲੇ—take care ; ਵਾਜੇ—resound ; ਨਾਦ—musical instruments ; ਅਨੇਕ—many ; ਅਸੰਖਾ—numberless ; ਕੇਤੇ—many ; ਵਾਵਣਹਾਰੇ—musicians ; ਰਾਗ—ragas, musical modes ; ਪਰੀ—fairy ; ਸਿਉ—with ; ਕਹੀਅਨਿ—described ; ਗਾਵਣਹਾਰੇ—singers ; ਗਾਵਹਿ—sing ; ਤੁਹਨੋ—Thee ; ਪਉਣੁ—wind ; ਪਾਣੀ—water ; ਬੈਸੰਤਰੁ—fire ; ਗਾਵੈ—sings ; ਰਾਜਾ ਧਰਮੁ—Dharmaraja, the King-Justiciar ; ਦੁਆਰੇ—at the door ; ਚਿਤੁ ਗੁਪਤੁ—the recording angels ; ਲਿਖਿ ਜਾਣਹਿ—know to write ; ਲਿਖਿ ਲਿਖਿ—continuously write ; ਧਰਮੁ—justiciar ; ਵੀਚਾਰੇ—adjudicates ;

ਈਸਰੁ—Shiva ; ਬਰਮਾ—Brahma ; ਦੇਵੀ—goddess ; ਸੋਹਨਿ—adorn ; ਸਦਾ—ever ; ਸਵਾਰੇ—bedecked ; ਇੰਦ—Indra ; ਇੰਦਾਸਣਿ—The Throne of Indra ; ਬੈਠੇ—seated ; ਦੇਵਤਿਆ—gods ; ਦਰਿ—gate ; ਨਾਲੇ—with ; ਸਿਧ—adept ; ਸਮਾਧੀ—abstract meditation ; ਅੰਦਰਿ—in ; ਗਾਵਨਿ—sing ; ਸਾਧ— saints ; ਵਿਚਾਰੇ—in (their) reflection ; ਜਤੀ—continent ; ਸਤੀ—true ; ਸੰਤੋਖੀ—contented ; ਵੀਰ—warriors ; ਕਰਾਰੇ—fearless ; ਪੰਡਿਤ—Pundit ; ਪੜਨਿ—reader, reading ; ਰਖੀਸਰ—sages ; ਜੁਗੁ—age ; ਵੇਦਾ—Vedas ; ਨਾਲੇ—with ; ਮੋਹਣੀਆ—enchanting damsels ; ਮਨੁ ਮੋਹਨਿ— captivating the mind ; ਸੁਰਗਾ—heavens ; ਮਛ—fish connoting creatures of this world ; ਪਇਆਲੇ—nether world ; ਰਤਨ—gems ; ਉਪਾਏ—created ; ਤੇਰੇ—Thine ; ਅਠਸਠਿ—sixty-eight ; ਤੀਰਥ—place of pilgrimage ; ਜੋਧ—warrior ; ਮਹਾਬਲ—mighty ; ਸੂਰਾ—hero ; ਖਾਣੀ— source of creation ; ਚਾਰੇ—four ; ਖੰਡ—region ; ਮੰਡਲ—sphere ; ਵਰਭੰਡਾ—universe ; ਕਰਿ ਕਰਿ—created ; ਰਖੇ ਧਾਰੇ—installed ; ਸੇਈ— they ; ਤੁਧਨੋ—Thee ; ਜੋ—who ; ਭਾਵਨਿ—please ; ਰਤੇ—absorbed, steeped ; ਭਗਤ—saints, devotees ; ਰਸਾਲੇ—lucid, absorbed in blissful love ; ਹੋਰਿ—others ; ਕੇਤੇ—many ; ਸੇ—they ; ਮੈ—to me ; ਚਿਤਿ—mind ; ਨ—not ; ਆਵਨਿ—come ; ਕਿਆ—what, how ; ਵੀਚਾਰੇ—think, reflect ; ਸੋਈ—that ; ਸਚੁ—true ; ਸਾਹਿਬੁ—Lord ; ਸਾਚਾ ਸਾਚੀ—true ; ਨਾਈ—Name ; ਹੈ ਭੀ—is ; ਹੋਸੀ—will be ; ਜਾਇ ਨ ਜਾਸੀ—will not perish ; ਰਚਨਾ—creation ; ਜਿਨਿ—who ; ਰਚਾਈ—created ; ਰੰਗੀ ਰੰਗੀ— of various colours ; ਭਾਤੀ—types, kinds ; ਕਰਿ ਕਰਿ—creating ; ਜਿਨਸੀ—whose ; ਮਾਇਆ—Maya, mammon ; ਜਿਨਿ—who ; ਉਪਾਈ—created ; ਵੇਖੈ—sees ; ਕੀਤਾ—creation ; ਆਪਣਾ—His ; ਜਿਵ—as ; ਤਿਸ ਦੀ—His ; ਵਡਿਆਈ—greatness, honour ; ਭਾਵੈ—pleases ; ਸੋਈ—that ; ਕਰਸੀ—will do ; ਹੁਕਮੁ—order ; ਨ ਕਰਣਾ ਜਾਈ—cannot be done ; ਸੋ—He ; ਪਾਤਿਸਾਹੁ—king ; ਸਾਹਾ ਪਾਤਿਸਾਹਿਬੁ—king of kings ; ਰਹਣੁ—remain ; ਰਜਾਈ—Will.

Translation :

In what type of Abode the Lord lives and what type of gate it has, wherein the Lord sits and takes care of all (the creation) ? Many and innumerable musical instruments resound there and many are the musicians. There are many musical modes described as fairies and there are many singers. O Lord, the wind, water and fire sing (Thy Praises) there. The god of justice sings Thy Praises at that Door. The recording angels (Citra and Gupta), who know the art of writing and who continuously write about the deeds of beings and whose accounts are adjudicated by the Justiciar, they also sing Thy Praises. Shiva, Brahma, and the goddess also sing, who adorn Thy Abode, always bedecked. Indras seated on their thrones alongwith gods sing

Thy Praises at Thy Gate. The adepts in trance and the saints in their reflection sing Thy Praises. The Celibates, the Truthful (or virtuous), the contented and fearless warriors sing Thy Praises. The studious Pundits and great sages alongwith Vedas of various ages also sing. The enchanting damsels who captivate the mind belonging to heavens, oceans and nether regions also sing. All the gems created by Thee and the sixty-eight places of pilgrimage also sing. The warriors, mighty heroes and all the four sources of creation also sing. The regions, spheres and universes created and installed by Thee also sing. All those who are liked by Thee sing Thy Praises. Thy Lucid devotees also sing. There are many others, who do not come into my mind, also sing Thee, what should I (Nanak) reflect ? That Lord is always True, the Name of the True Lord is also True. He is and also will be, He, the creator of the world, will never perish. He has created His own Maya of diverse kinds and colours. After creating, He scans His own creation, the emblem of His own Greatness. He will do, whatever Pleases Him, He cannot be ordered. He is the Sovereign, the monarch of monarchs, we have to remain under His Will, sayeth Nanak.

Comments :

This stanza brings forth the vision of the Great Guru about the Abode of the Lord. The Guru sees all the gods, goddesses, adepts, celibates, Pundits, musicians, singers, heroes, warriors, saints, devotees, the recording angels and even those who do not come into his mind—all standing at the Gate of the Lord and singing the Praises of His Greatness. The searching eye of the Guru even sees, the elements, the Vedas, the worlds, heaven, nether regions, the places of pilgrimage—all joining the chorus of the singers of Lord's praises. The vast creation, in its entirety, comes within the Perception of the Lord. The Lord is Immortal. All else will perish, but the Lord is ever-existent. The wonder of wonders is that the Lord takes care of all his created beings, wherever they are.

TWENTY-EIGHTH STANZA

Text :

ਮੁੰਦਾ ਸੰਤੋਖੁ ਸਰਮੁ ਪਤੁ ਝੋਲੀ ਧਿਆਨ ਕੀ ਕਰਹਿ ਬਿਭੂਤਿ ॥
ਖਿੰਥਾ ਕਾਲੁ ਕੁਆਰੀ ਕਾਇਆ ਜੁਗਤਿ ਡੰਡਾ ਪਰਤੀਤਿ ॥

ਆਈ ਪੰਥੀ ਸਗਲ ਜਮਾਤੀ ਮਨਿ ਜੀਤੈ ਜਗੁ ਜੀਤੁ ॥
ਆਦੇਸੁ ਤਿਸੈ ਆਦੇਸੁ ॥
ਆਦਿ ਅਨੀਲੁ ਅਨਾਦਿ ਅਨਾਹਤਿ ਜੁਗੁ ਜੁਗੁ ਏਕੋ ਵੇਸੁ ॥੨੮॥

Transliteration :

Muṁdā saṁtokhu saramu patu jholī dhiān kī karahi bibhūti.
Khiṁthā kālu kuārī kāiā jugati ḍaṁḍā partīti.
Āī paṁthī sagal jamātī mani jītai jagu jītu.
Ādesu tisai ādesu.
Ādi anīlu anādi anāhati jugu jugu eko vesu.28.

Glossary :

ਮੁੰਦਾ—ear-ring ; ਸੰਤੋਖੁ—contentment ; ਸਰਮੁ—effort ; ਪਤੁ—the begging bowl ; ਝੋਲੀ—wallet ; ਧਿਆਨ—meditation ; ਕੀ—of ; ਕਰਹਿ—to make ; ਬਿਭੂਤਿ—ashes ; ਖਿੰਥਾ—patched coat ; ਕਾਲੁ—death ; ਕੁਆਰੀ—chaste ; ਕਾਇਆ—body ; ਜੁਗਤਿ—way, device, method ; ਡੰਡਾ—staff ; ਪਰਤੀਤਿ—faith ; ਆਈ ਪੰਥੀ—the highest sect of Yogis ; ਸਗਲ—all ; ਜਮਾਤੀ—the class or brotherhood of Yogis ; ਮਨਿ—mind ; ਜੀਤੈ—conquesting ; ਜਗੁ—world ; ਜੀਤੁ—conquest ; ਆਦੇਸੁ—obeisance, salutation ; ਤਿਸੈ—Him ; ਆਦਿ— primal ; ਅਨੀਲੁ—pure ; ਅਨਾਦਿ—without beginning ; ਅਨਾਹਤਿ—indestructible ; ਜੁਗੁ—age ; ਏਕੋ—the same ; ਵੇਸੁ—guise, vesture.

Translation :

O Yogi, make your ear-rings of contentment, the begging-bowl and wallet of effort, the ashes of meditation, the patched coat of death, the discipline of chastity, the staff of faith, consider all your sects equally high and thus conquer your mind and consequently the whole world. Make obeisance to that Lord, who is the Primal, the Pure, without beginning, indestructible and who is of the same vesture in all the ages.

Comments :

In this stanza and also in the three stanzas that follow, Guru Nanak Dev has addressed the Yogis in respect of their discipline. For the conquest of the mind and the world it is necessary to leave the practice of begging and lead an active and chaste life, full of contentment and faith and always remembering death. He should forsake his ego of superiority and meditate on the Immortal and Changeless Lord.

Twenty-ninth Stanza

Text :

ਭੁਗਤਿ ਗਿਆਨੁ ਦਇਆ ਭੰਡਾਰਣਿ ਘਟਿ ਘਟਿ ਵਾਜਹਿ ਨਾਦ ॥
ਆਪਿ ਨਾਥੁ ਨਾਥੀ ਸਭ ਜਾ ਕੀ ਰਿਧਿ ਸਿਧਿ ਅਵਰਾ ਸਾਦ ॥
ਸੰਜੋਗੁ ਵਿਜੋਗੁ ਦੁਇ ਕਾਰ ਚਲਾਵਹਿ ਲੇਖੇ ਆਵਹਿ ਭਾਗ ॥
ਆਦੇਸੁ ਤਿਸੈ ਆਦੇਸੁ ॥
ਆਦਿ ਅਨੀਲੁ ਅਨਾਦਿ ਅਨਾਹਤਿ ਜੁਗੁ ਜੁਗੁ ਏਕੋ ਵੇਸੁ ॥੨੯॥

Transliteration :

Bhugati giānu diā bhaṁdāraṇi ghaṭi ghaṭi vājahi nād.
Āpi nāthu nāthī sabh jā kī ridhi sidhi avarā sād.
Saṁjogu vijogu dui kār calāvahi lekhe āvahi bhāg.
Ādesu tisai ādesu.
Ādi anīlu anādi anāhati jugu jugu eko vesu.29.

Glossary :

ਭੁਗਤਿ—food ; ਗਿਆਨੁ—knowledge ; ਦਇਆ—mercy ; ਭੰਡਾਰਣਿ—female storekeeper ; ਘਟਿ ਘਟਿ—in every heart ; ਵਾਜਹਿ—resounds ; ਨਾਦ—sound, music ; ਆਪਿ—Himself ; ਨਾਥੁ—Lord ; ਨਾਥੀ—controlled, snaffled ; ਸਭ—all ; ਜਾ ਕੀ—whose ; ਰਿਧਿ—riches ; ਸਿਧਿ—miracles ; ਅਵਰਾ—other ; ਸਾਦ—relish ; ਸੰਜੋਗੁ—union ; ਵਿਜੋਗੁ—separation ; ਦੁਇ—both ; ਕਾਰ—work, business ; ਚਲਾਵਹਿ—run, regulate ; ਲੇਖੇ—account, share ; ਆਵਹਿ—obtain ; ਭਾਗ—destiny.

Translation :

Mercy is the storekeeper of the Lord, the food is of knowledge and in every heart resounds the divine music. The whole world is controlled by the Lord Himself. O Yogi, then performance of miracles has not the divine relish. The work of union and separation is run according to Writ of the Lord, whom we should make obeisance and who is the Primal, the Pure, without beginning and indestructible Lord and who is of the same vesture in all the ages.

Comments :

When everything is controlled by the Lord Himself, who is compassionate and Giver of knowledge, then the ego of a yogi resulting in the performance of miracles is working against the Will of the Lord, which is not liked by Him. Performance of miracles is thus not in consonance with the Will of the Lord, hence it is forbidden by guru Nanak Dev. The union and separation occur only according to the Will of the Lord.

THIRTIETH STANZA

Text :

ਏਕਾ ਮਾਈ ਜੁਗਤਿ ਵਿਆਈ ਤਿਨਿ ਚੇਲੇ ਪਰਵਾਣੁ ॥
ਇਕੁ ਸੰਸਾਰੀ ਇਕੁ ਭੰਡਾਰੀ ਇਕੁ ਲਾਏ ਦੀਬਾਣੁ ॥
ਜਿਵ ਤਿਸੁ ਭਾਵੈ ਤਿਵੈ ਚਲਾਵੈ ਜਿਵ ਹੋਵੈ ਫੁਰਮਾਣੁ ॥
ਓਹੁ ਵੇਖੈ ਓਨਾ ਨਦਰਿ ਨ ਆਵੈ ਬਹੁਤਾ ਏਹੁ ਵਿਡਾਣੁ ॥
ਆਦੇਸੁ ਤਿਸੈ ਆਦੇਸੁ ॥
ਆਦਿ ਅਨੀਲੁ ਅਨਾਦਿ ਅਨਾਹਤਿ ਜੁਗੁ ਜੁਗੁ ਏਕੋ ਵੇਸੁ ॥੩੦॥

Transliteration :

Ekā māī jugati viāī tini cele paravāṇu.
Iku saṁsārī iku bhaṁḍārī iku lāe dībāṇu.
Jiv tisu bhāvai tivai calāvai jiv hovai phurmāṇu.
Ohu vekhai onā nadari na āvai bahutā ehu viḍāṇu.
Ādesu tisai ādesu.
Ādi anīlu anādi anāhati jugu jugu eko vesu.30.

Glossary :

ਏਕਾ—the one ; ਮਾਈ—maya, mother ; ਜੁਗਤਿ—method, plan ; ਵਿਆਈ—became pregnant ; ਤਿਨਿ—three ; ਚੇਲੇ—disciples ; ਪਰਵਾਣੁ—approved ; ਇਕੁ—one ; ਸੰਸਾਰੀ—creator of the world ; ਭੰਡਾਰੀ—sustainer of the world ; ਲਾਏ ਦੀਬਾਣੁ—holds His court for judgment ; ਜਿਵ—as ; ਤਿਸੁ—Him ; ਭਾਵੈ—pleases ; ਤਿਵੈ—in the same manner ; ਚਲਾਵੈ—runs, drives, directs ; ਹੋਵੈ—to come about ; ਫੁਰਮਾਣੁ—command, order ; ਓਹੁ—He ; ਵੇਖੈ—sees ; ਓਨਾ—they ; ਨਦਰਿ ਨ ਆਵੈ—do not see, is not seen ; ਬਹੁਤਾ—great ; ਏਹੁ—this ; ਵਿਡਾਣੁ—wonder.

Translation :

The one maya became pregnant according to Lord's Plan and gave birth to three approved disciples, the one creates the world, the other sustains it and third one holds the court (for judgment). The Lord directs them and commands them as it pleases Him. He sees them but He is not perceived by them, this is a great wonder. We should make obeisance to that Lord who is the Primal, the Pure, without beginning and Indestructible and who is of the same vesture in all ages.

Comments :

Maya according to the Lord's Plan, conceived three modes

represented by Brahma the Creator, Vishnu the Preserver and Shiva the Adjudicator. These modes work according to the direction and Will of the Lord. The Lord scans them, but they cannot see Him, a very wonderful thing. Guru Nanak Dev in this stanza, clearly states that all the gods or forces act under the direction and Will of the Lord.

THIRTY-FIRST STANZA

Text :

ਆਸਣੁ ਲੋਇ ਲੋਇ ਭੰਡਾਰ ॥
ਜੋ ਕਿਛੁ ਪਾਇਆ ਸੁ ਏਕਾ ਵਾਰ ॥
ਕਰਿ ਕਰਿ ਵੇਖੈ ਸਿਰਜਣਹਾਰੁ ॥
ਨਾਨਕ ਸਚੇ ਕੀ ਸਾਚੀ ਕਾਰ ॥
ਆਦੇਸੁ ਤਿਸੈ ਆਦੇਸੁ ॥
ਆਦਿ ਅਨੀਲੁ ਅਨਾਦਿ ਅਨਾਹਤਿ ਜੁਗੁ ਜੁਗੁ ਏਕੋ ਵੇਸੁ ॥੩੧॥

Transliteration :

Āsaṇu loi loi bhanḍār.
Jo kichu pāiā su ekā vār.
Kari kari vekhai Sirjaṇhāru.
Nānak sace kī sācī kār.
Ādesu tisai ādesu.
Ādi anīlu anādi anāhati jugu jugu eko vesu.31.

Glossary :

ਆਸਣੁ—seat ; ਲੋਇ—world ; ਭੰਡਾਰ—store-house ; ਜੋ ਕਿਛੁ— whatever ; ਪਾਇਆ—obtained ; ਸੁ—that ; ਏਕਾ ਵਾਰ—once ; ਕਰਿ ਕਰਿ—create ; ਵੇਖੈ—sees ; ਸਿਰਜਣਹਾਰੁ—creator ; ਸਚੇ—The True Lord ; ਕੀ—of ; ਸਾਚੀ—true ; ਕਾਰ—work.

Translation :

All the worlds are the seats and store-houses of the Lord, which he has filled once for all. The Creator Lord Himself scans them. The True Lord's working is also True. We should make obeisance to Him, who is the Primal, the Pure, the beginningless and Indestructible and who is of the same vesture in all the ages.

Comments :

Guru Nanak Dev in this stanza makes a mention of the two-fold importance of the worlds. Firstly they are the abodes of the Lord and secondly they are also the store-houses under the over-all care of the Lord. The Lord Himself scans all His doing which is a Reality and not an Illusion.

THIRTY-SECOND STANZA

Text :

ਇਕ ਦੂ ਜੀਭੌ ਲਖ ਹੋਹਿ ਲਖ ਹੋਵਹਿ ਲਖ ਵੀਸ ॥
ਲਖੁ ਲਖੁ ਗੇੜਾ ਆਖੀਅਹਿ ਏਕੁ ਨਾਮੁ ਜਗਦੀਸ ॥
ਏਤੁ ਰਾਹਿ ਪਤਿ ਪਵੜੀਆ ਚੜੀਐ ਹੋਇ ਇਕੀਸ ॥
ਸੁਣਿ ਗਲਾ ਆਕਾਸ ਕੀ ਕੀਟਾ ਆਈ ਰੀਸ ॥
ਨਾਨਕ ਨਦਰੀ ਪਾਈਐ ਕੂੜੀ ਕੂੜੈ ਠੀਸ ॥੩੨॥

Transliteration :

Ik dū jībhau lakh hohi lakh hovahi lakh vīs.
Lakhu lakhu geṛā ākhīahi eku nāmu jagadīs.
Etu rāhi pati pavaṛīā caṛīai hoi ikīs.
Suṇi galā ākās kī kīṭā āī rīs.
Nānak nadarī pāīai kūṛī kūṛai ṭhīs.32.

Glossary :

ਇਕ ਦੂ—from one ; ਜੀਭੌ—tongue ; ਲਖ—lakh ; ਹੋਹਿ—become ; ਹੋਵਹਿ—become ; ਵੀਸ—twenty ; ਗੇੜਾ—times ; ਆਖੀਅਹਿ—repeated ; ਏਕੁ—one ; ਨਾਮੁ—Name (of the Lord) ; ਜਗਦੀਸ—Lord, Master of the World ; ਏਤੁ—in this ; ਰਾਹਿ—way ; ਪਤਿ—honour, husband ; ਪਵੜੀਆ—rungs of the ladder ; ਚੜੀਐ—ascend ; ਹੋਇ—become ; ਇਕੀਸ—one with the Lord ; ਸੁਣਿ—hearing ; ਗਲਾ—talk ; ਆਕਾਸ— sky, heaven ; ਕੀ—of ; ਕੀਟਾ—worms ; ਆਈ ਰੀਸ—wanted to emulate ; ਨਦਰੀ—through grace ; ਪਾਈਐ—obtain ; ਕੂੜੀ—false ; ਕੂੜੈ—false (person) ; ਠੀਸ—boast.

Translation :

If one tongue increases to one lakh tongues and one lakh tongues become twenty lakhs. Then with each tongue the Name of the Lord is repeated one lakh times. In this way, one may ascend the rungs of the ladder of honour and become one with the Lord. But the insects try to imitate after listening to the talk of heaven. The boast of false persons is false, only the attainment is through Grace (of the Lord), saith Nanak.

Comments :

In this stanza, Guru Nanak Dev tells us about the merit of repeating the Name of the Lord. It ultimately leads the devotee towards the unity with the Lord. One who imitates the true devotee and boasts falsely, achieves nothing. There can be no achievement without the Grace of the Lord.

Thirty-third Stanza

Text :

ਆਖਣਿ ਜੋਰੁ ਚੁਪੈ ਨਹ ਜੋਰੁ ॥
ਜੋਰੁ ਨ ਮੰਗਣਿ ਦੇਣਿ ਨ ਜੋਰੁ ॥
ਜੋਰੁ ਨ ਜੀਵਣਿ ਮਰਣਿ ਨਹ ਜੋਰੁ ॥
ਜੋਰੁ ਨ ਰਾਜਿ ਮਾਲਿ ਮਨਿ ਸੋਰੁ ॥
ਜੋਰੁ ਨ ਸੁਰਤੀ ਗਿਆਨਿ ਵੀਚਾਰਿ ॥
ਜੋਰੁ ਨ ਜੁਗਤੀ ਛੁਟੈ ਸੰਸਾਰੁ ॥
ਜਿਸੁ ਹਥਿ ਜੋਰੁ ਕਰਿ ਵੇਖੈ ਸੋਇ ॥
ਨਾਨਕ ਉਤਮੁ ਨੀਚੁ ਨ ਕੋਇ ॥੩੩॥

Transliteration :

Ākhaṇi joru cupai nah joru.
Joru na mamgaṇi deṇi na joru.
Joru na jīvaṇi maraṇi na joru.
Joru na rāji māli mani soru.
Joru na suratī giāni vīcāri.
Joru na jugatī chuṭai samsāru.
Jisu hathi joru kari vekhai soi.
Nānak utamu nīcu na koi.33.

Glossary :

ਆਖਣਿ—speak ; ਜੋਰੁ—power, strength ; ਚੁਪੈ—to remain silent ; ਨ—not ; ਮੰਗਣਿ—beg , ਦੇਣਿ—give ; ਜੀਵਣਿ—life, live ; ਮਰਣਿ—death, die ; ਰਾਜਿ—rule ; ਮਾਲਿ—wealth, property ; ਮਨਿ—mind ; ਸੋਰੁ—commotion ; ਸੁਰਤੀ—understanding ; ਗਿਆਨਿ—knowledge ; ਵੀਚਾਰਿ—reflection ; ਜੁਗਤੀ— method ; ਛੁਟੈ—to be free ; ਸੰਸਾਰੁ—world ; ਜਿਸੁ—in whose ; ਹਥਿ—hand ; ਕਰਿ—exercise ; ਵੇਖੈ—see ; ਸੋਇ—He ; ਉਤਮੁ—superior ; ਨੀਚੁ—inferior ; ਕੋਇ—any.

Translation :

One cannot speak with his own strength and also cannot observe silence with his own effort. One cannot beg or give with his own strength. One cannot live or die with his own effort. One cannot rule, gain wealth or undergo commotion in his mind with his own strength. One cannot have the understanding of knowledge or reflect on it with his own effort. One cannot know the method of attaining release from the noose of the world with his own strength. He who has the strength in His own Hand, exercises and sees it. Thus there is none superior or inferior.

Comments :

All the power of doing anything is in the Hands of the Lord alone. Everything is being done in the world with the power given by the Lord. Therefore none should boast of one's own strength. It is the Lord alone who makes one superior or inferior.

THIRTY-FOURTH STANZA

Text :

ਰਾਤੀ ਰੁਤੀ ਥਿਤੀ ਵਾਰ ॥
ਪਵਣ ਪਾਣੀ ਅਗਨੀ ਪਾਤਾਲ ॥
ਤਿਸੁ ਵਿਚਿ ਧਰਤੀ ਥਾਪਿ ਰਖੀ ਧਰਮਸਾਲ ॥
ਤਿਸੁ ਵਿਚਿ ਜੀਅ ਜੁਗਤਿ ਕੇ ਰੰਗ ॥
ਤਿਨ ਕੇ ਨਾਮ ਅਨੇਕ ਅਨੰਤ ॥
ਕਰਮੀ ਕਰਮੀ ਹੋਇ ਵੀਚਾਰੁ ॥
ਸਚਾ ਆਪਿ ਸਚਾ ਦਰਬਾਰੁ ॥
ਤਿਥੈ ਸੋਹਨਿ ਪੰਚ ਪਰਵਾਣੁ ॥
ਨਦਰੀ ਕਰਮਿ ਪਵੈ ਨੀਸਾਣੁ ॥
ਕਚ ਪਕਾਈ ਓਥੈ ਪਾਇ ॥
ਨਾਨਕ ਗਇਆ ਜਾਪੈ ਜਾਇ ॥੩੪॥

Transliteration :

Rātī rutī thitī vār.
Pavaṇ pāṇī aganī pātāl.
Tisu vici dharatī thapi rakhī dharamasāl.
Tisu vici jīa jugati ke raṁg.

Tin ke nāṁ anek anaṁt.
Karamī karamī hoi vīcāru.
Sacā āpi sacā darbāru.
Tithai sohani paṁc paravāṇu.
Nadarī karami pavai nīsāṇu.
Kac pakāī othai pāi.
Nānak giā jāpai jāi.34.

Glossary :

ਰਾਤੀ—night ; ਰੁਤੀ—season ; ਥਿਤੀ—lunar day ; ਵਾਰ—week day ; ਪਵਣ—wind ; ਪਾਣੀ—water ; ਅਗਨੀ—fire ; ਪਾਤਾਲ—nether-world ; ਤਿਸੁ—that ; ਵਿਚਿ—in ; ਧਰਤੀ—earth ; ਥਾਪਿ ਰਖੀ—established ; ਧਰਮਸਾਲ—the house for practising piety ; ਜੀਅ—jiva, being ; ਜੁਗਤਿ—type ; ਕੇ—and ; ਰੰਗ—colour ; ਤਿਨ ਕੇ—their ; ਨਾਮ—names ; ਅਨੇਕ—many ; ਅਨੰਤ—infinite ; ਕਰਮੀ—action ; ਹੋਇ ਵੀਚਾਰੁ—judged ; ਸਚਾ—True ; ਆਪਿ—Himself ; ਦਰਬਾਰੁ—court ; ਤਿਥੈ—there ; ਸੋਹਨਿ—look graceful ; ਪੰਚ—chiefs, saints ; ਪਰਵਾਣੁ—approved ; ਨਦਰੀ—Graceful Lord ; ਕਰਮਿ—grace ; ਪਵੈ—obtained ; ਨੀਸਾਣੁ—mark ; ਕਚ—raw ; ਪਕਾਈ—mature ; ਓਥੈ—there ; ਪਾਇ—assayed ; ਗਇਆ—on going ; ਜਾਪੈ—seem ; ਜਾਇ—reaching.

Translation :

The earth as the abode of *Dharma*, has been established within the complex of time i.e. nights, seasons, lunar days and week days, elements i.e.wind, water and fire and also the nether world. Within this earth are beings of various types and colours, having innumerable names. These beings are judged by their actions by the True Lord in His True Court, where only the approved saints look graceful. The mark is obtained through the Grace of the Graceful Lord. The rawness and maturity are assayed and seen on reaching there, saith Nanak.

Comments :

In this stanza, Guru Nanak Dev has described the real status of the earth, in which we live. It is temporal and elemental. Its space works and moves within various phases and combinations of time and elements. It is not the only creation of God, many worlds are there beneath it. It has, in fact, been created as the abode of piety and righteousness. There are several categories of beings who reside in it. Their names are innumerable. Their actions are judged with the yard-sticks of Piety and Truth. In the True court of the True Lord, only Truth and Piety prevail and only the saints who are saturated with Truth and Piety, look graceful there. They are the mature beings, while there are many who are moving from rawness to maturity and are in the gradual state of development, according to their actions and the Grace of the Graceful Lord. This region has been named by the great Guru as the region of Piety.

THIRTY-FIFTH STANZA

Text :

ਧਰਮ ਖੰਡ ਕਾ ਏਹੋ ਧਰਮੁ ॥
ਗਿਆਨ ਖੰਡ ਕਾ ਆਖਹੁ ਕਰਮੁ ॥
ਕੇਤੇ ਪਵਣ ਪਾਣੀ ਵੈਸੰਤਰ ਕੇਤੇ ਕਾਨ ਮਹੇਸ ॥
ਕੇਤੇ ਬਰਮੇ ਘਾੜਤਿ ਘੜੀਅਹਿ ਰੂਪ ਰੰਗ ਕੇ ਵੇਸ ॥
ਕੇਤੀਆ ਕਰਮ ਭੂਮੀ ਮੇਰ ਕੇਤੇ ਕੇਤੇ ਧੂ ਉਪਦੇਸ ॥
ਕੇਤੇ ਇੰਦ ਚੰਦ ਸੂਰ ਕੇਤੇ ਕੇਤੇ ਮੰਡਲ ਦੇਸ ॥
ਕੇਤੇ ਸਿਧ ਬੁਧ ਨਾਥ ਕੇਤੇ ਕੇਤੇ ਦੇਵੀ ਵੇਸ ॥
ਕੇਤੇ ਦੇਵ ਦਾਨਵ ਮੁਨਿ ਕੇਤੇ ਕੇਤੇ ਰਤਨ ਸਮੁੰਦ ॥
ਕੇਤੀਆ ਖਾਣੀ ਕੇਤੀਆ ਬਾਣੀ ਕੇਤੇ ਪਾਤ ਨਰਿੰਦ ॥
ਕੇਤੀਆ ਸੁਰਤੀ ਸੇਵਕ ਕੇਤੇ ਨਾਨਕ ਅੰਤੁ ਨ ਅੰਤੁ ॥੩੫॥

Transliteration :

Dharam khaṁḍ kā eho dharamu.
Giān khaṁḍ kā ākhahu karamu.
Kete pavaṇ pāṇī vaisaṁtar kete kān mahes.
Kete Barame ghaṛati ghaṛīahi rūp raṁg ke ves.
Ketīā karam bhūmī mer kete kete dhū updes.
Kete Iṁd caṁd sūr kete kete maṁḍal des.
Kete sidh budh nāth kete kete devī ves.
Kete dev dānav muni kete kete ratan samuṁd.
Ketīā khāṇī ketīā bāṇī kete pāt nariṁd.
Ketīā suratī sewak kete Nānak aṁtu na aṁtu.35.

Glossary :

ਧਰਮ ਖੰਡ—the region of Piety ; ਕਾ—of ; ਏਹੋ—this ; ਧਰਮੁ—duty, characteristic ; ਗਿਆਨ ਖੰਡ—the region of knowledge ; ਆਖਹੁ—describe ,

ਕਰਮੁ—action, doing ; ਕੇਤੇ—many ; ਪਵਣ—wind ; ਪਾਣੀ—water ; ਵੈਸੰਤਰ—fire ; ਕਾਨ—Krishna, Vishnu ; ਮਹੇਸ—Shiva ; ਬਰਮੇ—Brahma ; ਘਾੜਤਿ—created forms ; ਘੜੀਅਹਿ—creating, making ; ਰੂਪ—beauty ; ਰੰਗ—colour ; ਕੇ—and ; ਵੇਸ—guise, garb ; ਕੇਤੀਆ— many ; ਕਰਮ ਭੂਮੀ—the earth of deeds ; ਮੇਰ—mountains ; ਧੂ—Dhruva (a saint) ; ਉਪਦੇਸ—instructions ; ਇੰਦ—Indra ; ਚੰਦ—moon ; ਸੂਰ—sun ; ਮੰਡਲ—sphere ; ਦੇਸ—country ; ਸਿਧ—adept ; ਬੁਧ—Buddha ; ਨਾਥ—Nath, Yogi ; ਦੇਵੀ—goddess ; ਦੇਵ—god ; ਦਾਨਵ—demon ; ਮੁਨਿ—Muni, sage ; ਰਤਨ—gem ; ਸਮੁੰਦ—sea, ocean ; ਖਾਣੀ—source of creation ; ਬਾਣੀ—source of speech ; ਪਾਤ—king ; ਨਰਿੰਦ—king ; ਸੁਰਤੀ—understanding, knowledge ; ਸੇਵਕ—servant ; ਅੰਤੁ ਨ ਅੰਤੁ—countless.

Translation :

Such is the characteristic of the region of Piety. Now I relate the functioning of the region of knowledge. In that region there are many winds, waters and fires, many Krishnas (Vishnus) and Shivas, many Brahmas creating creations of diverse forms, colours and guises, many action-oriented worlds and mountains, many Dhruvas engaged in instructions, many Indras, moons and suns, many spheres and countries, many Siddhas (adepts), Buddhas (wise men), and nāthas (yogis), many goddesses in diverse guises, many gods, demons, sages (*munis*), many gems of the ocean, many sources of creation, many types of speech, many kings and emperors and many knowledgeable servants. There is no end of them, says Nanak.

Comments :

In this stanza Guru Nanak Dev gives a view of the region of knowledge. It is a view of an unending cosmos, containing various universes consisting of many gods, goddesses, demons, sages, sources of creation, types of speech, kings and action-oriented worlds. Many elements work in many spheres and there are many creations and created beings of diverse forms, colours and guises. Such a vast panorama giving knowledge of various kinds makes one individual-self looking like an infinitesimal dot, wonder about the sublimity of the Supreme Being whose doings can never be comprehended in totality. There is a feeling of the Infinity on one hand and a very limited being on the other, giving rise to a state of egolessness.

THIRTY-SIXTH STANZA

Text :

ਗਿਆਨ ਖੰਡ ਮਹਿ ਗਿਆਨੁ ਪਰਚੰਡੁ ॥
ਤਿਥੈ ਨਾਦ ਬਿਨੋਦ ਕੋਡ ਅਨੰਦੁ ॥
ਸਰਮ ਖੰਡ ਕੀ ਬਾਣੀ ਰੂਪੁ ॥
ਤਿਥੈ ਘਾੜਤਿ ਘੜੀਐ ਬਹੁਤੁ ਅਨੂਪੁ ॥
ਤਾ ਕੀਆ ਗਲਾ ਕਥੀਆ ਨਾ ਜਾਹਿ ॥
ਜੇ ਕੋ ਕਹੈ ਪਿਛੈ ਪਛੁਤਾਇ ॥
ਤਿਥੈ ਘੜੀਐ ਸੁਰਤਿ ਮਤਿ ਮਨਿ ਬੁਧਿ ॥
ਤਿਥੈ ਘੜੀਐ ਸੁਰਾ ਸਿਧਾ ਕੀ ਸੁਧਿ ॥੩੬॥

Transliteration :

Giān khaṁḍ mahi giānu paracaṁḍu.
Tithai nād binod koḍ anaṁdu.
Saram khaṁḍ kī bāṇī rūpu.
Tithai ghāṛati ghaṛīai bahutu anūpu.
Tā kīā galā kathīā na jāhi.
Je ko kahai pichai pachutāi.
Tithai ghaṛīai surati mati mani budhi.
Tithai ghaṛīai surā sidhā kī sudhi.36.

Glossary :

ਗਿਆਨ ਖੰਡ—the region of knowledge ; ਮਹਿ—in ; ਪਰਚੰਡੁ—powerful ; ਤਿਥੈ—there ; ਨਾਦ—music, musical instrument ; ਬਿਨੋਦ—amusement ; ਕੋਡ—entertainment ; ਅਨੰਦੁ—joy, bliss ; ਸਰਮ ਖੰਡ—the region of effort ; ਕੀ—of ; ਬਾਣੀ—language, formation ; ਰੂਪੁ—beauty ; ਤਿਥੈ—there ; ਘਾੜਤਿ—created thing ; ਘੜੀਐ—created, made ; ਬਹੁਤੁ—greatly ; ਅਨੂਪੁ—incomparable ; ਤਾ—that ; ਕੀਆ—of ; ਗਲਾ—facts ; ਕਥੀਆ ਨ ਜਾਹਿ—cannot be described ; ਜੇ—if ; ਕੋ—anyone ; ਕਹੈ—speak, describe ; ਪਿਛੈ—afterwards ; ਪਛੁਤਾਇ— repents ; ਸੁਰਤਿ—consciousness ; ਮਤਿ—understanding ; ਮਨਿ—mind ; ਬੁਧਿ—intellect ; ਸੁਰਾ—gods ; ਸਿਧਾ—adepts ; ਕੀ—of ; ਸੁਧਿ—consciousness.

Translation :

In the region of knowledge, the Power of knowledge is apparent, where there is musical amusement and blissful entertainment. Then there is region of effort, which is beauty-incarnate and where very queer creation is created. Its facts cannot be described. Anyone who describes repents afterwards. There the consciousness, understanding, mind and intellect are created. There the consciousness of gods and adepts is created.

Comments :

The region of knowledge gives knowledge and the amusement, entertainment and bliss attending it. But the region of effort beautifies the mind and intellect . It is a region of practice, where the beauty of the soul becomes evident. In this region the knowledged person attains the status of a god or an adept. He is purified.

THIRTY-SEVENTH STANZA

Text :

ਕਰਮ ਖੰਡ ਕੀ ਬਾਣੀ ਜੋਰੁ ॥
ਤਿਥੈ ਹੋਰੁ ਨ ਕੋਈ ਹੋਰੁ ॥
ਤਿਥੈ ਜੋਧ ਮਹਾ ਬਲ ਸੂਰ ॥
ਤਿਨ ਮਹਿ ਰਾਮੁ ਰਹਿਆ ਭਰਪੂਰਿ ॥
ਤਿਥੈ ਸੀਤੋ ਸੀਤਾ ਮਹਿਮਾ ਮਾਹਿ ॥
ਤਾ ਕੇ ਰੂਪ ਨ ਕਥਨੇ ਜਾਹਿ ॥
ਨਾ ਓਹਿ ਮਰਹਿ ਨ ਠਾਗੇ ਜਾਹਿ ॥
ਜਿਨ ਕੈ ਰਾਮੁ ਵਸੈ ਮਨ ਮਾਹਿ ॥
ਤਿਥੈ ਭਗਤ ਵਸਹਿ ਕੇ ਲੋਅ ॥
ਕਰਹਿ ਅਨੰਦੁ ਸਚਾ ਮਨਿ ਸੋਇ ॥
ਸਚ ਖੰਡਿ ਵਸੈ ਨਿਰੰਕਾਰੁ ॥
ਕਰਿ ਕਰਿ ਵੇਖੈ ਨਦਰਿ ਨਿਹਾਲ ॥
ਤਿਥੈ ਖੰਡ ਮੰਡਲ ਵਰਭੰਡ ॥
ਜੇ ਕੋ ਕਥੈ ਤ ਅੰਤ ਨ ਅੰਤ ॥
ਤਿਥੈ ਲੋਅ ਲੋਅ ਆਕਾਰ ॥
ਜਿਵ ਜਿਵ ਹੁਕਮੁ ਤਿਵੈ ਤਿਵ ਕਾਰ ॥
ਵੇਖੈ ਵਿਗਸੈ ਕਰਿ ਵੀਚਾਰੁ ॥
ਨਾਨਕ ਕਥਨਾ ਕਰੜਾ ਸਾਰੁ ॥੩੭॥

Transliteration :

Karam khaṁḍ kī bāṇī joru.
Tithai horu na koī horu.

Tithai jodh mahā bal sūr.
Tin mahi Rāmu rahiā bharapūri.
Tithai sīto sītā mahimā māhi.
Tā ke rūp na kathane jāhi.
Na ohi marahi na ṭhāge jāhi.
Jin kai Rāmu vasai man māhi.
Tithai bhagat vasahi ke loa.
Karahi anaṁdu sacā mani soi.
Sac khaṁḍ vasai Niraṁkāru.
Kari kari vekhai nadari nihāl.
Tithai khaṁḍ maṁḍal varbhaṁḍ.
Je ko kathai ta aṁt na aṁt.
Tithai loa loa ākār.
Jiv jiv hukamu tivai tiv kār.
Vekhai vigasai kari vīcāru.
Nānak kathanā karaṛā sāru.37.

Glossary :

ਕਰਮ ਖੰਡ—the region of grace ; ਕੀ—of ; ਬਾਣੀ—language, formation ; ਜੋਰੁ—power, force ; ਤਿਥੈ—there ; ਹੋਰੁ—other ; ਨ—not ; ਕੋਈ—any ; ਜੋਧ—warrior ; ਮਹਾ ਬਲ—mighty ; ਸੂਰ—hero ; ਤਿਨ—them ; ਮਹਿ—in ; ਰਾਮੁ—God ; ਰਹਿਆ—remains ; ਭਰਪੂਰਿ—full ; ਸੀਤੋ—coldness, passionless state ; ਸੀਤਾ—sewn ; ਮਹਿਮਾ—praise (of the Lord) ; ਮਾਹਿ—in ; ਤਾ ਕੇ—their ; ਰੂਪ—beauty ; ਨ ਕਥਨੇ ਜਾਹਿ—cannot be described ; ਓਹਿ—they ; ਮਰਹਿ—die ; ਠਾਗੇ ਜਾਹਿ—cheated ; ਜਿਨ ਕੈ—whose ; ਵਸੈ—abides ; ਮਨ—mind, heart ; ਭਗਤ—devotee ; ਵਸਹਿ—abide, dwell ; ਕੇ—of ; ਲੋਅ—world ; ਕਰਹਿ ਅਨੰਦੁ—experience bliss ; ਸਚਾ—True Lord ; ਸੋਇ—He ; ਸਚ ਖੰਡਿ—the region of Truth ; ਨਿਰੰਕਾਰੁ—The Transcendent Lord ; ਕਰਿ—create ; ਵੇਖੈ—sees ; ਨਦਰਿ—grace ; ਨਿਹਾਲ—make happy ; ਖੰਡ—region ; ਮੰਡਲ—sphere ; ਵਰਭੰਡ—universe ; ਜੇ—if ; ਕੋ—anyone ; ਕਥੈ—describe ; ਤ—then ; ਅੰਤ ਨ ਅੰਤ—endless, limitless ; ਲੋਅ—world ; ਆਕਾਰ—creation ; ਜਿਵ—as ; ਹੁਕਮੁ—order ; ਤਿਵੈ—so ; ਕਾਰ—doing, function ; ਵਿਗਸੈ—be happy ; ਕਰਿ ਵੀਚਾਰੁ—contemplate ; ਕਥਨਾ—describe ; ਕਰੜਾ—hard ; ਸਾਰੁ—steel.

Translation :

Then we enter the region of grace after the region of effort. This region is power-incarnate. There is none else than the powerful ones. There are mighty spiritual warriors and heroes there who are fully saturated with the love of the Lord. There the residents are always in cool composure and drenched with the Praises of the Lord. Their beauty is inexpressible. They are immortal and undeceivable, because the Lord abides in their mind. In that region there are abodes of saints, where they experience in their minds the bliss of the True Lord.

The next region is the region of Truth, where the transcendental Lord abides, and from that region He creates and scans His creation with Grace. There are indescribable and limitless (infinite) regions, spheres and universes there. There are many worlds and creations, which work according to the Will of the Lord. He scans His creation, contemplates about it and feels happy. Its description is like chewing the hard steel.

Comments :

In this stanza two regions have been described, the region of Grace and the region of Truth. The effort done spontaneously results in Grace and Grace leads towards the unity with Truth i.e. God. When mind and intellect are purified in the region of effort, the Lord's Grace is achieved. The All-Pervading Lord catches the Pure one's arm and lifts him up. Within the Region of Truth, the Infinity becomes evident. There are innumerable universes there which are supervised by the Beneficent, Merciful, Graceful and Blissful Lord Himself. This state is inexpressible.

Guru Nanak Dev has given us a glimpse of the five spiritual stages, beginning from the stage of Piety and passing through the stages of knowledge, effort, Grace, the devotee enters the final stage of Truth. This spiritual ascent is comparable to the spiritual ascent of Sufi's where Shariat seems to be the stage of Piety, M'aarfat the stage of knowledge and Haqiqat the stage of Truth. Their state of *Malakut* may be equalised with the state of effort and the state of *Jabarut* with the state of Grace. The state of *Malakut* is the stage of angels or adepts and the state of *Jabarut* is the stage of the Power or *Jor*.

THIRTY-EIGHTH STANZA

Text :

ਜਤੁ ਪਾਹਾਰਾ ਧੀਰਜੁ ਸੁਨਿਆਰੁ ॥
ਅਹਰਣਿ ਮਤਿ ਵੇਦੁ ਹਥੀਆਰੁ ॥

ਭਉ ਖਲਾ ਅਗਨਿ ਤਪ ਤਾਉ ॥
ਭਾਂਡਾ ਭਾਉ ਅੰਮ੍ਰਿਤੁ ਤਿਤੁ ਢਾਲਿ ॥
ਘੜੀਐ ਸਬਦੁ ਸਚੀ ਟਕਸਾਲ ॥
ਜਿਨ ਕਉ ਨਦਰਿ ਕਰਮੁ ਤਿਨ ਕਾਰ ॥
ਨਾਨਕ ਨਦਰੀ ਨਦਰਿ ਨਿਹਾਲ ॥੩੮॥

Transliteration :

Jatu pāhārā dhīraju suniāru.
Aharaṇi mati vedu hathiāru.
Bhau khalā agani tap tāu.
Bhāṁḍā bhāu Aṁritu titu ḍhāli.
Ghaṛīai sabadu sacī ṭakasāl.
Jin kau nadari karamu tin kār.
Nānak nadarī nadari nihāl.38.

Glossary :

ਜਤੁ—continence ; ਪਾਹਾਰਾ—furnace ; ਧੀਰਜੁ—patience ; ਸੁਨਿਆਰੁ—goldsmith ; ਅਹਰਣਿ—anvil ; ਮਤਿ—intellect ; ਵੇਦੁ—knowledge ; ਹਥੀਆਰੁ—hammer, tool ; ਭਉ—fear ; ਖਲਾ—bellows ; ਅਗਨਿ—fire ; ਤਪ ਤਾਉ—practising austerity ; ਭਾਂਡਾ—vessel ; ਭਾਉ—love ; ਅੰਮ੍ਰਿਤੁ—nectar ; ਤਿਤੁ—in which ; ਢਾਲਿ—filter ; ਘੜੀਐ—fashion, make ; ਸਬਦੁ—Word ; ਸਚੀ—true ; ਟਕਸਾਲ—mint ; ਜਿਨ ਕਉ—to whom ; ਨਦਰਿ—sight, glare ; ਕਰਮੁ—grace ; ਤਿਨ—whose ; ਕਾਰ—work, deed ; ਨਦਰੀ—the Graceful Lord ; ਨਦਰਿ—grace ; ਨਿਹਾਲ—happy.

Translation :

The patience is the goldsmith whose furnace is of continence, the anvil of intellect, the hammer of knowledge, the bellows of Lord's Fear, the fire of austerity and the vessel of love, in which the nectar is filtered. In such a true mint the Word is fashioned. This work is done by those, who come under the graceful glances of the Lord. The Grace of the Graceful Lord keeps them in bliss.

Comments :

On the face of it this stanza gives a brief description of a goldsmith's workshop, but in fact it sums up the way of life to be led by a devotee, as envisaged by Guru Nanak Dev. The spiritual path is to be traversed with patience. The Grace of the Lord will come only when the devotee follows whole-heartedly the discipline enunciated by the Guru. This discipline is the discipline of the Name of the

Lord, which is also called the WORD given by the Guru. In the workshop of continence, when the hammer of knowledge falls on the anvil of intellect, when the fear and love of the Lord bring in His utter devotion, the Word of the Guru emerges as the elixir, whose repetition by the devotee brings in the Grace of the Lord who lifts the devotee to His Bosom as His very dear child. This is, in short, the crux of Guru Nanak Dev's religion.

THE SHLOKA AT THE END

Text :

ਸਲੋਕੁ ॥
ਪਵਣੁ ਗੁਰੂ ਪਾਣੀ ਪਿਤਾ ਮਾਤਾ ਧਰਤਿ ਮਹਤੁ ॥
ਦਿਵਸੁ ਰਾਤਿ ਦੁਇ ਦਾਈ ਦਾਇਆ ਖੇਲੈ ਸਗਲ ਜਗਤੁ ॥
ਚੰਗਿਆਈਆ ਬੁਰਿਆਈਆ ਵਾਚੈ ਧਰਮੁ ਹਦੂਰਿ ॥
ਕਰਮੀ ਆਪੋ ਆਪਣੀ ਕੇ ਨੇੜੈ ਕੇ ਦੂਰਿ ॥
ਜਿਨੀ ਨਾਮੁ ਧਿਆਇਆ ਗਏ ਮਸਕਤਿ ਘਾਲਿ ॥
ਨਾਨਕ ਤੇ ਮੁਖ ਉਜਲੇ ਕੇਤੀ ਛੁਟੀ ਨਾਲਿ ॥੧॥

Transliteration :

Saloku.
Pavaṇu gurū pāṇī pitā mātā dharati mahatu.
Divasu rāti dui dāī dāiā khelai sagal jagatu.
Caṃgiāīā buriāīā vācai dharamu hadūri.
Karamī āpo āpaṇī ke neṛe ke dūri.
Jinī nāmu dhiāiā gae masakati ghāli.
Nānak te mukh ujale ketī chuṭī nāli.1.

Glossary :

ਪਵਣੁ—Air ; ਗੁਰੂ—Guru ; ਪਾਣੀ—water ; ਪਿਤਾ—father ; ਮਾਤਾ—mother ; ਧਰਤਿ—earth ; ਮਹਤੁ—consciousness ; ਦਿਵਸੁ—day ; ਰਾਤਿ—night ; ਦੁਇ—both ; ਦਾਈ—female nurse ; ਦਾਇਆ—male nurse ; ਖੇਲੈ—plays ; ਸਗਲ—whole ; ਜਗਤੁ—world ; ਚੰਗਿਆਈਆ—good deeds, merits ; ਬੁਰਿਆਈਆ—vices, demerits ; ਵਾਚੈ—reads ; ਧਰਮੁ—Dharamraja, Justiciar ; ਹਦੂਰਿ—in presence ; ਕਰਮੀ—actions, deeds ; ਆਪੋਆਪਣੀ—one's own ; ਕੇ—some ; ਨੇੜੈ—near ; ਦੂਰਿ— distant, far away ; ਜਿਨੀ—who ; ਨਾਮੁ—The Name of the Lord ; ਧਿਆਇਆ—repeat, remember ; ਗਏ—went away, departed ; ਮਸਕਤਿ—hard work ; ਘਾਲਿ—putting in ; ਤੇ—those ;

ਮੁਖ—faces, persons ; ਉਜਲੇ—bright ; ਕੇਤੀ—many ; ਛੁਟੀ—freed ; ਨਾਲਿ—with.

Translation :

The air is the preceptor, the water is the father and the earth is the mother which combine to pulsate with consciousness, on account of which the whole world plays under the care of the male and female nurses of night and day. The good and bad deeds of the beings are seen by the Justiciar and on account of these actions, some gain nearness of the Lord and some move far away from Him. Those who have repeated the Name of the Lord, they have really put in hard work. Their faces are bright and many others are freed with them.

Comments :

This Shloka is an epilogue of the poem *Japu,* which presents a conclusion. In this concluding stanza, Guru Nanak Dev talks about the evolution of the world, which is a combination of elements and the consciousness of the soul. All the beings perform actions. Some are good actions and some are bad. The human beings who are conscious about their source either gain nearness of their source through their good actions or are led away from their source by their bad actions. But the best action according to the Guru, is the remembrance of the Name of the Lord and through this action they not only ferry across the ocean of *Samsara* themselves, but also take many others alongwith them.

RAHRĀSI

(VOCATION)

THE EVENING PRAYER

ਹਰਿ ਕੀਰਤਿ ਹਮਰੀ ਰਹਰਾਸਿ ॥

(THE PRAISE OF THE LORD IS OUR VOCATION)

ਸੋ ਦਰੁ

(SO DARU—THAT DOOR)

ਰਾਗੁ ਆਸਾ ਮਹਲਾ ੧ ॥

Rāgu Āsā Mahlā 1

ੴ ਸਤਿਗੁਰਪ੍ਰਸਾਦਿ ॥

IK AUMKĀR SATIGURPRASĀDI

Text :

ਸੋ ਦਰੁ ਤੇਰਾ ਕੇਹਾ ਸੋ ਘਰੁ ਕੇਹਾ ਜਿਤੁ ਬਹਿ ਸਰਬ ਸਮਾਲੇ ॥
ਵਾਜੇ ਤੇਰੇ ਨਾਦ ਅਨੇਕ ਅਸੰਖਾ ਕੇਤੇ ਤੇਰੇ ਵਾਵਣਹਾਰੇ ॥
ਕੇਤੇ ਤੇਰੇ ਰਾਗ ਪਰੀ ਸਿਉ ਕਹੀਅਹਿ ਕੇਤੇ ਤੇਰੇ ਗਾਵਣਹਾਰੇ ॥
ਗਾਵਨਿ ਤੁਧ ਨੋ ਪਵਣੁ ਪਾਣੀ ਬੈਸੰਤਰੁ ਗਾਵੈ ਰਾਜਾ ਧਰਮੁ ਦੁਆਰੇ ॥
ਗਾਵਨਿ ਤੁਧ ਨੋ ਚਿਤੁ ਗੁਪਤੁ ਲਿਖਿ ਜਾਣਨਿ ਲਿਖਿ ਲਿਖਿ ਧਰਮੁ ਬੀਚਾਰੇ ॥
ਗਾਵਨਿ ਤੁਧ ਨੋ ਈਸਰੁ ਬ੍ਰਹਮਾ ਦੇਵੀ ਸੋਹਨਿ ਤੇਰੇ ਸਦਾ ਸਵਾਰੇ ॥
ਗਾਵਨਿ ਤੁਧ ਨੋ ਇੰਦ੍ਰ ਇੰਦ੍ਰਾਸਣਿ ਬੈਠੇ ਦੇਵਤਿਆ ਦਰਿ ਨਾਲੇ ॥
ਗਾਵਨਿ ਤੁਧ ਨੋ ਸਿਧ ਸਮਾਧੀ ਅੰਦਰਿ ਗਾਵਨਿ ਤੁਧ ਨੋ ਸਾਧ ਬੀਚਾਰੇ ॥
ਗਾਵਨਿ ਤੁਧ ਨੋ ਜਤੀ ਸਤੀ ਸੰਤੋਖੀ ਗਾਵਨਿ ਤੁਧ ਨੋ ਵੀਰ ਕਰਾਰੇ ॥
ਗਾਵਨਿ ਤੁਧ ਨੋ ਪੰਡਿਤ ਪੜਨਿ ਰਖੀਸੁਰ ਜੁਗੁ ਜੁਗੁ ਵੇਦਾ ਨਾਲੇ ॥
ਗਾਵਨਿ ਤੁਧਨੋ ਮੋਹਣੀਆ ਮਨੁ ਮੋਹਨਿ ਸੁਰਗੁ ਮਛੁ ਪਇਆਲੇ ॥
ਗਾਵਨਿ ਤੁਧ ਨੋ ਰਤਨ ਉਪਾਏ ਤੇਰੇ ਅਠਸਠਿ ਤੀਰਥ ਨਾਲੇ ॥
ਗਾਵਨਿ ਤੁਧ ਨੋ ਜੋਧ ਮਹਾਬਲ ਸੂਰਾ ਗਾਵਨਿ ਤੁਧ ਨੋ ਖਾਣੀ ਚਾਰੇ ॥
ਗਾਵਨਿ ਤੁਧ ਨੋ ਖੰਡ ਮੰਡਲ ਬ੍ਰਹਮੰਡਾ ਕਰਿ ਕਰਿ ਰਖੇ ਤੇਰੇ ਧਾਰੇ ॥
ਸੇਈ ਤੁਧ ਨੋ ਗਾਵਨਿ ਜੋ ਤੁਧੁ ਭਾਵਨਿ ਰਤੇ ਤੇਰੇ ਭਗਤ ਰਸਾਲੇ ॥

ਹੋਰਿ ਕੇਤੇ ਤੁਧ ਨੋ ਗਾਵਨਿ ਸੇ ਮੈ ਚਿਤਿ ਨ ਆਵਨਿ ਨਾਨਕੁ ਕਿਆ ਬੀਚਾਰੇ ॥
ਸੋਈ ਸੋਈ ਸਦਾ ਸਚੁ ਸਾਹਿਬੁ ਸਾਚਾ ਸਾਚੀ ਨਾਈ ॥
ਹੈ ਭੀ ਹੋਸੀ ਜਾਇ ਨ ਜਾਸੀ ਰਚਨਾ ਜਿਨਿ ਰਚਾਈ ॥
ਰੰਗੀ ਰੰਗੀ ਭਾਤੀ ਕਰਿ ਕਰਿ ਜਿਨਸੀ ਮਾਇਆ ਜਿਨਿ ਉਪਾਈ ॥
ਕਰਿ ਕਰਿ ਦੇਖੈ ਕੀਤਾ ਆਪਣਾ ਜਿਉ ਤਿਸ ਦੀ ਵਡਿਆਈ ॥
ਜੋ ਤਿਸੁ ਭਾਵੈ ਸੋਈ ਕਰਸੀ ਫਿਰਿ ਹੁਕਮੁ ਨ ਕਰਣਾ ਜਾਈ ॥
ਸੋ ਪਾਤਿਸਾਹੁ ਸਾਹਾ ਪਤਿ ਸਾਹਿਬੁ ਨਾਨਕ ਰਹਣੁ ਰਜਾਈ ॥੧॥

For *transliteration* see the Twenty-Seventh Stanza of *JAPU* which has been made the first stanza of *Rahirās* the only difference being :

1. The addition of ਤੇਰਾ (Terā) in the first verse.
2. The addition of ਤੇਰੇ (Tere) twice in the second verse.
3. The addition of ਤੇਰੇ (Tere) twice in the third verse.
4. Change of ਗਾਵਨਿ ਤੁਧ ਨੋ (Gāvani tudh no) instead of ਗਾਵਹਿ ਤੁਹਨੋ (Gāvahi tuhano) in the fourth verse.
5. Change of ਗਾਵਨਿ ਤੁਧ ਨੋ (Gāvani tudh no) and ਜਾਣਨਿ (Jāṇani) instead of ਗਾਵਹਿ (Gāvahi) and ਜਾਣਹਿ (Jāṇahi) in the fifth verse.
6. Change of ਗਾਵਨਿ ਤੁਧ ਨੋ (gāvani tudh no) instead of ਗਾਵਹਿ (gāvahi) and addition of ਤੇਰੇ (Tere) in the sixth verse.
7. Change of ਗਾਵਨਿ ਤੁਧ ਨੋ ਇੰਦ੍ਰ ਇੰਦ੍ਰਾਸਣਿ (gāvani tudh no Iṁdra Iṁdrāsaṇi) instead of ਗਾਵਹਿ ਇੰਦ ਇੰਦਾਸਣਿ (gāvahi Iṁd Iṁdāsaṇi) in the seventh verse.
8. Change of ਗਾਵਨਿ ਤੁਧ ਨੋ (gāvani tudh no) instead of ਗਾਵਹਿ (gāvahi) and the addition of ਤੁਧ ਨੋ (tudh no) again in the eighth verse.
9. Change of ਗਾਵਨਿ ਤੁਧ ਨੋ (gāvani tudh no) twice for ਗਾਵਨਿ (gāvani) in the first case and ਗਾਵਹਿ (gāvahi) in the second case of ninth verse.
10. Addition of ਤੁਧ ਨੋ (tudh no) in the tenth verse.
11. Change of ਗਾਵਨਿ ਤੁਧ ਨੋ (gāvani tudh no) instead of ਗਾਵਹਿ (gāvahi) and change of ਸੁਰਗੁ (suragu) for ਸੁਰਗਾ (surgā) in the eleventh verse.
12. Addition of ਤੁਧ ਨੋ (tudh no) in the twelfth verse.
13. Change of ਗਾਵਨਿ ਤੁਧ ਨੋ (gāvani tudh no) for ਗਾਵਹਿ (gāvahi) in the thirteenth verse.
14. Change of ਗਾਵਨਿ ਤੁਧ ਨੋ (gāvani tudh no) twice instead

of ਗਾਵਹਿ (gāvahi) in the fourteenth verse.

15. Change of ਗਾਵਨਿ ਤੁਧ ਨੋ ਖੰਡ ਮੰਡਲ ਬ੍ਰਹਮੰਡਾ instead of ਗਾਵਹਿ ਖੰਡ ਮੰਡਲ ਵਰਭੰਡਾ and also addition of ਤੇਰੇ in the fifteenth verse.

16. Change of ਗਾਵਨਿ (gāvani) instead of ਗਾਵਹਿ (gāvahi) in the sixteenth verse.

17. Addition of ਤੁਧ ਨੋ (tudh no) in the seventeenth verse and change of ਬੀਚਾਰੇ (bicāre) instead of ਵੀਚਾਰੇ (vicāre) in the seventeenth verse.

18. Change of ਦੇਖੈ (dekhai) instead of ਵੇਖੈ (vekhai) in the twentieth verse.

19. Addition of ਫਿਰਿ (phiri) in the twenty-first verse.

Though there are a few changes and additions of words, the sense of the stanza remains the same.

See the meanings of words in the twenty-seventh stanza of *Japu*.

A few additional or changed words :

ਤੇਰਾ—Thine ; ਤੇਰੇ—Thine ; ਤੁਧ ਨੋ—Thee ; ਗਾਵਨਿ—sing ; ਜਾਣਨਿ—know ; ਇੰਦ੍ਰ—Imdra ; ਇੰਦ੍ਰਾਸਣਿ—The Throne of Imdra ; ਸੁਰਗੁ—heaven ; ਬ੍ਰਹਮੰਡਾ—universe ; ਬੀਚਾਰੇ—think, reflect ; ਦੇਖੈ—see ; ਫਿਰਿ—then.

Comments :

This hymn of Guru Nanak Dev in Asa Raga is also a part of the *Japu* with a minor change of words here and there. There is no change in the thought-content. The importance of such a hymn which forms part of both the morning as well as the evening prayer, cannot be denied. The devotee is required to remember that Creator Lord who is the real sovereign and who is remembered by every species created by Him. He is Immortal and Eternal. Everything moves and works under His Will.

ਆਸਾ ਮਹਲਾ ੧
Āsā Mahlā 1

Text :

ਸੁਣਿ ਵਡਾ ਆਖੈ ਸਭੁ ਕੋਇ ॥
ਕੇਵਡੁ ਵਡਾ ਡੀਠਾ ਹੋਇ ॥
ਕੀਮਤਿ ਪਾਇ ਨ ਕਹਿਆ ਜਾਇ ॥
ਕਹਣੈ ਵਾਲੇ ਤੇਰੇ ਰਹੇ ਸਮਾਇ ॥੧॥
ਵਡੇ ਮੇਰੇ ਸਾਹਿਬਾ ਗਹਿਰ ਗੰਭੀਰਾ ਗੁਣੀ ਗਹੀਰਾ ॥

ਕੋਇ ਨ ਜਾਣੈ ਤੇਰਾ ਕੇਤਾ ਕੇਵਡੁ ਚੀਰਾ ॥੧॥ ਰਹਾਉ ॥
ਸਭਿ ਸੁਰਤੀ ਮਿਲਿ ਸੁਰਤਿ ਕਮਾਈ ॥
ਸਭਿ ਕੀਮਤਿ ਮਿਲਿ ਕੀਮਤਿ ਪਾਈ ॥
ਗਿਆਨੀ ਧਿਆਨੀ ਗੁਰ ਗੁਰ ਹਾਈ ॥
ਕਹਣੁ ਨ ਜਾਈ ਤੇਰੀ ਤਿਲੁ ਵਡਿਆਈ ॥੨॥
ਸਭਿ ਸਤ ਸਭਿ ਤਪ ਸਭਿ ਚੰਗਿਆਈਆ ॥
ਸਿਧਾ ਪੁਰਖਾ ਕੀਆ ਵਡਿਆਈਆ ॥
ਤੁਧੁ ਵਿਣੁ ਸਿਧੀ ਕਿਨੈ ਨ ਪਾਈਆ ॥
ਕਰਮਿ ਮਿਲੈ ਨਾਹੀ ਠਾਕਿ ਰਹਾਈਆ ॥੩॥
ਆਖਣ ਵਾਲਾ ਕਿਆ ਵੇਚਾਰਾ ॥
ਸਿਫਤੀ ਭਰੇ ਤੇਰੇ ਭੰਡਾਰਾ ॥
ਜਿਸੁ ਤੂ ਦੇਹਿ ਤਿਸੈ ਕਿਆ ਚਾਰਾ ॥
ਨਾਨਕ ਸਚੁ ਸਵਾਰਣਹਾਰਾ ॥੪॥੨॥

Transliteration :

Suṇi vaḍā ākhai sabhu koi.
Kevaḍu vaḍā ḍiṭhā hoi.
Kīmati pāe na kahiā jāi.
Kahaṇai vāle tere rahe samāi.1.
Vaḍe mere sāhibā gahir gambhīrā guṇī gahīrā.
Koi na jāṇai terā ketā kevaḍu cīrā.1. *Rahāu.*
Sabhi suratī mili surati kamāī.
Sabhi kīmati mili kīmati pāī.
Giānī dhiānī gur gur hāī.
Kahaṇu na jāī terī tilu vaḍiāī.2.
Sabhi sat sabhi tapu sabhi camgiāīā.
Sidhā purakhā kiā vaḍiāīā.
Tudhu viṇu sidhī kinai na pāīā.
Karami milai nāhī ṭhāki rahāīā.3.
Ākhaṇ wālā kiā vecārā.
Siphatī bhare tere bhamḍārā.
Jisu tū dehi tisai kiā cārā.
Nānak sacu savāraṇhārā.4.2.

Glossary :

ਸੁਣਿ—hear ; ਵਡਾ—great ; ਆਖੈ—say, describe ; ਸਭੁ ਕੋਇ—every-one ; ਕੇਵਡੁ—how great ; ਡੀਠਾ ਹੋਇ—on seeing ; ਕੀਮਤਿ ਪਾਇ—evaluating ; ਨ ਕਹਿਆ ਜਾਇ—cannot be described ; ਕਹਣੈ

ਵਾਲੇ—describers ; ਤੇਰੇ— Thine ; ਰਹੇ ਸਮਾਇ—be absorbed ; ਵਡੇ—great ; ਮੇਰੇ—my ; ਸਾਹਿਬਾ—Lord ; ਗਹਿਰ—depth ; ਗੰਭੀਰਾ—great, umfathomable ; ਗੁਣੀ—qualities, merits ; ਗਹੀਰਾ—ocean ; ਕੋਇ ਨ ਜਾਣੈ—no one knows ; ਕੇਤਾ—how much ; ਚੀਰਾ—expanse ; ਸਭਿ—all ; ਸੁਰਤੀ—contemplative persons ; ਮਿਲਿ—meet together ; ਸੁਰਤਿ—contemplation ; ਕਮਾਈ—practised ; ਕੀਮਤਿ—appraiser (ਕੀ+ਮਤਿ—the intellect of) ; ਕੀਮਤਿ ਪਾਈ—appraised ; ਗਿਆਨੀ—knowers ; ਧਿਆਨੀ—visualisers ; ਗੁਰ ਗੁਰ ਹਾਈ—preacher of preachers ; ਕਹਣੁ ਨ ਜਾਈ—cannot be described ; ਤੇਰੀ—Thine ; ਤਿਲੁ—a very small sesame seed, very small ; ਵਡਿਆਈ—greatness ; ਸਤ—truth ; ਤਪ—austerity ; ਚੰਗਿਆਈਆ—virtues ; ਸਿਧਾ—adepts ; ਪੁਰਖਾ—men ; ਕੀਆ—of ; ਵਡਿਆਈਆ—magnificences ; ਤੁਧੁ—thee ; ਵਿਣੁ—without ; ਸਿਧੀ—occult power ; ਕਿਨੈ ਨ ਪਾਈਆ—none attained ; ਕਰਮਿ—grace ; ਮਿਲੈ—attained ; ਨਾਹੀ—not ; ਠਾਕਿ ਰਹਾਈਆ—obstructed ; ਆਖਣ ਵਾਲਾ—describer, narrator ; ਕਿਆ—what ; ਵੇਚਾਰਾ—helpless ; ਸਿਫਤੀ—praise ; ਭਰੇ—full ; ਤੇਰੇ—Thine ; ਭੰਡਾਰਾ—stores ; ਜਿਸੁ—to whom ; ਤੂ—Thou ; ਦੇਹਿ—give ; ਤਿਸੈ—him ; ਕਿਆ—what ; ਚਾਰਾ—means ; ਸਚੁ—true Lord ; ਸਵਾਰਣਹਾਰਾ—decorator.

Translation :

Everyone who hears about the Lord, talks about His Greatness. But how great He is ? His Greatness can be known only on seeing Him. If one wants to evaluate Him, He cannot be described. Those who can describe, remain absorbed in Thee, O my Great Lord, profound, unfathomable and ocean of qualities. No one knows how much and how great is Thy expanse ? All the contemplative persons have met together and practised contemplation. The intellect of all have collectively tried to appraise Thee. The knowers, visualisers and preachers of preachers have not been able to describe an iota of Thy Greatness. All truths, all austerities and all virtues, the magnificences of the adepts, all the occult powers could not be attained without Thee and Thy Grace and could not be obstructed. What a helpless person is the describer because the stores of Thy Praises are full to the brim. He on whom you bestow Thy Praises, what other means he can adopt ? The True Lord is the only decorator, says Nanak.

Comments :

In this hymn, Guru Nanak Dev talks about the Greatness of

the Lord. His Greatness cannot be described and evaluated by anyone. Even an iota of the Lord's Greatness cannot be described. The stores of the Praise of the Lord are so great that the describer is helpless.

ਆਸਾ ਮਹਲਾ ੧

Āsā Mahlā 1

Text :

ਆਖਾ ਜੀਵਾ ਵਿਸਰੈ ਮਰਿ ਜਾਉ ॥
ਆਖਣਿ ਅਉਖਾ ਸਾਚਾ ਨਾਉ ॥
ਸਾਚੇ ਨਾਮ ਕੀ ਲਾਗੈ ਭੂਖ ॥
ਉਤੁ ਭੂਖੈ ਖਾਇ ਚਲੀਅਹਿ ਦੂਖ ॥੧॥
ਸੋ ਕਿਉ ਵਿਸਰੈ ਮੇਰੀ ਮਾਇ ॥
ਸਾਚਾ ਸਾਹਿਬੁ ਸਾਚੈ ਨਾਇ ॥੧॥ ਰਹਾਉ ॥
ਸਾਚੇ ਨਾਮ ਕੀ ਤਿਲੁ ਵਡਿਆਈ ॥
ਆਖਿ ਥਕੇ ਕੀਮਤਿ ਨਹੀ ਪਾਈ ॥
ਜੇ ਸਭਿ ਮਿਲਿ ਕੈ ਆਖਣ ਪਾਹਿ ॥
ਵਡਾ ਨ ਹੋਵੈ ਘਾਟਿ ਨ ਜਾਇ ॥੨॥
ਨਾ ਓਹੁ ਮਰੈ ਨ ਹੋਵੈ ਸੋਗੁ ॥
ਦੇਦਾ ਰਹੈ ਨ ਚੂਕੈ ਭੋਗੁ ॥
ਗੁਣੁ ਏਹੋ ਹੋਰੁ ਨਾਹੀ ਕੋਇ ॥
ਨਾ ਕੋ ਹੋਆ ਨਾ ਕੋ ਹੋਇ ॥੩॥
ਜੇਵਡੁ ਆਪਿ ਤੇਵਡ ਤੇਰੀ ਦਾਤਿ ॥
ਜਿਨਿ ਦਿਨੁ ਕਰਿ ਕੈ ਕੀਤੀ ਰਾਤਿ ॥
ਖਸਮੁ ਵਿਸਾਰਹਿ ਤੇ ਕਮਜਾਤਿ ॥
ਨਾਨਕ ਨਾਵੈ ਬਾਝੁ ਸਨਾਤਿ ॥੪॥੩॥

Transliteration :

Ākhā jīvā visarai mari jāu.
Ākhaṇi aukhā sācā nāu.
Sāce nām kī lāgai bhūkh.
Utu bhūkhai khāi calīahi dūkh.1.
So kiu visarai merī māi.
Sācā sāhibu sācai nāi.1.*Rahāu.*
Sāce nām kī tilu vaḍiāī.
Ākhi thake kīmati nahī pāī.

Je sabhi mili kai ākhaṇ pāhi.
Vaḍā na hovai ghāṭi na jāi.2.
Nā ohu marai na hovai sogu.
Dedā rahai na cūkai bhogu.
Guṇu eho horu nāhī koi.
Nā ko hoā nā ko hoi.3.
Jevaḍu āpi tevaḍ terī dāti.
Jini dinu kari kai kītī rāti.
Khasamu visārahi te kamjāti.
Nānak nāvai bājhu sanāti.4.3.

Glossary :

ਆਖਾ—say, utter ; ਜੀਵਾ—live ; ਵਿਸਰੈ—forget ; ਮਰਿ ਜਾਉ—die ; ਆਖਣਿ—utterance ; ਅਉਖਾ—difficult ; ਸਾਚਾ—true ; ਨਾਉ—Name of the Lord ; ਸਾਚੇ ਨਾਮ ਕੀ—of the True Name ; ਲਾਗੈ ਭੂਖ—hunger is felt ; ਉਤੁ—that ; ਭੂਖੈ—hunger ; ਖਾਇ—eat ; ਚਲੀਅਹਿ—go away, leave ; ਦੂਖ—sorrow, pain ; ਸੋ—He ; ਕਿਉ—why ; ਵਿਸਰੈ—forgotten ; ਮੇਰੀ—my ; ਮਾਇ—mother ; ਸਾਚਾ—true ; ਸਾਹਿਬੁ—Lord ; ਸਾਚੈ—True ; ਨਾਇ—Name ; ਸਾਚੇ ਨਾਮ ਕੀ—of True Name ; ਤਿਲੁ—a very small sesame seed ; ਵਡਿਆਈ—greatness ; ਆਖਿ—describe ; ਥਕੇ—tired ; ਕੀਮਤਿ ਨਹੀ ਪਾਈ—could not evaluate ; ਜੇ—if ; ਸਭਿ—all ; ਮਿਲਿ ਕੈ—together ; ਆਖਣਿ ਪਾਹਿ—describe ; ਵਡਾ—great ; ਨ ਹੋਵੈ—does not become ; ਘਾਟਿ ਨ ਜਾਇ—does not become lesser ; ਨਾ ਓਹੁ ਮਰੈ—He does not die ; ਨ ਹੋਵੈ ਸੋਗੁ—there is no mourning ; ਦੇਦਾ ਰਹੈ—continues to give ; ਨ ਚੂਕੈ—does not run short ; ਭੋਗੁ—eatables ; ਗੁਣੁ—merit ; ਏਹੋ—this is ; ਹੋਰੁ ਨਾਹੀ ਕੋਇ—there is none other ; ਨਾ ਕੋ ਹੋਆ—there has been none ; ਨਾ ਕੋ ਹੋਇ—there will be none ; ਜੇਵਡੁ—as great ; ਆਪਿ—Thou ; ਤੇਵਡ—so great ; ਤੇਰੀ—Thine ; ਦਾਤਿ—gift ; ਜਿਨਿ— who ; ਦਿਨੁ—day ; ਕਰਿ ਕੈ—made ; ਕੀਤੀ—made ; ਰਾਤਿ—night ; ਖਸਮੁ—Master, Lord ; ਵਿਸਾਰਹਿ—forget ; ਤੇ—they ; ਕਮਜਾਤਿ—ignoble, degenerate ; ਨਾਵੈ—Name ; ਬਾਝੁ—without ; ਸਨਾਤਿ—outcaste wretch.

Translation :

I live only when I remember Thy Name and I die when I forget it. It is very difficult to utter the True Name. When we feel hungry for the True Name, the sorrows go away on eating for that hunger. O my mother ! why should we forget Him who is the True Lord whose Name is also True ? The describers got tired of describing an iota of the Praises of the Lord but could not evaluate it. If all meet together and describe His Praises, He neither becomes Great nor small. He does not die and there is no mourning ; He keeps on giving and the eatables do not run short. His quality is this that there is none other. There has been none and there will be none. O Lord, as great Thou are, so Great is Thy Gift. Thou who has made the day and also made the night. They who forget the Lord, they are ignoble; without the Name they are outcaste wretches.

Comments :

In this hymn, Guru Nanak Dev mentions the importance of the remembrance of the Name of the Lord. For a true devotee the Name is his food and the very life. One may get tired in describing the Praises of the Lord, but the Lord cannot be evaluated. He is Immortal, Ever-Existent, unparalleled and the Greatest. He gives and continues giving, therefore one should always remain grateful to Him. His Name should always be remembered. Those who forget Him, they are ignoble and outcaste wretches.

ਰਾਗੁ ਗੂਜਰੀ ਮਹਲਾ ੪

Rāgu Gūjarī Mahlā 4

Text :

ਹਰਿ ਕੇ ਜਨ ਸਤਿਗੁਰ ਸਤਪੁਰਖਾ ਬਿਨਉ ਕਰਉ ਗੁਰ ਪਾਸਿ ॥
ਹਮ ਕੀਰੇ ਕਿਰਮ ਸਤਿਗੁਰ ਸਰਣਾਈ ਕਰਿ ਦਇਆ ਨਾਮੁ ਪਰਗਾਸਿ ॥੧॥
ਮੇਰੇ ਮੀਤ ਗੁਰਦੇਵ ਮੋ ਕਉ ਰਾਮ ਨਾਮੁ ਪਰਗਾਸਿ ॥
ਗੁਰਮਤਿ ਨਾਮੁ ਮੇਰਾ ਪ੍ਰਾਨ ਸਖਾਈ ਹਰਿ ਕੀਰਤਿ ਹਮਰੀ ਰਹਰਾਸਿ ॥੧॥ਰਹਾਉ॥
ਹਰਿ ਜਨ ਕੇ ਵਡ ਭਾਗ ਵਡੇਰੇ ਜਿਨ ਹਰਿ ਹਰਿ ਸਰਧਾ ਹਰਿ ਪਿਆਸ ॥
ਹਰਿ ਹਰਿ ਨਾਮੁ ਮਿਲੈ ਤ੍ਰਿਪਤਾਸਹਿ ਮਿਲਿ ਸੰਗਤਿ ਗੁਣ ਪਰਗਾਸਿ ॥੨॥
ਜਿਨ ਹਰਿ ਹਰਿ ਹਰਿ ਰਸੁ ਨਾਮੁ ਨ ਪਾਇਆ ਤੇ ਭਾਗਹੀਣ ਜਮ ਪਾਸਿ ॥
ਜੋ ਸਤਿਗੁਰ ਸਰਣਿ ਸੰਗਤਿ ਨਹੀ ਆਏ ਧ੍ਰਿਗੁ ਜੀਵੇ ਧ੍ਰਿਗੁ ਜੀਵਾਸਿ ॥੩॥
ਜਿਨ ਹਰਿ ਜਨ ਸਤਿਗੁਰ ਸੰਗਤਿ ਪਾਈ ਤਿਨ ਧੁਰਿ ਮਸਤਕਿ ਲਿਖਿਆ ਲਿਖਾਸਿ ॥
ਧਨੁ ਧੰਨੁ ਸਤਸੰਗਤਿ ਜਿਤੁ ਹਰਿ ਰਸੁ ਪਾਇਆ
ਮਿਲਿ ਜਨ ਨਾਨਕ ਨਾਮੁ ਪਰਗਾਸਿ ॥੪॥੪॥

Transliteration :

Hari ke jan Satigur Satpurakhā binau karau Gur pāsi.
Ham kīre kiram Satigur sarṇāī kari diā nāmu pargāsi.1
Mere mīt Gurdev mo kau Rām nāmu pargāsi.

Gurmati nāmu merā prān sakhāī hari kīrati
hamarī Rahrāsi.1.*Rahāu*.
Harī jan ke vaḍbhāg vaḍere jin Hari Hari sardhā Hari piās.
Hari Hari nāmu milai triptāsahi mili saṁgati guṇ pargāsi.2.
Jin Hari Hari Hari rasu nāmu na pāiā te bhāghīṇ jam pāsi.
Jo Satigur saraṇi saṁgati nahī āe dhrigu jīve dhrigu jīvāsi.3.
Jin Hari jan Satigur saṁgati pāī tin dhuri
mastaki likhiā likhāsi.
Dhanu dhaṁnu satsaṁgati jitu Hari rasu pāiā
mili jan Nānak nāmu pargāsi.4.4.

Glossary :

ਹਰਿ—Hari, God ; ਕੇ—of ; ਜਨ—man ; ਸਤਿਗੁਰ—True Guru ; ਸਤਪੁਰਖਾ—True Person ; ਬਿਨਉ ਕਰਉ—request ; ਗੁਰ ਪਾਸਿ—before the Guru ; ਹਮ—I ; ਕੀਰੇ—insect ; ਕਿਰਮ—worm ; ਸਰਣਾਈ—shelter ; ਕਰਿ ਦਇਆ—have mercy ; ਨਾਮੁ—Name ; ਪਰਗਾਸਿ—bestow the light ; ਮੇਰੇ—my ; ਮੀਤ—friend ; ਗੁਰਦੇਵ—Guru ; ਮੋ ਕਉ—to me ; ਰਾਮ—Lord ; ਗੁਰਮਤਿ—Guru's instruction ; ਪ੍ਰਾਨ—breath, life ; ਸਖਾਈ—friend ; ਕੀਰਤਿ—praise ; ਹਮਰੀ—my ; ਰਹਰਾਸਿ—vocation ; ਵਡ ਭਾਗ— good fortune ; ਵਡੇਰੇ—greatest ; ਜਿਨ—who ; ਸਰਧਾ—faith ; ਪਿਆਸ—thirst ; ਮਿਲੈ—obtain ; ਤ੍ਰਿਪਤਾਸਹਿ—satisfied ; ਮਿਲਿ—meet ; ਸੰਗਤਿ—company, society ; ਗੁਣ—virtue ; ਰਸੁ—elixir ; ਪਾਇਆ—obtained ; ਤੇ—they ; ਭਾਗਹੀਣ—unfortunate ; ਜਮ—angel of death ; ਪਾਸਿ—near ; ਜੋ—those ; ਸਰਣਿ—refuge ; ਆਏ—came ; ਧ੍ਰਿਗੁ—fie ; ਜੀਵੇ—life ; ਜੀਵਾਸਿ—the hope of living ; ਧੁਰਿ—beginning ; ਮਸਤਕਿ—forehead ; ਲਿਖਿਆ—written ; ਲਿਖਾਸਿ—writ ; ਧਨੁ—blessed ; ਸਤ—true ; ਜਿਤੁ—from which ; ਪਾਇਆ—obtained, procured.

Translation :

O, the man of God, the True Guru is the True Person. I make this request before the Guru, We are the insects and worms, O True Guru, we are in your shelter, be merciful to us and bestow the light of the Name on us. O my friend Gurudev, bestow on me the light of the Name of the Lord. The Name given in Guru's instruction is my breath and friend and the Praise of the Lord is my vocation. It is the good and the greatest fortune of the man of God who has the faith in God and thirst for God. When they obtain the Name of the Lord, they are satisfied. On meeting the holy congregation, their virtues are manifested. Those who have not obtained the elixir of the Name of the Lord, they are unfortunate near the angel of death. Those who have not come in the shelter and company of the True Guru, fie on their life and the hope of living. Those men of God, who attained the company of the True Guru, the Writ was recorded on their foreheads from the beginning. Blessed is that true company in which the elixir of the Lord is obtained and where the light of the Name is manifested, says Nanak.

Comments :

In this hymn, the fourth Guru, Guru Ramdas makes the man of God conscious about the importance of the True Guru (Preceptor). The man of God is order to know the ultimate Reality, must approach and request the Guru to bestow on him the light of the Name. The man of God has to join the holy congregation, which is the school of the true Guru, where he makes the spiritual progress in the company of other men of God and absorbs himself in meditation on the Name. Others who do not join the holy company and do not remember the Name of the Lord, waste away their precious birth.

ਰਾਗੁ ਗੂਜਰੀ ਮਹਲਾ ੫
Rāgu Gūjarī Mahlā 5

Text :

ਕਾਹੇ ਰੇ ਮਨ ਚਿਤਵਹਿ ਉਦਮੁ ਜਾ ਆਹਰਿ ਹਰਿ ਜੀਉ ਪਰਿਆ ॥
ਸੈਲ ਪਥਰ ਮਹਿ ਜੰਤ ਉਪਾਏ ਤਾ ਕਾ ਰਿਜਕੁ ਆਗੈ ਕਰਿ ਧਰਿਆ ॥੧॥
ਮੇਰੇ ਮਾਧਉ ਜੀ ਸਤਸੰਗਤਿ ਮਿਲੇ ਸੁ ਤਰਿਆ ॥
ਗੁਰ ਪਰਸਾਦਿ ਪਰਮ ਪਦੁ ਪਾਇਆ ਸੂਕੇ ਕਾਸਟ ਹਰਿਆ ॥੧॥ਰਹਾਉ॥
ਜਨਨਿ ਪਿਤਾ ਲੋਕ ਸੁਤ ਬਨਿਤਾ ਕੋਇ ਨ ਕਿਸ ਕੀ ਧਰਿਆ ॥
ਸਿਰਿ ਸਿਰਿ ਰਿਜਕੁ ਸੰਬਾਹੇ ਠਾਕੁਰੁ ਕਾਹੇ ਮਨ ਭਉ ਕਰਿਆ ॥੨॥
ਊਡੇ ਊਡਿ ਆਵੈ ਸੈ ਕੋਸਾ ਤਿਸੁ ਪਾਛੈ ਬਚਰੇ ਛਰਿਆ ॥
ਤਿਨ ਕਵਣੁ ਖਲਾਵੈ ਕਵਣੁ ਚੁਗਾਵੈ ਮਨ ਮਹਿ ਸਿਮਰਨੁ ਕਰਿਆ ॥੩॥
ਸਭਿ ਨਿਧਾਨ ਦਸ ਅਸਟ ਸਿਧਾਨ ਠਾਕੁਰ ਕਰ ਤਲ ਧਰਿਆ ॥
ਜਨ ਨਾਨਕ ਬਲਿ ਬਲਿ ਸਦ ਬਲਿ ਜਾਈਐ
ਤੇਰਾ ਅੰਤੁ ਨ ਪਾਰਾਵਰਿਆ ॥੪॥੫॥

Transliteration :

Kāhe re man citavahi udamu jā āhari Hari jīu pariā.
Sail pathar mahi jamt upāe tā kā rijaku āgai kari dhariā.1.

Mere mādhau jī satsaṁgat mile su tariā.
Gur parsādi param padu pāiā sūke kāsaṭ hariā.1.*Rahāu.*
Janani pitā lok sut banitā koi na kis kī dhariā.
Siri siri rijaku saṁbāhe ṭhākuru kāhe man bhau kariā.2.
Ūḍe ūḍi āvai sai kosā tisu pāchai bacare chariā.
Tin kavaṇu khalāvai kavaṇu cugāvai
man mahi simranu kariā.3.
Sabhi nidhān das asaṭ sidhān ṭhākur kar tal dhariā.
Jan Nānak bali bali sad bali jāīai terā aṁtu na pārāvariā.4.5.

Glossary :

ਕਾਹੇ—why ; ਰੇ—thou ; ਮਨ—mind ; ਚਿਤਵਹਿ—think ; ਉਦਮੁ—effort, enterprise ; ਜਾ—when ; ਆਹਰਿ—activity ; ਹਰਿ ਜੀਉ—Beloved Lord ; ਪਰਿਆ—engaged ; ਸੈਲ—rock ; ਪਥਰ—stone ; ਜੰਤ—being ; ਉਪਾਏ—created ; ਤਾ ਕਾ—whose ; ਰਿਜਕੁ—sustenance ; ਆਗੈ ਕਰਿ ਧਰਿਆ—puts before them ; ਮੇਰੇ—my ; ਮਾਧਉ—the husband of Lakshmi, Lord ; ਜੀ—a term of respect ; ਸਤਸੰਗਤਿ—true company ; ਮਿਲੇ—meet ; ਸੁ—that ; ਤਰਿਆ—swim across ; ਗੁਰ—Guru ; ਪਰਸਾਦਿ—grace ; ਪਰਮ ਪਦੁ—the highest spiritual state ; ਪਾਇਆ—attained ; ਸੂਕੇ—dry ; ਕਾਸਟ—wood ; ਹਰਿਆ—bloom ; ਜਨਨਿ—mother ; ਪਿਤਾ—father ; ਲੋਕ—people ; ਸੁਤ—son ; ਬਨਿਤਾ—wife ; ਕੋਇ—any : ਨ—not ; ਕਿਸ ਕੀ—any one's ; ਧਰਿਆ—support ; ਸਿਰਿ ਸਿਰਿ—on every head ; ਰਿਜਕੁ—sustenance ; ਸੰਬਾਹੇ—provides ; ਠਾਕੁਰੁ—Lord ; ਭਉ ਕਰਿਆ—fear ; ਊਡੇ ਊਡਿ—fly continuously ; ਆਵੈ— come ; ਸੈ—hundred ; ਕੋਸਾ—Kos, miles ; ਤਿਸੁ—her ; ਪਾਛੈ—behind ; ਬਚਰੇ—young ones ; ਛਰਿਆ—leave ; ਤਿਨ—them ; ਕਵਣੁ—who ; ਖਲਾਵੈ— feeds ; ਚੁਗਾਵੈ—to cause to peck ; ਮਹਿ—in ; ਸਿਮਰਨੁ ਕਰਿਆ—remember ; ਸਭਿ—all ; ਨਿਧਾਨ—treasures ; ਦਸ ਅਸਟ—eighteen ; ਸਿਧਾਨ—occult powers ; ਠਾਕੁਰ—The Lord ; ਕਰ—hand ; ਤਲ—palm ; ਧਰਿਆ—hold, put ; ਜਨ—person ; ਸਦ—always ; ਬਲਿ ਜਾਈਐ—be a sacrifice ; ਤੇਰਾ—thine ; ਅੰਤੁ—limit ; ਪਾਰਾਵਰਿਆ—bound.

Translation :

O mind, why do you think of the effort on your part, when the Beloved Lord Himself is engaged on directing your activity. He has created the beings in stones and has put before them their sustenance. O my Lord, whosoever meets the true company, swims across (the ocean of saṁsāra). With the grace of the Guru he attains the highest spiritual state and the dry wood blooms.

The mother, father, people, son and wife, none of them comes to the support of anyone; the Lord provides sustenance for every head, then O mind, why do you fear ? The (cranes) come flying hundreds of miles leaving their young ones behind them, they ruminate in their minds as to who feeds the young ones and causes them to peck (the foodgrains). All the treasures and eighteen occult powers are held by the Lord in the palm of His Hand. O Lord, Nanak, the person is always a sacrifice to Thee, none knows Thy limits and bounds.

Comments :

In this hymn, Guru Arjan Dev, the fifth Guru says that the Lord, who has created all the beings, also cares for their sustenance. Therefore, one should not unnecessarily worry about it. He has given two examples. The beings created in stones have also been provided their sustenance. The young ones of cranes, whose parents have taken long flights, are also fed and cared for. It is the Lord, who cares for all His creation. It is also He, who through His Grace, provides the beings with True company in order to attain the highest spiritual state. None of the relatives comes to the support of anyone. It is only the Lord, who provides sustenance to everyone.

ਰਾਗੁ ਆਸਾ ਮਹਲਾ ੪
Ragū Āsā Mahla 4
ਸੋ ਪੁਰਖੁ (SO PURAKHU)

ੴ ਸਤਿਗੁਰਪ੍ਰਸਾਦਿ ॥

IK AUMKĀR SATIGURPRASĀDI

Text :

ਸੋ ਪੁਰਖੁ ਨਿਰੰਜਨੁ ਹਰਿ ਪੁਰਖੁ ਨਿਰੰਜਨੁ ਹਰਿ ਅਗਮਾ ਅਗਮ ਅਪਾਰਾ ॥
ਸਭਿ ਧਿਆਵਹਿ ਸਭਿ ਧਿਆਵਹਿ ਤੁਧੁ ਜੀ ਹਰਿ ਸਚੇ ਸਿਰਜਣਹਾਰਾ ॥
ਸਭਿ ਜੀਅ ਤੁਮਾਰੇ ਜੀ ਤੂੰ ਜੀਆ ਕਾ ਦਾਤਾਰਾ ॥
ਹਰਿ ਧਿਆਵਹੁ ਸੰਤਹੁ ਜੀ ਸਭਿ ਦੂਖ ਵਿਸਾਰਣਹਾਰਾ ॥
ਹਰਿ ਆਪੇ ਠਾਕੁਰੁ ਹਰਿ ਆਪੇ ਸੇਵਕੁ ਜੀ ਕਿਆ ਨਾਨਕ ਜੰਤ ਵਿਚਾਰਾ ॥੧॥
ਤੂੰ ਘਟ ਘਟ ਅੰਤਰਿ ਸਰਬ ਨਿਰੰਤਰਿ ਜੀ ਹਰਿ ਏਕੋ ਪੁਰਖੁ ਸਮਾਣਾ ॥
ਇਕਿ ਦਾਤੇ ਇਕਿ ਭੇਖਾਰੀ ਜੀ ਸਭਿ ਤੇਰੇ ਚੋਜ ਵਿਡਾਣਾ ॥
ਤੂੰ ਆਪੇ ਦਾਤਾ ਆਪੇ ਭੁਗਤਾ ਜੀ ਹਉ ਤੁਧੁ ਬਿਨੁ ਅਵਰੁ ਨ ਜਾਣਾ ॥
ਤੂੰ ਪਾਰਬ੍ਰਹਮੁ ਬੇਅੰਤੁ ਬੇਅੰਤੁ ਜੀ ਤੇਰੇ ਕਿਆ ਗੁਣ ਆਖਿ ਵਖਾਣਾ ॥

ਜੋ ਸੇਵਹਿ ਜੋ ਸੇਵਹਿ ਤੁਧੁ ਜੀ ਜਨੁ ਨਾਨਕੁ ਤਿਨ ਕੁਰਬਾਣਾ ॥੨॥
ਹਰਿ ਧਿਆਵਹਿ ਹਰਿ ਧਿਆਵਹਿ ਤੁਧੁ ਜੀ ਸੇ ਜਨ ਜੁਗ ਮਹਿ ਸੁਖਵਾਸੀ ॥
ਸੇ ਮੁਕਤੁ ਸੇ ਮੁਕਤੁ ਭਏ ਜਿਨ ਹਰਿ ਧਿਆਇਆ ਜੀ ਤਿਨ ਤੂਟੀ ਜਮ ਕੀ ਫਾਸੀ ॥
ਜਿਨ ਨਿਰਭਉ ਜਿਨ ਹਰਿ ਨਿਰਭਉ ਧਿਆਇਆ ਜੀ ਤਿਨ ਕਾ ਭਉ ਸਭੁ ਗਵਾਸੀ ॥
ਜਿਨ ਸੇਵਿਆ ਜਿਨ ਸੇਵਿਆ ਮੇਰਾ ਹਰਿ ਜੀ ਤੇ ਹਰਿ ਹਰਿ ਰੂਪਿ ਸਮਾਸੀ ॥
ਸੇ ਧੰਨੁ ਸੇ ਧੰਨੁ ਜਿਨ ਹਰਿ ਧਿਆਇਆ ਜੀ ਜਨੁ ਨਾਨਕੁ ਤਿਨ ਬਲਿ ਜਾਸੀ ॥੩॥
ਤੇਰੀ ਭਗਤਿ ਤੇਰੀ ਭਗਤਿ ਭੰਡਾਰ ਜੀ ਭਰੇ ਬਿਅੰਤ ਬੇਅੰਤਾ ॥
ਤੇਰੇ ਭਗਤ ਤੇਰੇ ਭਗਤ ਸਲਾਹਨਿ ਤੁਧੁ ਜੀ ਹਰਿ ਅਨਿਕ ਅਨੇਕ ਅਨੰਤਾ ॥
ਤੇਰੀ ਅਨਿਕ ਤੇਰੀ ਅਨਿਕ ਕਰਹਿ ਹਰਿ ਪੂਜਾ ਜੀ ਤਪੁ ਤਾਪਹਿ ਜਪਹਿ ਬੇਅੰਤਾ ॥
ਤੇਰੇ ਅਨੇਕ ਤੇਰੇ ਅਨੇਕ ਪੜਹਿ ਬਹੁ ਸਿਮ੍ਰਿਤਿ ਸਾਸਤ ਜੀ
ਕਰਿ ਕਿਰਿਆ ਖਟੁ ਕਰਮ ਕਰੰਤਾ ॥
ਸੇ ਭਗਤ ਸੇ ਭਗਤ ਭਲੇ ਜਨ ਨਾਨਕ ਜੀ ਜੋ ਭਾਵਹਿ ਮੇਰੇ ਹਰਿ ਭਗਵੰਤਾ ॥੪॥
ਤੂੰ ਆਦਿ ਪੁਰਖੁ ਅਪਰੰਪਰੁ ਕਰਤਾ ਜੀ ਤੁਧੁ ਜੇਵਡੁ ਅਵਰੁ ਨ ਕੋਈ ॥
ਤੂੰ ਜੁਗੁ ਜੁਗੁ ਏਕੋ ਸਦਾ ਸਦਾ ਤੂੰ ਏਕੋ ਜੀ ਤੂੰ ਨਿਹਚਲੁ ਕਰਤਾ ਸੋਈ ॥
ਤੁਧੁ ਆਪੇ ਭਾਵੈ ਸੋਈ ਵਰਤੈ ਜੀ ਤੂੰ ਆਪੇ ਕਰਹਿ ਸੁ ਹੋਈ ॥
ਤੁਧੁ ਆਪੇ ਸ੍ਰਿਸਟਿ ਸਭ ਉਪਾਈ ਜੀ ਤੁਧੁ ਆਪੇ ਸਿਰਜਿ ਸਭ ਗੋਈ ॥
ਜਨੁ ਨਾਨਕੁ ਗੁਣ ਗਾਵੈ ਕਰਤੇ ਕੇ ਜੀ ਜੋ ਸਭਸੈ ਕਾ ਜਾਣੋਈ ॥੫॥੧॥

Transliteration :

So purakhu niramjanu Hari purakhu niramjanu
Hari agamā agam apārā.
Sabhi dhiāvahi sabhi dhiāvahi tudhu jī Hari sace sirjaṇhārā.
Sabhi jīa tumāre jī tūṁ jīā kā dātārā.
Hari dhiāvahu saṁtahu jī sabhi dūkh visāraṇhārā.
Hari āpe ṭhākuru Hari āpe sevaku jī kiā Nānak jaṁt vicārā.1.
Tūṁ ghaṭ ghaṭ aṁtari sarab niraṁtari jī
Hari eko purakhu samāṇā.
Iki dāte iki bhekhārī jī sabhi tere coj viḍāṇā.
Tūṁ āpe dātā āpe bhugtā jī hau tudhu binu avaru na jāṇā.
Tūṁ Pārabrahamu beaṁtu beaṁtu jī tere kiā guṇ ākhi vakhāṇā.
Jo sevahi jo sevahi tudhu jī janu Nānaku tin qurbāṇā 2.
Hari dhiāvahi Hari dhiāvahi tudhu jī
se jan jug mahi sukhvāsī.
Se mukatu se mukatu bhae jin Hari dhiāiā jī
tin tūṭī jam kī phāsī.
Jin nirbhau jin Hari nirbhau dhiāiā jī
tin kā bhau sabhu gavāsī.

Jin seviā jin seviā merā Hari jī te Hari Hari rūpi samāsī.
Se dhaṁnu se dhaṁnu jin Hari dhiāiā jī
janu Nānaku tin bali jāsī.3.
Terī bhagati terī bhagati bhaṁḍār jī bhare beaṁt beaṁtā.
Tere bhagat tere bhagat salāhani tudhu jī
Hari anik anek anaṁtā.
Terī anik terī anik karahi Hari pūjā jī
tapu tāpahi japahi beaṁtā.
Tere anek tere anek paṛahi bahu simriti sāsat jī
kari kiriā khaṭu karam karaṁtā.
Se bhagat se bhagat bhale jan Nānak jī
jo bhāvahi mere Hari Bhagavaṁtā.4.
Tūṁ ādi purakhu apraṁparu kartā jī
tudhu jevaḍu avaru na koī.
Tūṁ jugu jugu eko sadā sadā tūṁ eko jī
tūṁ nihacalu kartā soī.
Tudhu āpe bhāvai soī vartai jī tūṁ āpe karahi su hoī.
Tudhu āpe srisaṭi sabh upāī jī tudhu āpe siraji sabh goī.
Janu Nānak guṇ gāvai karte ke jī jo sabhsai kā jāṇoī.5.1.

Glossary :

ਸੋ ਪੁਰਖੁ—That Lord ; ਨਿਰੰਜਨੁ—pure ; ਹਰਿ—Hari ; ਅਗਮਾ ਅਗਮ—unapproachable ; ਅਪਾਰਾ—infinite ; ਸਭਿ—all ; ਧਿਆਵਹਿ—meditate ; ਸਚੇ—true ; ਸਿਰਜਣਹਾਰਾ—creator ; ਜੀਅ—jivas ; ਤੁਮਾਰੇ—Thine ; ਕਾ—of ; ਦਾਤਾਰਾ—giver, donor ; ਸੰਤਹੁ—O saints ; ਦੁਖ—sorrows ; ਵਿਸਾਰਣਹਾਰਾ—dispeller ; ਆਪੇ—Himself ; ਠਾਕੁਰੁ—master ; ਸੇਵਕੁ—servant ; ਕਿਆ—what ; ਜੰਤ—being ; ਵਿਚਾਰਾ—poor, insignificant ; ਤੂੰ—Thou ; ਘਟ—heart ; ਅੰਤਰਿ—within ; ਸਰਬ—all ; ਨਿਰੰਤਰਿ—within ; ਏਕੋ—the one ; ਸਮਾਣਾ—absorbed, contained ; ਇਕਿ—some ; ਦਾਤੇ—donors ; ਭੇਖਾਰੀ—beggar ; ਚੋਜ—frolic ; ਵਿਡਾਣਾ—wondrous ; ਦਾਤਾ—donor ; ਭੁਗਤਾ—enjoyer ; ਹਉ—I ; ਤੁਧੁ ਬਿਨੁ—without Thee ; ਅਵਰੁ ਨ ਜਾਣਾ—not know any other ; ਪਾਰਬ੍ਰਹਮੁ—Transcendent Lord ; ਬੇਅੰਤੁ—limitless ; ਗੁਣ—merit ; ਆਖਿ ਵਖਾਣਾ—describe ; ਜੋ—those ; ਸੇਵਹਿ—serve ; ਕੁਰਬਾਣਾ—sacrifice ; ਜੁਗ—age ; ਮਹਿ—in ; ਸੁਖਵਾਸੀ—living in peace ; ਸੇ—they ; ਮੁਕਤੁ— liberated ; ਭਏ—become ; ਤੂਟੀ—broken ; ਜਮ—angel of death ; ਕੀ—of ; ਫਾਸੀ—noose ; ਨਿਰਭਉ—fearless ; ਭਉ—fear ; ਗਵਾਸੀ—will be lost ; ਸੇਵਿਆ—served ; ਹਰਿ ਰੂਪਿ—form of God ; ਸਮਾਸੀ—will be absorbed ; ਧੰਨੁ—blest ; ਭਗਤਿ—devotion ; ਭੰਡਾਰ—store, treasure ; ਭਰੇ—full ; ਬਿਅੰਤ—infinite ; ਸਲਾਹਨਿ—praise ; ਅਨਿਕ ਅਨੇਕ—many ; ਅਨੰਤਾ—numberless ; ਪੂਜਾ—worship ; ਤਪੁ ਤਾਪਹਿ—practise austerity ; ਜਪਹਿ—repeat ; ਪੜਹਿ—read ; ਬਹੁ—many ; ਸਿਮ੍ਰਿਤਿ—Simritis ; ਸਾਸਤ—Shastras ; ਕਰਿ ਕਿਰਿਆ—perform rituals ; ਕਰੰਤਾ—perform ; ਖਟੁ ਕਰਮ—six religious rites ; ਭਲੇ—good ; ਭਾਵਹਿ—please ; ਭਗਵੰਤਾ—Auspicious Lord ; ਆਦਿ ਪੁਰਖੁ—Primal Being ; ਅਪਰੰਪਰੁ—disassociated ; ਕਰਤਾ—creator ; ਜੇਵਡੁ—as great ; ਜੁਗੁ—age ; ਨਿਹਚਲੁ—stable ; ਵਰਤੈ—comes to pass ; ਸ੍ਰਿਸਟਿ—world ; ਉਪਾਈ—created ; ਸਿਰਜਿ—created ; ਗੋਈ—destroyed ; ਸਭਸੈ—of all ; ਜਾਣੋਈ—knower.

Translation :

O Thou Pure, Unapproachable and Infinite Lord, O True Creator, all meditate on Thee; all the beings are Thine and Thou art the Donor. O Saint, meditate on the Lord, the dispeller of all sorrows. The Lord Himself is the Master and Himself the servant. What an insignificant being Nanak is !

O Lord, Thou art within every heart and within all, the one Lord, pervading everything. Some are donors and some beggars, wonderful are all Thy frolics. Thou are the donor yourself and the enjoyer yourself. I do not know anyone else except Thee. Thou art the transcendent and limitless Lord. Which of your merits should I describe ? Whosoever serve Thee, I Nanak, am a sacrifice to them.

O Lord, those who meditate on Thee, they live in peace in the Age. Those who have meditated on Thee, they are liberated, their noose of the angel of death has broken. Those who have meditated on the Fearless Lord, all their fears will be lost. Those who have served my Lord, they will be absorbed in the Form of the Lord. Blessed are they who have meditated on the Lord, Nanak will be a sacrifice to them.

O Infinite Lord, the stores of Thy devotion are full. Many and numberless devotees of Thine Praise Thee. O Lord, many are engaged in Thy worship, O infinite Lord, they practise austerities and repeat Thy Name. Many read Smritis and Shastras, and perform rituals and six religious rites. Only those devotees are good, says Nanak, who are liked by my Lord.

O Lord, Thou art the Primal Being and disassociated creator, none is as great as Thee. Thou art the one and only one in all the Ages, Thou art the same stable creator. Everything occurs according to Thy desire. Whatever Thou doest, happens. Thou hast created all the world and after Creation Thou hast destroyed it. Nanak, the person, sings the qualities of the Creator, who is the knower of all.

Comments :

Guru Ramdas, the fourth Sikh Guru, in this hymn entitled 'So Purakhu' (That Purusha) mentions the qualities of that one and only one Lord, who is the Pure, Unapproachable and Infinite Lord, The True Creator, the real Donor, the Dispeller of all sorrows, the All-pervading Lord, the primal Being and the Transcendent Lord. He is the master as well as the servant. He is the Donor as well as the Enjoyer. The True devotees love Him for His affection and kindness. Many people perform rituals and read scriptures in order to please Him but the real devotees are those who are liked and loved by Him. The qualities of the Lord are inexpressible. Those who meditate on Him and repeat His Name are recipients of His Grace. They attain emancipation. They become Fearless because their Lord is Fearless. The Lord creates all, does everything and knows everything. It is the duty of the created beings to meditate on Him and attain unity with Him.

ਆਸਾ ਮਹਲਾ ੪
Āsā Mahlā 4

Text :

ਤੂੰ ਕਰਤਾ ਸਚਿਆਰੁ ਮੈਡਾ ਸਾਂਈ ॥
ਜੋ ਤਉ ਭਾਵੈ ਸੋਈ ਥੀਸੀ ਜੋ ਤੂੰ ਦੇਹਿ ਸੋਈ ਹਉ ਪਾਈ ॥੧॥ਰਹਾਉ॥
ਸਭ ਤੇਰੀ ਤੂੰ ਸਭਨੀ ਧਿਆਇਆ ॥
ਜਿਸ ਨੋ ਕ੍ਰਿਪਾ ਕਰਹਿ ਤਿਨਿ ਨਾਮ ਰਤਨੁ ਪਾਇਆ ॥
ਗੁਰਮੁਖਿ ਲਾਧਾ ਮਨਮੁਖਿ ਗਵਾਇਆ ॥
ਤੁਧੁ ਆਪਿ ਵਿਛੋੜਿਆ ਆਪਿ ਮਿਲਾਇਆ ॥੧॥
ਤੂੰ ਦਰੀਆਉ ਸਭ ਤੁਝ ਹੀ ਮਾਹਿ ॥
ਤੁਝ ਬਿਨੁ ਦੂਜਾ ਕੋਈ ਨਾਹਿ ॥
ਜੀਅ ਜੰਤ ਸਭਿ ਤੇਰਾ ਖੇਲੁ ॥
ਵਿਜੋਗਿ ਮਿਲਿ ਵਿਛੁੜਿਆ ਸੰਜੋਗੀ ਮੇਲੁ ॥੨॥
ਜਿਸ ਨੋ ਤੂ ਜਾਣਾਇਹਿ ਸੋਈ ਜਨੁ ਜਾਣੈ ॥
ਹਰਿ ਗੁਣ ਸਦ ਹੀ ਆਖਿ ਵਖਾਣੈ ॥
ਜਿਨਿ ਹਰਿ ਸੇਵਿਆ ਤਿਨਿ ਸੁਖੁ ਪਾਇਆ ॥

ਸਹਜੇ ਹੀ ਹਰਿ ਨਾਮਿ ਸਮਾਇਆ ॥੩॥
ਤੂ ਆਪੇ ਕਰਤਾ ਤੇਰਾ ਕੀਆ ਸਭੁ ਹੋਇ ॥
ਤੁਧੁ ਬਿਨੁ ਦੂਜਾ ਅਵਰੁ ਨ ਕੋਇ ॥
ਤੂ ਕਰਿ ਕਰਿ ਵੇਖਹਿ ਜਾਣਹਿ ਸੋਇ ॥
ਜਨ ਨਾਨਕ ਗੁਰਮੁਖਿ ਪਰਗਟੁ ਹੋਇ ॥੪॥੨॥

Transliteration :

Tūṁ kartā saciāru maiḍā sāṅī.
Jo tau bhāvai soī thīsī jo tūṁ dehi soī hau pāī.1.*Rahāu*.
Sabh terī tūṁ sabhanī dhiāiā.
Jis no kripā karahi tini nām ratanu pāiā.
Gurmukhi lādhā manmukhi gavāiā.
Tudhu āpi vichoṛiā āpi milāiā.1.
Tūṁ darīāu sabh tujh hī māhi.
Tujh binu dūjā koī nāhi.
Jīa jaṁt sabhi terā khelu.
Vijogi mili vichuṛiā saṁjogī melu.2.
Jis no tū jāṇāihi soī janu jāṇai.
Hari guṇ sad hī ākhi vakhāṇai.
Jini Hari seviā tini sukhu pāiā.
Sahaje hī Hari nāmi samāiā.3.
Tū āpe kartā terā kīā sabhu hoi.
Tudhu binu dūjā avaru na koi.
Tū kari kari vekhahi jāṇahi soi.
Jan Nānak gurmukhi paragaṭu hoi.4.2.

Glossary :

ਤੂੰ—Thou ; ਕਰਤਾ—creator ; ਸਚਿਆਰੁ—True ; ਮੈਡਾ—mine ; ਸਾਂਈ—master ; ਜੋ—what ; ਤਉ—to Thee ; ਭਾਵੈ—pleases ; ਸੋਈ—same ; ਥੀਸੀ—will happen ; ਦੇਹਿ—give ; ਹਉ—I ; ਪਾਈ—obtain ; ਸਭ—all ; ਤੇਰੀ—Thine ; ਸਭਨੀ—all ; ਧਿਆਇਆ—meditated ; ਜਿਸ ਨੋ—to whom ; ਕ੍ਰਿਪਾ ਕਰਹਿ—show grace ; ਤਿਨਿ—they ; ਨਾਮ ਰਤਨੁ—the jewel of the Name ; ਪਾਇਆ—obtained ; ਗੁਰਮੁਖਿ—Guruward, the enlightened person ; ਲਾਧਾ—obtained ; ਮਨਮੁਖਿ—the self-willed ; ਗਵਾਇਆ—lost ; ਤੁਧੁ—Thou ; ਆਪਿ—Thyself ; ਵਿਛੋੜਿਆ—separated ; ਮਿਲਾਇਆ—united ; ਦਰੀਆਉ—river ; ਤੁਝ ਹੀ ਮਾਹਿ—in Thee ; ਤੁਝ ਬਿਨੁ—without Thee ; ਦੂਜਾ—second ; ਕੋਈ ਨਾਹਿ—none ; ਜੀਅ—jiva ; ਜੰਤ—beings ; ਤੇਰਾ—Thine ; ਖੇਲੁ—sport ; ਵਿਜੋਗਿ—separation ; ਮਿਲਿ—meet ; ਵਿਛੁੜਿਆ—separated ;

ਸੰਜੋਗੀ—through destiny ; ਮੇਲੁ—union ; ਜਿਸ ਨੋ—to whom ; ਜਾਣਾਇਹਿ—cause to know ; ਸੋਈ—the same ; ਜਾਣੈ—knows ; ਹਰਿ ਗੁਣ—attributes of the Lord ; ਸਦ ਹੀ—ever ; ਆਖਿ ਵਖਾਣੈ—utters ; ਸੇਵਿਆ—served ; ਜਿਨਿ—those ; ਤਿਨਿ—they ; ਸੁਖੁ ਪਾਇਆ—attained peace ; ਸਹਜੇ ਹੀ—with ease ; ਸਮਾਇਆ—absorbed ; ਕਰਤਾ—creator ; ਕੀਆ—doing ; ਸਭੁ ਹੋਇ—all occurs ; ਅਵਰੁ—other ; ਕਰਿ—create ; ਵੇਖਹਿ—see ; ਜਾਣਹਿ—know ; ਸੋਇ—same ; ਜਨ—person ; ਪਰਗਟੁ ਹੋਇ—is revealed.

Translation :

O Lord, Thou art True Creator and my Master, whatever pleases Thee, will happen. I obtain, whatever Thou givest. All is Thine and all meditate on Thee. On whomsoever Thou showerest Thy Grace, he obtains the jewel of the Name. The Guruward enlightened person gains, but the self-willed loses. Thou Thyself have separated and Thyself united. Thou art the river and everything is within Thee. There is none other without Thee. The jivas and beings are all Thy sport. In separation the united are separated and through destiny they are again united. That person only knows, whom Thou causest to know. He always utters the attributes of the Lord. Those who have served the Lord, they have attained peace. They are absorbed with ease in the Name of the Lord. Thou art the creator Thyself and everything occurs at Thy doing. There is none other except Thee. Thou createst, seeest and knowest the same. The Guruward enlightened person is revealed, says Nanak.

Comments :

In this hymn, Guru Ramdas, the fourth Guru talks about the Will of the Lord. His Will is Supreme. Whatever God Wills, happens. On whomsoever He showers His Grace, he gets the jewel of the Name of the Lord. Those who are Guruward and enlightened persons, they sing the Praises of the Lord and ultimately attain unity with Him. But those who are self-willed persons they suffer in separation. The Lord who has created the world sees and knows everything and through His Grace the Guruward enlightened person is granted a high status.

ਆਸਾ ਮਹਲਾ ੧
Āsā Mahlā 1

Text :

ਤਿਤੁ ਸਰਵਰੜੈ ਭਈਲੇ ਨਿਵਾਸਾ ਪਾਣੀ ਪਾਵਕੁ ਤਿਨਹਿ ਕੀਆ ॥
ਪੰਕਜੁ ਮੋਹ ਪਗੁ ਨਹੀ ਚਾਲੈ ਹਮ ਦੇਖਾ ਤਹ ਡੂਬੀਅਲੇ ॥੧॥
ਮਨ ਏਕੁ ਨ ਚੇਤਸਿ ਮੂੜ ਮਨਾ ॥
ਹਰਿ ਬਿਸਰਤ ਤੇਰੇ ਗੁਣ ਗਲਿਆ ॥੧॥ਰਹਾਉ॥
ਨਾ ਹਉ ਜਤੀ ਸਤੀ ਨਹੀ ਪੜਿਆ ਮੂਰਖ ਮੁਗਧਾ ਜਨਮੁ ਭਇਆ ॥
ਪ੍ਰਣਵਤਿ ਨਾਨਕ ਤਿਨ ਕੀ ਸਰਣਾ ਜਿਨ ਤੂੰ ਨਾਹੀ ਵੀਸਰਿਆ ॥੨॥੩॥

Transliteration :

Titu sarvararai bhaīle nivāsā pāṇī pāvaku tinahi kīā.
Pamkaju moh pagu nahī cālai ham dekhā tah ḍūbīale.1.
Man eku na cetasi mūṛ manā.
Hari bisrat tere guṇ galiā.1.*Rahāu.*
Nā hau jatī satī nahī paṛiā mūrakh mugdhā janamu bhaiā.
Praṇvati Nānak tin kī sarṇā jin tūṁ nāhī vīsariā.2.3.

Glossary :

ਤਿਤੁ—that ; ਸਰਵਰੜੈ—pool ; ਭਈਲੇ—become ; ਨਿਵਾਸਾ—abode ; ਪਾਣੀ—water ; ਪਾਵਕੁ—fire ; ਤਿਨਹਿ—He ; ਕੀਆ—did ; ਪੰਕ—mud ; ਜੁ—that ; ਮੋਹ—attachment ; ਪਗੁ—foot ; ਨਹੀ—not ; ਚਾਲੈ— move ; ਹਮ—I ; ਦੇਖਾ—see ; ਤਹ—then ; ਡੂਬੀਅਲੇ—drowning ; ਮਨ—mind, man ; ਏਕੁ—one Lord ; ਨ—not ; ਚੇਤਸਿ—remember ; ਮੂੜ—foolish ; ਮਨਾ—mind ; ਹਰਿ—God ; ਬਿਸਰਤ—forgetting ; ਤੇਰੇ—your ; ਗੁਣ—merit ; ਗਲਿਆ—wasted away ; ਹਉ—I ; ਜਤੀ—continent ; ਸਤੀ—true ; ਪੜਿਆ—educated ; ਮੂਰਖ—foolish ; ਮੁਗਧਾ—ignorant ; ਜਨਮੁ ਭਇਆ—been born ; ਪ੍ਰਣਵਤਿ—pray ; ਤਿਨ ਕੀ—their, them ; ਸਰਣਾ—shelter ; ਜਿਨ—whom ; ਵੀਸਰਿਆ—forgotten.

Translation :

In that pool (of the world) I have got the abode where He, the Lord has created both water and fire. In the mud of attachment, my foot does not move, I see (the people) drowning there. O foolish mind, why do you not remember the One Lord. By forgetting Him, you have wasted away your merit. I am neither a man of continence, nor of truth nor of education. I have been born foolish and ignorant. Nanak prays that he has taken shelter of those persons, whom Thou could not be forgotten.

Comments :

This hymn of Guru Nanak Dev is an instance of a humble prayer. In the pool of the world, where the water and fire work side by side, he sees people sinking in the mud of attachment. He warns his mind to be cautious and remain in the company of chaste, truthful and wise persons who always remember the Lord and thus make the best use of this precious birth.

ਆਸਾ ਮਹਲਾ ੫
Āsā Mahlā 5

Text :

ਭਈ ਪਰਾਪਤਿ ਮਾਨੁਖ ਦੇਹੁਰੀਆ ॥
ਗੋਬਿੰਦ ਮਿਲਣ ਕੀ ਇਹ ਤੇਰੀ ਬਰੀਆ ॥
ਅਵਰਿ ਕਾਜ ਤੇਰੈ ਕਿਤੈ ਨ ਕਾਮ ॥
ਮਿਲੁ ਸਾਧ ਸੰਗਤਿ ਭਜੁ ਕੇਵਲ ਨਾਮ ॥੧॥
ਸਰੰਜਾਮਿ ਲਾਗੁ ਭਵਜਲ ਤਰਨ ਕੈ ॥
ਜਨਮੁ ਬ੍ਰਿਥਾ ਜਾਤ ਰੰਗਿ ਮਾਇਆ ਕੈ ॥੧॥ ਰਹਾਉ ॥
ਜਪੁ ਤਪੁ ਸੰਜਮੁ ਧਰਮੁ ਨ ਕਮਾਇਆ ॥
ਸੇਵਾ ਸਾਧ ਨ ਜਾਨਿਆ ਹਰਿ ਰਾਇਆ ॥
ਕਹੁ ਨਾਨਕ ਹਮ ਨੀਚ ਕਰੰਮਾ ॥
ਸਰਣਿ ਪਰੇ ਕੀ ਰਾਖਹੁ ਸਰਮਾ ॥੨॥੪॥

Transliteration :

Bhaī parāpati mānukh dehuriā.
Gobimd milaṇ kī ih terī bariā.
Avari kāj terai kitai na kām.
Milu sādh samgati bhaju keval nām-1.
Saramjāmi lāgu bhavjal taran kai.
Janamu brithā jāt ramgi māiā kai-1.*Rahāu.*
Japu tapu samjamu dharamu na kamāiā.
Sevā sādh na jāniā Hari rāiā.
Kahu Nānak ham nīc karammā.
Saraṇī pare kī rākhahu sarmā.2.4.

Glossary :

ਭਈ ਪਰਾਪਤਿ—has been obtained ; ਮਾਨੁਖ—human ; ਦੇਹੁਰੀਆ—body ; ਗੋਬਿੰਦ—God ; ਮਿਲਣ—meeting ; ਕੀ—of ; ਇਹ—this ; ਤੇਰੀ—yours ; ਬਰੀਆ—chance, time, turn ; ਅਵਰਿ—other ; ਕਾਜ— work ; ਤੇਰੈ—to you ;

ਕਿਤੈ ਨ ਕਾਮ—of no avail ; ਮਿਲੁ—meet ; ਸਾਧ ਸੰਗਤਿ—company of the saints ; ਭਜੁ—worship, remember ; ਕੇਵਲ—only ; ਨਾਮ—Name of the Lord ; ਸਰੰਜਾਮਿ—effort ; ਲਾਗੁ—make ; ਭਵਜਲ—dreadful world-ocean ; ਤਰਨ ਕੈ—for crossing ; ਜਨਮੁ—birth ; ਬ੍ਰਿਥਾ ਜਾਤ—passes in vain ; ਰੰਗਿ—love ; ਮਾਇਆ ਕੈ—of maya, of worldliness ; ਜਪੁ—meditation ; ਤਪੁ—austerity ; ਸੰਜਮੁ—self-restraint ; ਧਰਮੁ—faith ; ਨ ਕਮਾਇਆ—not practised ; ਸੇਵਾ—service ; ਸਾਧ—saint ; ਨ ਜਾਨਿਆ—not known ; ਹਰਿ ਰਾਇਆ—God, the King ; ਕਹੁ—says ; ਹਮ—I, we ; ਨੀਚ—mean ; ਕਰੰਮਾ—actions ; ਸਰਣਿ ਪਰੇ ਕੀ—of shelter-seeker ; ਰਾਖਹੁ—protect, preserve ; ਸਰਮਾ—honour.

Translation :

The human body has been obtained and this is the only chance of meeting the Lord. Other works are of no avail, meet the company of the saints and remember only the Name of the Lord. For crossing the dreadful world-ocean make effort. The birth is being wasted in the love of maya (worldliness). I have not practised meditation, austerity, self-restraint and faith, I have not served the saints and have not known God, the king, Nanak says, I am a man of lowly actions. O Lord, I seek Thy shelter, protect my honour.

Comments :

In this hymn, the fifth Guru, Guru Arjan Dev, talks about the precious human birth, which is the only chance of meeting the Lord. Our emphasis should be on the remembrance of the Name of the Lord in this world of maya. Since we have not traversed the path of religion having been without devotion, piety, self-restraint and service of the saints, we should seek the refuge of the Lord.

CHAUPAĪ (QUATRAIN)

ਪਾ: ੧੦ ਕਬਿਯੋ ਬਾਚ ਬੇਨਤੀ ॥ ਚੌਪਈ ॥

(UTTERANCE OF THE POET—PRAYER)

Text :

ਹਮਰੀ ਕਰੋ ਹਾਥ ਦੈ ਰੱਛਾ ॥
ਪੂਰਨ ਹੋਇ ਚਿਤ ਕੀ ਇੱਛਾ ॥
ਤਵ ਚਰਨਨ ਮਨ ਰਹੈ ਹਮਾਰਾ ॥
ਅਪਨਾ ਜਾਨ ਕਰੋ ਪ੍ਰਤਿਪਾਰਾ ॥੧॥
ਹਮਰੇ ਦੁਸਟ ਸਭੈ ਤੁਮ ਘਾਵਹੁ ॥

ਆਪੁ ਹਾਥ ਦੈ ਮੋਹਿ ਬਚਾਵਹੁ ॥
ਸੁਖੀ ਬਸੈ ਮੋਰੋ ਪਰਿਵਾਰਾ ॥
ਸੇਵਕ ਸਿਖ ਸਭੈ ਕਰਤਾਰਾ ॥੨॥
ਮੋ ਰੱਛਾ ਨਿਜ ਕਰ ਦੈ ਕਰਿਯੈ ॥
ਸਭ ਬੈਰਨ ਕੋ ਆਜ ਸੰਘਰਿਯੈ ॥
ਪੂਰਨ ਹੋਇ ਹਮਾਰੀ ਆਸਾ ॥
ਤੋਰ ਭਜਨ ਕੀ ਰਹੈ ਪਿਆਸਾ ॥੩॥
ਤੁਮਹਿ ਛਾਡਿ ਕੋਈ ਅਵਰ ਨ ਧਯਾਊਂ ॥
ਜੋ ਬਰ ਚਹੋਂ ਸੁ ਤੁਮ ਤੇ ਪਾਊਂ ॥
ਸੇਵਕ ਸਿੱਖ ਹਮਾਰੇ ਤਾਰੀਅਹਿ ॥
ਚੁਨਿ ਚੁਨਿ ਸਤ੍ਰ ਹਮਾਰੇ ਮਾਰੀਅਹਿ ॥੪॥
ਆਪ ਹਾਥ ਦੈ ਮੁਝੈ ਉਬਰਿਯੈ ॥
ਮਰਨ ਕਾਲ ਕਾ ਤ੍ਰਾਸ ਨਿਵਰਿਯੈ ॥
ਹੂਜੋ ਸਦਾ ਹਮਾਰੇ ਪੱਛਾ ॥
ਸ੍ਰੀ ਅਸਿਧੁਜ ਜੂ ਕਰਿਯਹੁ ਰੱਛਾ ॥੫॥

Transliteration :

Hamrī karo hāth dai racchā.
Pūran hoi cit kī icchā.
Tav charanan man rahai hamārā.
Apnā jān karo pratipārā.1.
Hamre dusṭ sabhai tum ghāvahu.
Āpu hāth dai mohi bacāvahu.
Sukhī basai moro parivārā.
Sewak sikkh sabhai kartārā.2.
Mo racchā nij kar dai karīyai.
Sabh bairan ko āj saṁgharīyai.
Pūran hoi hamārī āsā.
Tor bhajan kī rahai piāsā.3.
Tumahi chāḍi koī avar na dhiāūṁ.
Jo bar chahoṁ su tum te pāūṁ.
Sewak sikkh hamāre tārīahi.
Cuni cuni satr hamāre mārīahi.4.
Āp hāth dai mujhai ubariyai.
Maran kāl kā trās nivariyai.
Hū jo sadā hamāre pacchā.
Srī asidhuj jū kariyahu racchā.5.

Glossary :

ਹਮਰੀ ਕਰੋ—do to us ; ਹਾਥ ਦੈ—giving hand ; ਰੱਛਾ—protection ; ਪੂਰਨ ਹੋਇ—be fulfilled ; ਚਿਤ ਕੀ—of the mind ; ਇੱਛਾ—desire ; ਤਵ—Thine ; ਚਰਨਨ—feet ; ਮਨ ਰਹੈ ਹਮਾਰਾ—our mind be absorbed ; ਅਪਨਾ ਜਾਨ—considering Thine own ; ਕਰੋ ਪ੍ਰਤਿਪਾਰਾ—do protect, preserve ; ਦੁਸਟ—vicious, wicked, evil-minded ; ਸਭੈ—all ; ਘਾਵਹੁ—kill, destroy ; ਮੋਹਿ—to me ; ਬਚਾਵਹੁ—protect ; ਸੁਖੀ ਬਸੈ—may live in comfort ; ਮੋਰੋ—mine ; ਪਰਿਵਾਰਾ—family ; ਸੇਵਕ—servants, dependants ; ਸਿੱਖ—disciples ; ਕਰਤਾਰਾ—O Lord, O Creator ; ਮੋ—me ; ਨਿਜ ਕਰ ਦੈ ਕਰਿਯੈ—do it with Thy own hands ; ਬੈਰਨ—enemies ; ਆਜ—today, now ; ਸੰਘਰਿਯੈ—killed, destroyed ; ਆਸਾ—hopes ; ਤੋਰ—Thine ; ਭਜਨ—meditation, worship ; ਰਹੈ ਪਿਆਸਾ—remain athirsty ; ਤੁਮਹਿ ਛਾਡਿ—leaving Thee ; ਕੋਈ ਅਵਰੁ—any other ; ਧਯਾਊਂ—meditate ; ਜੋ—whatever ; ਬਰ—boon ; ਚਹੋਂ—want, desire ; ਪਾਊਂ—obtain ; ਤਾਰੀਅਹਿ—came to swim, to free from transmigration ; ਚੁਨਿ ਚੁਨਿ—select, pick ; ਸਤ੍ਰੁ—enemy ; ਮਾਰੀਅਹਿ—kill ; ਮੁਝੈ ਉਬਰਿਯੈ—save me ; ਮਰਨ ਕਾਲ ਕਾ—the time of death ; ਤ੍ਰਾਸ—fear ; ਨਿਵਰਿਯੈ—remove ; ਹੂਜੋ ਸਦਾ—be always ; ਪੱਛਾ—side ; ਸ੍ਰੀ ਅਸਿਧੁਜ ਜੂ—He on whose banner the insignia is the Sword ; Lord-God, the Great Destroyer.

Translation :

Protect me, O Lord ! with Thy own Hands. The desire of my mind be fulfilled. My mind may remain at Thy Feet. Preserve me, considering me Thy own.

Destroy all my vicious adversaries and save me with Thy own Hands. Let my family live in peace, O Creator-Lord, alongwith all servants, dependants and disciples.

Protect me with Thy own Hands and destroy now all my enemies. May my desire be fulfilled and I may remain athirsty of your worship.

I may not worship any other except You and receive the desired boon from Thee alone. Make all my dependants and disciples free from transmigration and picking all my enemies kill them.

Save me with Thy own Hands and remove the fear of the time of death. Remain always on my side, O Lord-God, protect me.

Comments :

In the above five stanzas of *Chaupai*, the Tenth Master has prayed to the Lord for his protection and also of his dependants and disciples from the enemies and wicked people.

Text :

ਰਾਖਿ ਲੇਹੁ ਮੁਹਿ ਰਾਖਨਹਾਰੇ ॥
ਸਾਹਿਬ ਸੰਤ ਸਹਾਇ ਪਿਆਰੇ ॥
ਦੀਨ ਬੰਧੁ ਦੁਸਟਨ ਕੇ ਹੰਤਾ ॥
ਤੁਮ ਹੋ ਪੁਰੀ ਚਤੁਰ ਦਸ ਕੰਤਾ ॥੬॥
ਕਾਲ ਪਾਇ ਬ੍ਰਹਮਾ ਬਪੁ ਧਰਾ ॥
ਕਾਲ ਪਾਇ ਸਿਵ ਜੂ ਅਵਤਰਾ ॥
ਕਾਲ ਪਾਇ ਕਰ ਬਿਸਨੁ ਪ੍ਰਕਾਸਾ ॥
ਸਕਲ ਕਾਲ ਕਾ ਕੀਆ ਤਮਾਸਾ ॥੭॥
ਜਵਨ ਕਾਲ ਜੋਗੀ ਸਿਵ ਕੀਓ ॥
ਬੇਦ ਰਾਜ ਬ੍ਰਹਮਾ ਜੂ ਥੀਓ ॥
ਜਵਨ ਕਾਲ ਸਭ ਲੋਕ ਸਵਾਰਾ ॥
ਨਮਸਕਾਰ ਹੈ ਤਾਹਿ ਹਮਾਰਾ ॥੮॥
ਜਵਨ ਕਾਲ ਸਭ ਜਗਤ ਬਨਾਯੋ ॥
ਦੇਵ ਦੈਤ ਜੱਛਨ ਉਪਜਾਯੋ ॥
ਆਦਿ ਅੰਤਿ ਏਕੈ ਅਵਤਾਰਾ ॥
ਸੋਈ ਗੁਰੂ ਸਮਝਿਯਹੁ ਹਮਾਰਾ ॥੯॥
ਨਮਸਕਾਰ ਤਿਸ ਹੀ ਕੋ ਹਮਾਰੀ ॥
ਸਕਲ ਪ੍ਰਜਾ ਜਿਨ ਆਪ ਸਵਾਰੀ ॥
ਸਿਵਕਨ ਕੋ ਸਿਵ ਗੁਨ ਸੁਖ ਦੀਓ ॥
ਸੱਤ੍ਰੁਨ ਕੋ ਪਲ ਮੋ ਬਧ ਕੀਓ ॥੧੦॥

Transliteration :

Rākhi lehu muhi rākhanhāre.
Sāhib saṁt sahāi piāre.
Dīn baṁdhu dusṭan ke haṁtā.
Tum ho purī catur das kaṁtā.6.
Kāl pāi Brahmā bapu dharā.
Kāl pāi Siv jū avtarā.
Kāl pāi kar Bisanu prakāsā.
Sakal kāl kā kīā tamāsā.7.
Javan kāl jogī siv kīo.
Bed rāj Brahmā jū thīo.
Javan kāl sabh lok savārā.
Namaskār hai tāhi hamārā.8.

Javan kāl sabh jagat banāyo.
Dev dait jacchan upjāyo.
Ādi aṁti ekai avtārā.
Soī Gurū samjhiyahu hamārā.9.
Namaskār tis hī ko hamārī.
Sakal prajā jin āp savārī.
Sivakan ko siv gun sukh dīo.
Sattrun ko pal mo badh kīo.10.

Glossary :

ਰਾਖਿ ਲੇਹੁ ਮੁਹਿ—protect me ; ਰਾਖਨਹਾਰੇ—protector ; ਸਾਹਿਬ—Lord ; ਸੰਤ ਸਹਾਇ—helper of the saints ; ਪਿਆਰੇ—beloved ; ਦੀਨ ਬੰਧੁ—friend of the lowly ; ਦੁਸਟਨ—evil-minded persons ; ਹੰਤਾ—killer ; ਤੁਮ ਹੋ—Thou art ; ਪੁਰੀ ਚਤੁਰ ਦਸ—the fourteen worlds ; ਕੰਤਾ—master ; ਕਾਲ—time, period ; ਬ੍ਰਹਮਾ—the God Brahma ; ਬਪੁ ਧਰਾ—was born ; ਸਿਵ ਜੂ—the God Shiva ; ਅਵਤਰਾ—was born ; ਬਿਸਨੁ—the God Vishnu ; ਪ੍ਰਕਾਸਾ—appeared ; ਸਕਲ—all ; ਕੀਆ—did display ; ਤਮਾਸਾ—spectacle ; ਜਵਨ—He, the Lord ; ਜੋਗੀ—yogi ; ਬੇਦ ਰਾਜ—the author of the Vedas ; ਥੀਓ—became manifest ; ਲੋਕ—worlds ; ਸਵਾਰਾ—created ; ਨਮਸਕਾਰ—salutation, bow in obeisance ; ਤਾਹਿ—to Him ; ਜਗਤ ਬਨਾਯੋ—created the world ; ਦੇਵ—gods ; ਦੈਤ—demons ; ਜੱਛਨ—yakshas ; ਉਪਜਾਯੋ—created ; ਆਦਿ—in the beginning ; ਅੰਤਿ—at the end ; ਏਕੈ—the one ; ਅਵਤਾਰਾ—manifested ; ਸੋਈ—the same ; ਗੁਰੂ—Guru, Preceptor ; ਸਮਝਿਯਹੁ—consider ; ਪ੍ਰਜਾ—subjects, people ; ਆਪ—Himself ; ਸਿਵਕਨ—servants, dependants ; ਸਿਵ ਗੁਨ—Beneficent qualities ; ਸੁਖ ਦੀਓ—gave comfort, gave peace ; ਸੱਤ੍ਰੁਨ—enemies ; ਪਲ ਮੋ—in an instant ; ਬਧ ਕੀਓ—killed.

Translation :

O my Protector, protect me. O Beloved Lord, Thou helpest the saints. O Friend of the lowly, the killer of the wicked people, Thou art the Master of the fourteen worlds.

In time Brahma was born. In time Siva was born. In time Vishnu appeared. All the spectacle has been displayed by time.

He, the Lord, in time, created the Yogi Siva. Brahma the author of the Vedas, became manifest. He, the Lord, in time, created all the worlds, I bow in obeisance to Him.

He, the Lord, in time, created all the worlds. He created gods, demons and yakshas. The One manifestation is there in the beginning and at the end. Consider Him as my Guru (Preceptor).

I bow in obeisance to Him, Who has Himself created all the subjects. He gave comfort and beneficent qualities to His dependants and, in an instant, killed the enemies.

Comments :

In the above five stanzas of *Chaupai*, the Tenth Master has mentioned very briefly the process of creation. The Lord created Brahma, Vishnu and Shiva, who represent the faculties of creation, preservation and destruction. The Lord, in time, not only created these gods, but also other gods, demons and yakshas. The Lord Himself is the same in all ages. The Guru bows before the Lord, who created all the worlds and subjects and gives comfort to the faithful and destroys the enemies.

Text :

ਘਟ ਘਟ ਕੇ ਅੰਤਰ ਕੀ ਜਾਨਤ ॥
ਭਲੇ ਬੁਰੇ ਕੀ ਪੀਰ ਪਛਾਨਤ ॥
ਚੀਟੀ ਤੇ ਕੁੰਚਰ ਅਸਥੂਲਾ ॥
ਸਭ ਪਰ ਕ੍ਰਿਪਾ ਦ੍ਰਿਸਟਿ ਕਰ ਫੂਲਾ ॥੧੧॥
ਸੰਤਨ ਦੁਖ ਪਾਏ ਤੇ ਦੁਖੀ ॥
ਸੁਖ ਪਾਏ ਸਾਧੁਨ ਕੇ ਸੁਖੀ ॥
ਏਕ ਏਕ ਕੀ ਪੀਰ ਪਛਾਨੈਂ ॥
ਘਟ ਘਟ ਕੇ ਪਟ ਪਟ ਕੀ ਜਾਨੈਂ ॥੧੨॥
ਜਬ ਉਦਕਰਖ ਕਰਾ ਕਰਤਾਰਾ ॥
ਪ੍ਰਜਾ ਧਰਤ ਤਬ ਦੇਹ ਅਪਾਰਾ ॥
ਜਬ ਆਕਰਖ ਕਰਤ ਹੋ ਕਬਹੂੰ ॥
ਤੁਮ ਮੈ ਮਿਲਤ ਦੇਹ ਧਰ ਸਭਹੂੰ ॥੧੩॥
ਜੇਤੇ ਬਦਨ ਸ੍ਰਿਸਟਿ ਸਭ ਧਾਰੈ ॥
ਆਪੁ ਆਪਨੀ ਬੂਝ ਉਚਾਰੈ ॥
ਤੁਮ ਸਭ ਹੀ ਤੇ ਰਹਤ ਨਿਰਾਲਮ ॥
ਜਾਨਤ ਬੇਦ ਭੇਦ ਅਰ ਆਲਮ ॥੧੪॥
ਨਿਰੰਕਾਰ ਨ੍ਰਿਬਿਕਾਰ ਨਿਰਲੰਭ ॥
ਆਦਿ ਅਨੀਲ ਅਨਾਦਿ ਅਸੰਭ ॥
ਤਾ ਕਾ ਮੂੜ੍ਹ ਉਚਾਰਤ ਭੇਦਾ ॥
ਜਾ ਕੌ ਭੇਵ ਨ ਪਾਵਤ ਬੇਦਾ ॥੧੫॥

Transliteration :

Ghaṭ ghaṭ ke aṁtar kī jānat.

Bhale bure kī pīr pachānat.
Ciṭī te kuṁcar asthūlā.
Sabh par kripā drisṭi kar phūlā-11.
Saṁtan dukh pāe te dukhī.
Sukh pāe sādhun ke sukhī.
Ek ek kī pīr pachānaiṅ.
Ghaṭ ghaṭ ke paṭ paṭ kī Jānaiṅ-12.
Jab udkarkh karā kartārā.
Prajā dharat tab deh apārā.
Jab ākarkh karat ho kabahūṁ.
Tum mai milat deh dhar sabhahūṁ-13.
Jete badan srisaṭi sabh dhārai.
Āpu āpanī būjh ucārai.
Tum sabh hī te rahat nirālam.
Jānat bed bhed ar ālam-14.
Niraṁkār nribikār nirlaṁbh.
Ādi anīl anādi asaṁbh.
Tā kā mūṛh ucārat bhedā.
Jā kau bhev na pāvat bedā-15.

Glossary :

ਘਟ ਘਟ ਕੇ—of each heart ; ਅੰਤਰ—inside ; ਜਾਨਤ—knows ; ਭਲੇ—good ; ਬੁਰੇ—bad ; ਪੀਰ—pain ; ਪਛਾਨਤ—recognises ; ਚੀਟੀ—the ant ; ਤੇ—to ; ਕੁੰਚਰ—elephant ; ਅਸਥੂਲਾ—of heavy body ; ਕ੍ਰਿਪਾ ਦ੍ਰਿਸਟਿ—the graceful sight ; ਫੂਲਾ—remained in bliss ; ਸੰਤਨ—the saints ; ਦੁਖ ਪਾਏ—suffered, experienced suffering ; ਦੁਖੀ—afflicted, aggrieved ; ਸੁਖ ਪਾਏ—remained comfortable ; ਸਾਧੁਨ—the saints ; ਸੁਖੀ—happy ; ਏਕ ਏਕ ਕੀ—of everyone ; ਪਛਾਨੈਂ—recognises ; ਜਾਨੈਂ—knows ; ਜਬ—when ; ਉਦਕਰਖ ਕਰਾ—created and expanded the world ; ਕਰਤਾਰਾ—Creator ; ਪ੍ਰਜਾ—the people ; ਧਰਤ—to assume, to bear ; ਦੇਹ—body ; ਅਪਾਰਾ—interminable, countless ; ਆਕਰਖ ਕਰਤ—to cause to shrink, to constringe ; ਕਬਹੂੰ—any time ; ਤੁਮ ਮੈ—within yourself ; ਮਿਲਤ—merge ; ਸਭਹੂੰ—all ; ਜੇਤੇ—as many ; ਬਦਨ—mouths, bodies ; ਸ੍ਰਿਸਟਿ—world ; ਧਾਰੈ—assume, bear ; ਆਪੁ ਆਪਨੀ—according to one's ; ਬੂਝ—understanding ; ਉਚਾਰੈ—speak ; ਰਹਤ—be ; ਨਿਰਾਲਮ—aloof, alone ; ਭੇਦ—division, secret ; ਆਲਮ—world ; ਨਿਰੰਕਾਰ—Transcendent Brahma, the Lord God who is Formless ; ਨ੍ਰਿਬਿਕਾਰ—The Lord who is without any vices ; ਨਿਰਲੰਭ—The Lord-God, who is without any prop or support ; ਆਦਿ—who is from the beginning of the world ; ਅਨੀਲ—taintless, without any colour and form ; ਅਨਾਦਿ—who has no beginning ; ਅਸੰਭ—who does not take birth ; ਤਾ ਕਾ—of Him ; ਮੂੜ—the fool ; ਉਚਾਰਤ—speaks ; ਭੇਦਾ—secret ; ਜਾ ਕੌ—whose ; ਭੇਵ—secret ; ਨ ਪਾਵਤ—do not get.

Translation :

The Lord knows everything whatever passes on within the hearts of all beings. He recognises the anguish of all the good and bad people. From an ant to a huge elephant, he showers His grace and remains in blissful mood.

He suffers if the saints suffer ; if the saints enjoy comfort, He is in bliss. He recognises the agony of all and knows whatever passes on within all the hearts.

When the Lord created and expanded the world, the subjects assumed countless bodies. When He causes the world to shrink, all the beings bearing bodies merge in Thee.

Many mouths that the world assumes, speak only according to their understanding. But, O Lord, Thou art aloof from all of them, the world and the divisions of the Vedas know this.

The Formless Lord, without any vices and support, is from the very beginning but He is also without any beginning. He is taintless and unborn. But the fool tries to speak about His secrets, whom even the Vedas could not know.

Comments :

In the above five stanzas of *Chaupai,* the Tenth Master describes some of the Attributes of the Lord. He is omniscient and inner-controller *(antaryamin)*. He knows everything of all beings whether they are human beings or animals, both small in size and huge. He is Graceful. He is the creator of the universe as well as its destroyer. Whatever limited intellect has been given to the human beings, they only talk about the Lord according to their understanding. None has been able to know the secrets of the Lord, though the fools try to talk about Him.

Text :

ਤਾ ਕੌ ਕਰਿ ਪਾਹਨ ਅਨੁਮਾਨਤ ॥
ਮਹਾ ਮੂੜ੍ਹ ਕਛੁ ਭੇਦ ਨ ਜਾਨਤ ॥
ਮਹਾਦੇਵ ਕੌ ਕਹਤ ਸਦਾ ਸਿਵ ॥
ਨਿਰੰਕਾਰ ਕਾ ਚੀਨਤ ਨਹਿ ਭਿਵ ॥੧੬॥

ਆਪੁ ਆਪਨੀ ਬੁਧਿ ਹੈ ਜੇਤੀ ॥
ਬਰਨਤ ਭਿੰਨ ਭਿੰਨ ਤੁਹਿ ਤੇਤੀ ॥
ਤੁਮਰਾ ਲਖਾ ਨ ਜਾਇ ਪਸਾਰਾ ॥
ਕਿਹ ਬਿਧਿ ਸਜਾ ਪ੍ਰਥਮ ਸੰਸਾਰਾ ॥੧੭॥
ਏਕੈ ਰੂਪ ਅਨੂਪ ਸਰੂਪਾ ॥
ਰੰਕ ਭਯੋ ਰਾਵ ਕਹੀ ਭੂਪਾ ॥
ਅੰਡਜ ਜੇਰਜ ਸੇਤਜ ਕੀਨੀ ॥
ਉਤਭੁਜ ਖਾਨਿ ਬਹੁਰ ਰਚਿ ਦੀਨੀ ॥੧੮॥
ਕਹੂੰ ਫੂਲ ਰਾਜਾ ਹ੍ਵੈ ਬੈਠਾ ॥
ਕਹੂੰ ਸਿਮਟਿ ਭਯੋ ਸੰਕਰ ਇਕੈਠਾ ॥
ਸਗਰੀ ਸ੍ਰਿਸਟਿ ਦਿਖਾਇ ਅਚੰਭਵ ॥
ਆਦਿ ਜੁਗਾਦਿ ਸਰੂਪ ਸੁਯੰਭਵ ॥੧੯॥
ਅਬ ਰੱਛਾ ਮੇਰੀ ਤੁਮ ਕਰੋ ॥
ਸਿੱਖ ਉਬਾਰਿ ਅਸਿੱਖ ਸੰਘਰੋ ॥
ਦੁਸ਼ਟ ਜਿਤੇ ਉਠਵਤ ਉਤਪਾਤਾ ॥
ਸਕਲ ਮਲੇਛ ਕਰੋ ਰਣ ਘਾਤਾ ॥੨੦॥

Transliteration :

Tā kau kari pāhan anumānat.
Mahā mūṛh kachu bhed na jānat.
Mahādev kau kahat sadā Siv.
Niraṁkār kā cīnat nahi bhiv.16.
Āpu āpanī budhi hai jetī.
Barnat bhiṁn bhiṁn tuhi tetī.
Tumrā lakhā na jāi pasārā.
Kih bidhi sajā pratham saṁsārā.17.
Ekai rūp anūp sarūpā.
Raṁk bhayo rāv kahi bhūpā.
Aṁḍaj jeraj setaj kīnī.
Utbhuj khāni bahur raci dīnī.18.
Kahūṁ phūl rājā hvai baiṭhā.
Kahūṁ simaṭi bhayo saṁkar ikaiṭhā.
Sagrī srisaṭi dikhāi acaṁbhav.
Ādi jugādi sarūp suyaṁbhav.19.
Ab rachhā merī tum karo.
Sikkh ubāri asikkh saṁgharo.
Dushṭ jite uṭhvat utpātā.
Sakal malech karo raṇ ghātā.20.

Glossary :

ਤਾ ਕੌ—to Him ; ਕਰਿ ਪਾਹਨ—as a stone ; ਅਨੁਮਾਨਤ—imagines ; ਮਹਾ ਮੂੜ੍ਹ—the great fool ; ਮਹਾਦੇਵ—the God Shiva ; ਸਦਾ ਸਿਵ—the eternal Lord ; ਚੀਨਤ—recognise ; ਭਿਵ—secret ; ਬੁਧਿ—intellect ; ਜੇਤੀ—whatever ; ਬਰਨਤ—describes ; ਭਿੰਨ ਭਿੰਨ—differently ; ਤੇਤੀ— in that way ; ਤੁਮਰਾ—yours ; ਲਖਾ—known ; ਪਸਾਰਾ—expanse ; ਕਿਹ ਬਿਧ—in what way ; ਸਜਾ—created ; ਪ੍ਰਥਮ—at first ; ਸੰਸਾਰਾ—the world ; ਏਕੈ ਰੂਪ—the one manifestation ; ਅਨੂਪ—wonderful, unique ; ਸਰੂਪਾ—manifestation ; ਰੰਕ—pauper, poor ; ਭਜੋ—becomes ; ਰਾਵ—the king ; ਕਹੀ—somewhere ; ਭੂਪਾ—the king ; ਅੰਡਜ—beings born from eggs ; ਜੇਰਜ—beings born from the umbilical cord of an animal together with the placenta ; ਸੇਤਜ—beings born from the sweat ; ਕੀਨੀ—created ; ਉਤਭੁਜ ਖਾਨਿ—the division of creation called vegetation ; ਬਹੁਰ—then ; ਰਚਿ ਦੀਨੀ—created ; ਕਹੂੰ—somewhere ; ਫੂਲ—blossoming, inflated, pleased ; ਰਾਜਾ—king ; ਹ੍ਵੈ ਬੈਠਾ—sits ; ਸਿਮਟਿ—shrink ; ਭਜੋ—became ; ਸੰਕਰ ਇਕੈਠਾ—to be condensed, to be collected together ; ਸਗਰੀ—all ; ਦਿਖਾਇ—to cause to be seen ; ਅਚੰਭਵ—wonderful ; ਜੁਗਾਦਿ—from the beginning of the ages ; ਸੁਯੰਭਵ—self-existent ; ਅਬ—now ; ਉਬਾਰਿ—protect ; ਅਸਿੱਖ—who do not follow the discipline of the Guru ; ਸੰਘਰੋ—destroy ; ਜਿਤੇ—all those ; ਉਠਵਤ ਉਤਪਾਤਾ—those who are the cause of heinous crimes ; ਮਲੇਛ—sinners ; ਕਰੋ ਰਣ ਘਾਤਾ—kill, destroy in the battlefield.

Translation :

To the Lord, the great fool imagines as a stone. He does not know even a little secret (about the Lord). He calls Mahadev (Siva) the eternal Lord and does not recognise the secret of the Formless Lord.

Whatever intellect one possesses himself, he describes Thee, O Lord, differently in that way. Thy expanse cannot be known. In what way the world was created, at first ?

Thine is the one unique manifestation, though Thou dost become a pauper and also a king. Thou hast created the divisions of creation, the beings created from eggs, the beings created from placenta, the beings created from sweat and then created vegetation.

Somewhere Thou dost sit inflated as a king, somewhere Thou dost shrink and become collected together. Thou does cause the world to be seen as wonderful. Thou art from the very beginning and from the beginning of the ages. Thy form is self-existent.

Now protect me, O Lord, save my disciples and destroy my adversaries. Kill all the sinners in the battlefield and those wicked people who are the cause of heinous crimes.

Comments :

In the above five stanzas of *Chaupai*, the Tenth Master has described the limited vision of the foolish people who consider the Lord as stone and do not know His Greatness. The Lord is the same one Lord, who manifests Himself as a pauper and also as a king. The Lord created all the four divisions of creation. He is wonderful, self-existent and eternal. The Tenth Guru prays to Him for his protection.

Text :

ਜੇ ਅਸਿਧੁਜ ਤਵ ਸਰਨੀ ਪਰੇ॥
ਤਿਨ ਕੇ ਦੁਸ਼ਟ ਦੁਖਿਤ ਹ੍ਵੈ ਮਰੇ॥
ਪੁਰਖ ਜਵਨ ਪਗ ਪਰੇ ਤਿਹਾਰੇ॥
ਤਿਨ ਕੇ ਤੁਮ ਸੰਕਟ ਸਭ ਟਾਰੇ॥੨੧॥
ਜੋ ਕਲਿ ਕੋ ਇਕ ਬਾਰ ਧਿਐ ਹੈ॥
ਤਾ ਕੇ ਕਾਲ ਨਿਕਟਿ ਨਹਿ ਐ ਹੈ॥
ਰੱਛਾ ਹੋਇ ਤਾਹਿ ਸਭ ਕਾਲਾ॥
ਦੁਸਟ ਅਰਿਸਟ ਟਰੇਂ ਤਤਕਾਲਾ॥੨੨॥
ਕ੍ਰਿਪਾ ਦ੍ਰਿਸਟਿ ਤਨ ਜਾਹਿ ਨਿਹਰਿਹੋ॥
ਤਾ ਕੇ ਤਾਪ ਤਨਕ ਮੋ ਹਰਿਹੋ॥
ਰਿੱਧਿ ਸਿੱਧਿ ਘਰ ਮੋ ਸਭ ਹੋਈ॥
ਦੁਸ਼ਟ ਛਾਹ ਛ੍ਵੈ ਸਕੈ ਨ ਕੋਈ॥੨੩॥
ਏਕ ਬਾਰ ਜਿਨੇ ਤੁਮੈ ਸੰਭਾਰਾ॥
ਕਾਲ ਫਾਸ ਤੇ ਤਾਹਿ ਉਬਾਰਾ॥
ਜਿਨ ਨਰ ਨਾਮ ਤਿਹਾਰੋ ਕਹਾ॥
ਦਾਰਿਦ ਦੁਸਟ ਦੋਖ ਤੇ ਰਹਾ॥੨੪॥
ਖੜਗ ਕੇਤ ਮੈ ਸਰਣਿ ਤਿਹਾਰੀ॥
ਆਪ ਹਾਥ ਦੈ ਲੇਹੁ ਉਬਾਰੀ॥
ਸਰਬ ਠੌਰ ਮੋ ਹੋਹੁ ਸਹਾਈ॥
ਦੁਸਟ ਦੋਖ ਤੇ ਲੇਹੁ ਬਚਾਈ॥੨੫॥

Transliteration :

Je asidhuj tav sarnī pare.
Tin ke dushṭ dukhit hvai mare.

Purakh jawan pag pare tihāre.
Tin ke tum saṁkaṭ sabh ṭāre.21.
Jo kali ko ik bār dhiai hai.
Tā ke kāl nikaṭ nahi ai hai.
Racchā hoi tāhi sabh kālā.
Dusṭ arisṭ ṭareṁ tatkālā.22.
Kripā drisṭi tan jāhi nihariho.
Tā ke tāp tanak mo hariho.
Riddhi siddhi ghar mo sabh hoī.
Dushṭ chāh chvai sakai na koī.23.
Ek bār jin tumai saṁbhārā.
Kāl phās te tāhi ubārā.
Jin nar nām tihāro kahā.
Dārid dusṭ dokh te rahā.24.
Kharag ket mai saraṇi tihārī.
Āp hāth dai lehu ubārī.
Sarab ṭhaur mo hohu sahāī.
Dusṭ dokh te lehu bacāī.25.

Glossary :

ਜੇ—Thou ; ਤਵ—Thine ; ਸਰਨੀ ਪਰੇ—took refuge ; ਦੁਖਿਤ—in suffering ; ਹ੍ਵੈ ਮਰੇ—have died ; ਪੁਰਖ—Purushas, beings ; ਪਗ ਪਰੇ— fallen at the feet ; ਤਿਹਾਰੇ—yours ; ਸੰਕਟ—sufferings ; ਟਾਰੇ—removed ; ਕਲਿ—Kaliyuga, the iron age ; ਇਕ ਬਾਰ—once ; ਧਿਐ ਹੈ—meditated, worshipped ; ਕਾਲ—the messengers of Yama ; ਨਿਕਟਿ ਨਹਿ ਐ ਹੈ—do not come near ; ਕਾਲਾ—time ; ਅਰਿਸਟ—suffering ; ਟਰੇਂ—removed, effaced ; ਤਤਕਾਲਾ—at once ; ਤਨ—body ; ਨਿਹਰਿਹੋ—cast glances, see ; ਤਾਪ—affliction, fever ; ਤਨਕ ਮੋ—in an instant ; ਹਰਿਹੋ—removed ; ਰਿੱਧਿ ਸਿੱਧਿ—the miraculous powers ; ਘਰ ਮੋ—in the house ; ਛਾਹ ਛ੍ਵੈ—destroy (ਛਾਹ—shade, ਛ੍ਵੈ—touch) ; ਸੰਭਾਰਾ—remembered ; ਕਾਲ ਫਾਸ—the noose of Yama ; ਨਰ—man ; ਨਾਮ—name ; ਕਹਾ—spoken ; ਦਾਰਿਦ—poverty ; ਦੋਖ—blemish ; ਤੇ ਰਹਾ—absolved ; ਖੜਗ ਕੇਤ—Lord God, the bearer of the sword ; ਤਿਹਾਰੀ—yours ; ਠੌਰ—place ; ਹੋਹੁ ਸਹਾਈ—be of help ; ਲੇਹੁ ਬਚਾਈ—save.

Translation :

Those persons, O Lord/ who have come under Thy refuge, their wicked adversaries have died in anguish. Those Purushas, who have fallen at Thy feet, Thou hast removed all their sufferings.

Those persons, who worship Thee even once, the messengers of Yama do not come near them. They are protected at all times, the suffering from wicked people is removed at once.

Those on whose bodies Thou does cast Thy Glances, Thou dost remove their afflictions in an instant. In their house abide all the miraculous powers and no wicked person can destroy them (no wicked person can touch even their shade).

Those who have remembered Thee even once, Thou hast saved them from the noose of Yama. Those who have uttered Thy Name, they were absolved from the impact of poverty, wickedness and blemish.

O Lord, the bearer of the sword, I have come under Thy refuge. Save me with Thy own Hands. Help me at all places and save me from wickedness and blemish.

Comments :

In the above five stanzas of *Chaupai*, the Tenth Master advises the people to take refuge in the Lord and come under His Grace because all the afflictions end in an instant, if He casts His Graceful glances on beings. He should always be remembered in order to save ourselves from the punishment of Yama.

ਸ੍ਵੈਯਾ ॥
SWAYYĀ

Text :

ਪਾਂਇ ਗਹੇ ਜਬ ਤੇ ਤੁਮਰੇ ਤਬ ਤੇ ਕੋਊ ਆਂਖ ਤਰੇ ਨਹੀਂ ਆਨ੍ਯੋ ॥
ਰਾਮ ਰਹੀਮ ਪੁਰਾਨ ਕੁਰਾਨ ਅਨੇਕ ਕਹੈਂ ਮਤ ਏਕ ਨ ਮਾਨ੍ਯੋ ॥
ਸਿੰਮ੍ਰਿਤਿ ਸਾਸਤ੍ਰ ਬੇਦ ਸਭੈ ਬਹੁ ਭੇਦ ਕਹੈਂ ਹਮ ਏਕ ਨ ਜਾਨ੍ਯੋ ॥
ਸ੍ਰੀ ਅਸਿਪਾਨ ਕ੍ਰਿਪਾ ਤੁਮਰੀ ਕਰਿ ਮੈ ਨ ਕਹ੍ਯੋ ਸਭ ਤੋਹਿ ਬਖਾਨ੍ਯੋ ॥

ਦੋਹਰਾ ॥

ਸਗਲ ਦੁਆਰ ਕਉ ਛਾਡਿ ਕੈ ਗਹਿਓ ਤੁਹਾਰੋ ਦੁਆਰ ॥
ਬਾਂਹਿ ਗਹੇ ਕੀ ਲਾਜ ਅਸ ਗੋਬਿੰਦ ਦਾਸ ਤੁਹਾਰ ॥

Transliteration :

Pānei gahe jab te tumre tab te koū ānkh tare nahiṅ ānyo.
Rām Rahīm Purān kurān anek kahaiṅ mat ek na mānyo.

Simmarati Sāstr Bed sabhai bahu bhed kahaiṅ
ham ek na jānyo.
Srī asipān kripā tumrī kari mai na kahyo
sabh tohi bakhānyo.

DOHRA

Sagal duār kau chāḍi kai gahio tuhāro duār.
Baṅhi gahe kī lāj as Gobiṁd dās tuhār.

Glossary :

ਪਾਂਇ—feet ; ਗਹੇ—caught ; ਜਬ ਤੇ—from the time ; ਤੁਮਰੇ—yours ; ਤਬ ਤੇ—since that time ; ਕੋਊ—any ; ਆਂਖ—eye ; ਤਰੇ—beneath ; ਨਹੀਂ ਆਨਜੋ—not brought ; ਰਾਮ—Hindu Name of God ; ਰਹੀਮ—Muslim Name of God ; ਪੁਰਾਨ—Hindu sacred texts, Puranas ; ਕੁਰਾਨ—Muslim scripture ; ਅਨੇਕ—many ; ਕਹੈਂ—utter; ਮਤ—advice ; ਏਕ ਨ ਮਾਨਜੋ—not accepted any ; ਸਿੰਮ੍ਰਿਤਿ—Hindu sacred texts—Simritis ; ਸਾਸਤ੍ਰ—six Hindu Shastras ; ਬੇਦ—four Vedas ; ਸਭੈ—all ; ਬਹੁ ਭੇਦ ਕਹੈਂ—speak of many differences ; ਜਾਨਜੋ—known ; ਸ੍ਰੀ ਅਸਿਪਾਨ—Lord God, The bearer of the sword ; ਕ੍ਰਿਪਾ—grace ; ਮੈ ਨ ਕਹਜੋ—I have not said ; ਸਭ ਤੋਹਿ ਬਖਾਨਜੋ—all have been narrated by Thee.

ਸਗਲ—all ; ਦੁਆਰ—doors, gates ; ਕਉ ਛਾਡਿ ਕੈ—forsaking ; ਗਹਿਓ—caught hold of ; ਤੁਹਾਰੋ ਦੁਆਰ—your door ; ਬਾਂਹਿ—arm ; ਲਾਜ—honour ; ਅਸ—such like ; ਗੋਬਿੰਦ—Lord ; ਦਾਸ ਤੁਹਾਰ—your servant.

Translation :

The time from which I have caught Thy Feet, I have not brought anyone else under my sight. They say about many faiths like Rama and Puranas of Hindus, Rahim and Koran of Muslims, but I do not accept any. The Simritis, Shastras and Vedas talk of many aspects, but I do not know any. O my Lord-God, the bearer of the sword, with Thy Grace, Thou hast narrated everything and nothing has been uttered by me.

I have forsaken all the gates and have caught only Thine. Keep Thy such like honour of holding my arm, O Lord, I am Thy servant.

Comments :

In the two stanzas given above, the Tenth Master says that he does not know or recognise anyone else except the Lord, who speaks through Him and who through His Grace, can grant him the honour, for which he supplicates.

ਰਾਮਕਲੀ ਮ: ੩ ਅਨੰਦੁ ॥

Rāmkalī Mahlā 3, Anaṁdu

ੴ ਸਤਿਗੁਰਪ੍ਰਸਾਦਿ ॥

IK AUMKĀR SATIGURPRASĀDI

(The Lord is one who can be realised by the Grace of the True Guru)

STANZA I

Text :

ਅਨੰਦੁ ਭਇਆ ਮੇਰੀ ਮਾਏ ਸਤਿਗੁਰੂ ਮੈ ਪਾਇਆ ॥
ਸਤਿਗੁਰੁ ਤ ਪਾਇਆ ਸਹਜ ਸੇਤੀ ਮਨਿ ਵਜੀਆ ਵਾਧਾਈਆ ॥
ਰਾਗ ਰਤਨ ਪਰਵਾਰ ਪਰੀਆ ਸਬਦ ਗਾਵਣ ਆਈਆ ॥
ਸਬਦੋ ਤ ਗਾਵਹੁ ਹਰੀ ਕੇਰਾ ਮਨਿ ਜਿਨੀ ਵਸਾਇਆ ॥
ਕਹੈ ਨਾਨਕੁ ਅਨੰਦੁ ਹੋਆ ਸਤਿਗੁਰੂ ਮੈ ਪਾਇਆ ॥੧॥

Transliteration :

Anaṁdu bhaiā merī māi Satigurū mai pāiā.
Satiguru ta pāiā sahaj setī mani vajīā vādhāīā.
Rāg ratan parvār parīā sabad gāvaṇ āīā.
Sabado ta gāvahu Harī kerā mani jinī vasāiā.
Kahai Nānaku anaṁdu hoā Satigurū mai pāiā.1.

Glossary :

ਅਨੰਦੁ—bliss ; ਭਇਆ—is experienced ; ਮੇਰੀ ਮਾਏ—my mother ; ਸਤਿਗੁਰੂ—True Guru ; ਮੈ ਪਾਇਆ—I have attained ; ਸਹਜ ਸੇਤੀ—with ease (spontaneity) ; ਮਨਿ—mind ; ਵਜੀਆ—resounded ; ਵਾਧਾਈਆ—congratulations ; ਰਾਗ—musical modes ; ਰਤਨ—jewels ; ਪਰਵਾਰ ਪਰੀਆ—the family of fairies ; ਸਬਦ—hymn, word ; ਗਾਵਣ ਆਈਆ—came to sing ; ਤ—then ; ਗਾਵਹੁ ਹਰੀ ਕੇਰਾ—sing the (hymns) of God ; ਜਿਨੀ—those ; ਵਸਾਇਆ—to cause to dwell ; ਕਹੈ ਨਾਨਕੁ—Nanak says.

Translation :

O my mother ! I have experienced bliss on realising the True Guru. I attained him spontaneously and my mind resounds with congratulations. The musical modes which are like jewels and the families of fairies have come to sing the divine hymn. Those who have enshrined the Lord in their mind, they sing the divine hymn of the Lord. Nanak says : I have experienced bliss on realising the True Guru.

Comments :

In his poem *Anandu* the third Sikh Guru, Guru Amar Das, has given his concept of bliss. In this first stanza, he says that he has experienced bliss on realising the True Guru. In the exuberance of divine bliss, he sings the divine hymn of the Lord and invites the lovers of the Lord also to come and sing the divine song.

STANZA II

Text :

ਏ ਮਨ ਮੇਰਿਆ ਤੂ ਸਦਾ ਰਹੁ ਹਰਿ ਨਾਲੇ ॥
ਹਰਿ ਨਾਲਿ ਰਹੁ ਤੂ ਮੰਨ ਮੇਰੇ ਦੂਖ ਸਭਿ ਵਿਸਾਰਣਾ ॥
ਅੰਗੀਕਾਰੁ ਓਹੁ ਕਰੇ ਤੇਰਾ ਕਾਰਜ ਸਭਿ ਸਵਾਰਣਾ ॥
ਸਭਨਾ ਗਲਾ ਸਮਰਥੁ ਸੁਆਮੀ ਸੋ ਕਿਉ ਮਨਹੁ ਵਿਸਾਰੇ ॥
ਕਹੈ ਨਾਨਕੁ ਮੰਨ ਮੇਰੇ ਸਦਾ ਰਹੁ ਹਰਿ ਨਾਲੇ ॥੨॥

Transliteration :

E man meriā tū sadā rahu Hari nāle.
Hari nāli rahu tū mamn mere dūkh sabhi visāraṇā.
Aṁgīkāru ohu kare terā kāraj sabhi savāraṇā.
Sabhanā galā samrathu suāmī so kio manahu visāre.
Kahai Nānaku mamn mere sadā rahu Hari nāle.2.

Glossary :

ਏ—O ; ਮਨ ਮੇਰਿਆ—my mind ; ਸਦਾ—always ; ਰਹੁ ਹਰਿ ਨਾਲੇ— live with God ; ਦੂਖ—sufferings ; ਵਿਸਾਰਣਾ—to forget ; ਅੰਗੀਕਾਰੁ ਓਹ ਕਰੇ ਤੇਰਾ—He will accept thee ; ਕਾਰਜ ਸਭਿ ਸਵਾਰਣਾ—He will make all your affairs successful ; ਸਭਨਾ—all ; ਗਲਾ—things, affairs ; ਸਮਰਥੁ—powerful ; ਸੁਆਮੀ—the Lord ; ਸੋ ਕਿਉ ਮਨਹੁ ਵਿਸਾਰੇ—why to forget him from the mind ?

Translation :

O my mind ! live aways with the Lord. Live with the Lord, O my mind ! and forget all sufferings. He (the Lord) will accept thee and make all your affairs successful. The Lord is Powerful to do all things, why should we forget Him from our mind ? Nanak says : O my mind ! live always with the Lord.

Comments :

In this second stanza, Guru Amar Das says that the Lord is all powerful and has the power to fulfil all your wishes and remove all sufferings, therefore he should always be remembered.

STANZA III

Text :

ਸਾਚੇ ਸਾਹਿਬਾ ਕਿਆ ਨਾਹੀ ਘਰਿ ਤੇਰੈ ॥
ਘਰਿ ਤ ਤੇਰੈ ਸਭੁ ਕਿਛੁ ਹੈ ਜਿਸੁ ਦੇਹਿ ਸੁ ਪਾਵਏ ॥
ਸਦਾ ਸਿਫਤਿ ਸਲਾਹ ਤੇਰੀ ਨਾਮੁ ਮਨਿ ਵਸਾਵਏ ॥
ਨਾਮੁ ਜਿਨ ਕੈ ਮਨਿ ਵਸਿਆ ਵਾਜੇ ਸਬਦ ਘਨੇਰੇ ॥
ਕਹੈ ਨਾਨਕੁ ਸਚੇ ਸਾਹਿਬ ਕਿਆ ਨਾਹੀ ਘਰਿ ਤੇਰੈ ॥੩॥

Transliteration :

Sāce sāhibā kiā nāhi ghari terai.
Ghari ta terai sabhu kichu hai jisu dehi su pāvae.
Sadā siphati salāh terī nāmu mani vasāvae.
Nāmu jin kai mani vasiā vāje sabad ghanere.
Kahai Nānaku sace sāhib kiā nāhī ghari terai.3.

Glossary :

ਸਾਚੇ ਸਾਹਿਬਾ—O True Lord ; ਕਿਆ—what ; ਘਰਿ ਤੇਰੈ—Thy Home ; ਜਿਸੁ ਦੇਹਿ—to whomsoever you give ; ਸੁ ਪਾਵਏ—he gets ; ਸਦਾ—always ; ਸਿਫਤਿ ਸਲਾਹ—Praise ; ਵਸਾਵਏ—to enshrine ; ਵਾਜੇ ਸਬਦ ਘਨੇਰੇ—many strains resound.

Translation :

O True Lord ! what things are not in Thy Home ? Thou hast everything in Thy Home and whomsoever Thou dost give, he only receives it. He is always busy in singing Thy Praises, who enshrines the Name in his mind. Those who enshrine the Name in their minds, many strains resound there. Nanak says : O True Lord, what things are not in Thy Home ?

Comments :

In this third stanza, Guru Amar Das talks about the Home of the Lord, which is full of everything. The men of God enshrine only His Name in their minds, where in due course many strains of divine music resound.

STANZA IV

Text :

ਸਾਚਾ ਨਾਮੁ ਮੇਰਾ ਆਧਾਰੋ ॥
ਸਾਚੁ ਨਾਮੁ ਅਧਾਰੁ ਮੇਰਾ ਜਿਨਿ ਭੁਖਾ ਸਭਿ ਗਵਾਈਆ ॥

ਕਰਿ ਸਾਂਤਿ ਸੁਖ ਮਨਿ ਆਇ ਵਸਿਆ ਜਿਨਿ ਇਛਾ ਸਭਿ ਪੁਜਾਈਆ ॥
ਸਦਾ ਕੁਰਬਾਣੁ ਕੀਤਾ ਗੁਰੂ ਵਿਟਹੁ ਜਿਸ ਦੀਆ ਏਹਿ ਵਡਿਆਈਆ ॥
ਕਹੈ ਨਾਨਕੁ ਸੁਣਹੁ ਸੰਤਹੁ ਸਬਦਿ ਧਰਹੁ ਪਿਆਰੋ ॥
ਸਾਚਾ ਨਾਮੁ ਮੇਰਾ ਆਧਾਰੋ ॥੪॥

Transliteration :

Sācā nāmu merā ādhāro.
Sācu nāmu adhāru merā jini bhukhā sabhi gavāīā.
Kari sāṁti sukh mani āi vasiā jini ichā sabhi pujāīā.
Sadā kurbāṇu kītā Gurū viṭahu jis dīā ehi vadiāīā.
Kahai Nānaku suṇahu saṁtahu sabadi dharahu piāro.
Sācā Nāmu merā ādhāro.4.

Glossary :

ਸਾਚਾ ਨਾਮੁ—The True Name ; ਮੇਰਾ ਆਧਾਰੋ—my support ; ਜਿਨਿ—which ; ਭੁਖਾ—hungers ; ਗਵਾਈਆ—finished, ended ; ਕਰਿ ਸਾਂਤਿ ਸੁਖ—gave peace ; ਇਛਾ ਸਭਿ ਪੁਜਾਈਆ—fulfilled all the wishes ; ਕੁਰਬਾਣੁ ਕੀਤਾ—became a sacrifice ; ਵਿਟਹੁ—from ; ਜਿਸ ਦੀਆ—whose ; ਏਹਿ ਵਡਿਆਈਆ—these excellences (greatnesses) ; ਸੁਣਹੁ—listen ; ਸੰਤਹੁ—O Saints ; ਸਬਦਿ ਧਰਹੁ ਪਿਆਰੋ—love the Word.

Translation :

My support is only the True Name. The True Name is my support which has finished all my hungers. It has enshrined peace and comfort in my mind and has fulfilled all my desires. I am ever a sacrifice to my Guru, who possesses these excellences. Nanak says : O Saints, listen, love the Name (word), the True Name is my only support.

Comments :

In this fourth stanza, Guru Amar Das says that his only support is the True Name which is the cause of mental peace and satisfaction. The Guru is the giver of the Name, therefore one should totally surrender before him.

STANZA V

Text :

ਵਾਜੇ ਪੰਚ ਸਬਦ ਤਿਤੁ ਘਰਿ ਸਭਾਗੈ ॥
ਘਰਿ ਸਭਾਗੈ ਸਬਦ ਵਾਜੇ ਕਲਾ ਜਿਤੁ ਘਰਿ ਧਾਰੀਆ ॥
ਪੰਚ ਦੂਤ ਤੁਧੁ ਵਸਿ ਕੀਤੇ ਕਾਲੁ ਕੰਟਕੁ ਮਾਰਿਆ ॥

ਧੁਰਿ ਕਰਮਿ ਪਾਇਆ ਤੁਧੁ ਜਿਨ ਕਉ ਸਿ ਨਾਮਿ ਹਰਿ ਕੈ ਲਾਗੇ ॥
ਕਹੈ ਨਾਨਕੁ ਤਹ ਸੁਖੁ ਹੋਆ ਤਿਤੁ ਘਰਿ ਅਨਹਦ ਵਾਜੇ ॥੫॥

Transliteration :

Vāje paṁc sabad titu ghari sabhāgai.
Ghari sabhāgai sabad vāje kalā jitu ghari dhārīā.
Paṁc dūt tudhu vasi kīte kālu kaṁṭaku māriā.
Dhuri karami pāiā tudhu jin kau si nāmi Hari kai lāge.
Kahai Nānaku tah sukhu hoā titu ghari anahad vāje.5.

Glossary :

ਵਾਜੇ—resounded ; ਪੰਚ ਸਬਦ—five kinds of sounds emanating from different musical instruments ; ਤਿਤੁ—that ; ਘਰਿ—house ; ਸਭਾਗੈ—fortunate ; ਕਲਾ—power ; ਜਿਤੁ—in which ; ਧਾਰੀਆ—sustained, taken on ; ਪੰਚ ਦੂਤ—the five vices (evil spirits) i.e. lust, anger, greed, attachment and ego ; ਵਸਿ ਕੀਤੇ—controlled ; ਕਾਲੁ ਕੰਟਕੁ—the thorn of Yama ; ਮਾਰਿਆ—killed ; ਧੁਰਿ—from the very beginning ; ਕਰਮਿ—blessed by grace ; ਨਾਮਿ ਹਰਿ ਕੈ ਲਾਗੇ—are engrossed (absorbed) in the Name of the Lord ; ਤਹ—there ; ਸੁਖੁ ਹੋਆ—peace was attained ; ਅਨਹਦ ਵਾਜੇ—the limitless celestial music resounded.

Translation :

That house is fortunate in which five types of music resound. In that fortunate house the strains of music resound in which the Lord has infused His Power. O Lord, Thou hast controlled the five demons and killed the thorn-like death. Those who have been blessed by Grace from the very beginning, they are engrossed in the Name of the Lord. Nanak says : They have attained peace and the limitless celestial music resounds in their house.

Comments :

In this fifth stanza, Guru Amar Das has talked about five types of music which resound in the mind of a fortunate individual. Such a mind is completely engrossed in the Name of the Lord. The five demons i.e. lust, anger, greed, attachment and ego are brought under control and the state of peace is attained.

FINAL STANZA OF *ANAṀDU* (i.e. 40th)

Text :

ਅਨਦੁ ਸੁਣਹੁ ਵਡਭਾਗੀਹੋ ਸਗਲ ਮਨੋਰਥ ਪੂਰੇ ॥
ਪਾਰਬ੍ਰਹਮੁ ਪ੍ਰਭੁ ਪਾਇਆ ਉਤਰੇ ਸਗਲ ਵਿਸੂਰੇ ॥

ਦੂਖ ਰੋਗ ਸੰਤਾਪ ਉਤਰੇ ਸੁਣੀ ਸਚੀ ਬਾਣੀ ॥
ਸੰਤ ਸਾਜਨ ਭਏ ਸਰਸੇ ਪੂਰੇ ਗੁਰ ਤੇ ਜਾਣੀ ॥
ਸੁਣਤੇ ਪੁਨੀਤ ਕਹਤੇ ਪਵਿਤੁ ਸਤਿਗੁਰੁ ਰਹਿਆ ਭਰਪੂਰੇ ॥
ਬਿਨਵੰਤਿ ਨਾਨਕੁ ਗੁਰ ਚਰਣ ਲਾਗੇ ਵਾਜੇ ਅਨਹਦ ਤੂਰੇ ॥੪੦॥੧॥

Transliteration :

Anadu suṇahu vaḍbhāgīho sagal manorath pūre.
Pārbrahm Prabhu pāiā utre sagal visūre.
Dūkh rog saṁtāp utare suṇī sacī bāṇī.
Saṁt sājan bhae sarse pūre gur te jāṇī.
Suṇte punīt kahte pavitu Satiguru rahiā bharpūre.
Binvaṁti Nānaku Gur caraṇ lāge vāje anhad tūre.40.1.

Glossary :

ਅਨਦੁ—the state of bliss, the name of the poem ; ਸੁਣਹੁ—listen ; ਵਡਭਾਗੀਹੋ—O fortunate persons ; ਸਗਲ—all ; ਮਨੋਰਥ—objectives ; ਪੂਰੇ—will be fulfilled ; ਪਾਰਬ੍ਰਹਮੁ ਪ੍ਰਭੁ—The Transcendental Brahma ; ਪਾਇਆ—realised ; ਉਤਰੇ—were removed ; ਵਿਸੂਰੇ—sufferings, afflictions ; ਦੂਖ—sufferings ; ਰੋਗ—diseases, maladies ; ਸੰਤਾਪ—grief, affliction ; ਉਤਰੇ—removed ; ਸੁਣੀ—heard ; ਸਚੀ ਬਾਣੀ—The True *Vani* (sacred utterance) ; ਸੰਤ—the saints ; ਸਾਜਨ—friends ; ਭਏ ਸਰਸੇ—feel pleased, became happy ; ਪੂਰੇ—perfect ; ਜਾਣੀ—known ; ਸੁਣਤੇ—listeners ; ਪੁਨੀਤ—pure ; ਕਹਤੇ—utterers ; ਪਵਿਤੁ—pure; ਸਤਿਗੁਰੁ—True Guru ; ਭਰਪੂਰੇ—all-Pervading ; ਬਿਨਵੰਤਿ—supplicate ; ਚਰਣ—feet ; ਲਾਗੇ—absorbed ; ਵਾਜੇ—resounded ; ਅਨਹਦ—limitless sound ; ਤੂਰੇ—bugles.

Translation :

O fortunate ones, listen about this state of bliss (Anaṁdu), all your objectives will be fulfilled. The Transcendent Lord has been realised and all the sufferings have ceased. Hearing this *True Bāṇī,* I am rid of afflictions, maladies and sufferings. The saints and friends feel pleased on coming to know of it from the perfect Guru. The listeners and the utterers are pure and they find the True Guru all-pervading. Nanak supplicates that those who are absorbed in the Feet of the Guru, the limitless celestial bugles play within them.

Comments :

In this last stanza of *Anaṁdu,* Guru Amar Das concludes that with the achievement of the state of bliss, the Transcendent Lord is realised. All the sufferings cease and the objectives are fulfilled. This state is realised through the help of the True Guru. In this state the limitless celestial music is heard.

ਮੁੰਦਾਵਣੀ ਮਹਲਾ ੫

Muṁdāvaṇī Mahlā 5

Text :

> ਥਾਲ ਵਿਚਿ ਤਿੰਨਿ ਵਸਤੂ ਪਈਓ ਸਤੁ ਸੰਤੋਖੁ ਵੀਚਾਰੋ ॥
> ਅੰਮ੍ਰਿਤ ਨਾਮੁ ਠਾਕੁਰ ਕਾ ਪਇਓ ਜਿਸ ਕਾ ਸਭਸੁ ਅਧਾਰੋ ॥
> ਜੇ ਕੋ ਖਾਵੈ ਜੇ ਕੋ ਭੁੰਚੈ ਤਿਸ ਕਾ ਹੋਇ ਉਧਾਰੋ ॥
> ਏਹ ਵਸਤੁ ਤਜੀ ਨਹ ਜਾਈ ਨਿਤ ਨਿਤ ਰਖੁ ਉਰਿ ਧਾਰੋ ॥
> ਤਮ ਸੰਸਾਰੁ ਚਰਨ ਲਗਿ ਤਰੀਐ ਸਭੁ ਨਾਨਕ ਬ੍ਰਹਮ ਪਸਾਰੋ ॥੧॥

Transliteration :

Thāl vici tiṁni vasatū paīo satu saṁtokhu vīcāro.

Aṁmrit Nāmu Ṭhākur kā paio jis kā sabhsu adhāro.

Je ko khāvai je ko bhuṁcai tisa kā hoi udhāro.

Eh vasatu tajī nah jāī nit nit rakhu uri dhāro.

Tam saṁsāru caran lagi tarīai

sabhu Nānak Braham pasāro.1.

Glossary :

ਥਾਲ—salver ; ਵਿਚਿ—in ; ਤਿੰਨਿ—three ; ਵਸਤੂ—things ; ਪਈਓ—placed, laid ; ਸਤੁ—truth ; ਸੰਤੋਖੁ—contentment ; ਵੀਚਾਰੋ—wisdom, reflection ; ਅੰਮ੍ਰਿਤ ਨਾਮੁ—Nectar of the Name ; ਠਾਕੁਰ—Lord ; ਜਿਸ ਕਾ—whose ; ਸਭਸੁ—for all ; ਅਧਾਰੋ—support, prop ; ਜੇ ਕੋ—if anyone ; ਖਾਵੈ—eats ; ਭੁੰਚੈ—relishes, eats ; ਤਿਸ ਕਾ—of him ; ਹੋਇ ਉਧਾਰੋ—emancipated, saved ; ਏਹ—this ; ਤਜੀ—forsaken ; ਨਿਤ—always ; ਉਰਿ—heart ; ਧਾਰੋ—keep, hold ; ਤਮ—dark ; ਸੰਸਾਰੁ—world ; ਚਰਨ—feet ; ਲਗਿ—absorbed ; ਤਰੀਐ—swim, cross, delivered ; ਸਭੁ—all ; ਬ੍ਰਹਮ—Brahman, God ; ਪਸਾਰੋ—expanse.

Translation :

In this salver *(of Guru Granth Sahib)* there are placed three things i.e. Truth, Contentment and Knowledge. The Nectar-Name of the Lord, who is the support of all, is also there. If one eats and relishes it, he is emancipated. This thing cannot be forsaken and always keep it enshrined in the heart. The dark world can be crossed by being absorbed in the Feet of the Lord. All (the world) is an expanse of the Lord.

Comments :

This hymn is the seal of the fifth Guru at the end of the *Adi Granth* wherein he considers the scripture as the salver consisting of three things i.e. Truth, Contentment and Knowledge alongwith the Name of the Lord. The Name of the Lord is the innermost Kernel which if enshrined in the heart, takes the seeker to spiritual heights.

ਸਲੋਕ ਮਹਲਾ ੫

Salok Mahlā V

Text :

ਤੇਰਾ ਕੀਤਾ ਜਾਤੋ ਨਾਹੀ ਮੈਨੋ ਜੋਗੁ ਕੀਤੋਈ ॥
ਮੈ ਨਿਰਗੁਣਿਆਰੇ ਕੋ ਗੁਣੁ ਨਾਹੀ ਆਪੇ ਤਰਸੁ ਪਇਓਈ ॥
ਤਰਸੁ ਪਇਆ ਮਿਹਰਾਮਤਿ ਹੋਈ ਸਤਿਗੁਰੁ ਸਜਣੁ ਮਿਲਿਆ ॥
ਨਾਨਕ ਨਾਮੁ ਮਿਲੈ ਤਾਂ ਜੀਵਾਂ ਤਨੁ ਮਨੁ ਥੀਵੈ ਹਰਿਆ ॥੧॥

Transliteration :

Terā kītā jāto nāhī maino jogu kītoī.
Mai nirguṇiāre ko guṇu nāhī āpe tarasu paioī.
Tarasu paiā miharāmati hoī Satiguru sajaṇu miliā.
Nānak nāmu milai tāṅ jīvāṅ tanu manu thīvai hariā.1.

Glossary :

ਤੇਰਾ—Thine, yours ; ਕੀਤਾ—doing, action ; ਜਾਤੋ—known, realised ; ਨਾਹੀ—not ; ਮੈਨੋ—to me ; ਜੋਗੁ—worthy, capable ; ਕੀਤੋਈ—made ; ਨਿਰਗੁਣਿਆਰੇ—meritless, without any qualities ; ਕੋ—any ; ਗੁਣੁ—quality ; ਆਪੇ—to Him ; ਤਰਸੁ ਪਇਓਈ—took pity, became merciful ; ਮਿਹਰਾਮਤਿ—merciful, kind ; ਹੋਈ—became ; ਸਤਿਗੁਰੁ—True Guru ; ਸਜਣੁ—friend ; ਮਿਲਿਆ—met ; ਮਿਲੈ—blessed with, receive ; ਤਾਂ—then ; ਜੀਵਾਂ—alive ; ਤਨੁ—body ; ਮਨੁ—mind ; ਥੀਵੈ—become ; ਹਰਿਆ—green, flourishing, blossoming.

Translation :

I have not realised (your kindness) in making me worthy (of this service). I am a meritless man without any quality. Thou has taken pity on me. Thy mercy towards me is Thy kindness which has enabled me to meet the True Guru, my friend. Nanak says,

O Lord, if I am blessed with the Name, then I consider myself alive and my body and mind flourish and blossom.

Comments :

In this concluding Shaloka, Guru Arjan Dev, in great humility, thanks the Lord for making him worthy of the service (of preparing *Granth Sahib*). It was solely due to the kindness and mercy of the Lord who caused him to meet the Perfect Guru and get absorbed with the Name of the Lord which resulted in the blossoming of his body and mind.

ARDĀS

FORMAL PRAYER

ਅਰਦਾਸ

ੴ ਵਾਹਿਗੁਰੂ ਜੀ ਕੀ ਫ਼ਤਹ॥

IK AUMKĀR WĀHEGURŪ JĪ KĪ FATEH

(The Lord is One and the Victory is of the Lord)

ਵਾਰ ਸ੍ਰੀ ਭਗੌਤੀ ਜੀ ਕੀ ਪਾਤਿਸ਼ਾਹੀ ੧੦॥

Vār (Ballad) of Srī Bhagautī Jī Kī (the Lord-God) Pātishāhī X

(Composed by the Tenth Guru)

Text :

ਪ੍ਰਿਥਮ ਭਗੌਤੀ ਸਿਮਰਿ ਕੈ ਗੁਰ ਨਾਨਕ ਲਈਂ ਧਿਆਇ।
ਫਿਰ ਅੰਗਦ ਗੁਰ ਤੇ ਅਮਰਦਾਸੁ ਰਾਮਦਾਸੈ ਹੋਈਂ ਸਹਾਇ।
ਅਰਜਨ ਹਰਿਗੋਬਿੰਦ ਨੋ ਸਿਮਰੌ ਸ੍ਰੀ ਹਰਿਰਾਇ।
ਸ੍ਰੀ ਹਰਿਕ੍ਰਿਸ਼ਨ ਧਿਆਈਐ ਜਿਸ ਡਿਠੇ ਸਭਿ ਦੁਖ ਜਾਇ।
ਤੇਗ ਬਹਾਦਰ ਸਿਮਰਿਐ ਘਰ ਨਉ ਨਿਧਿ ਆਵੈ ਧਾਇ।
ਸਭ ਥਾਈਂ ਹੋਇ ਸਹਾਇ।
ਦਸਵੇਂ ਪਾਤਸ਼ਾਹ ਸ੍ਰੀ ਗੁਰੂ ਗੋਬਿੰਦ ਸਿੰਘ ਸਾਹਿਬ ਜੀ!
ਸਭ ਥਾਈਂ ਹੋਇ ਸਹਾਇ।
ਦਸਾਂ ਪਾਤਿਸ਼ਾਹੀਆਂ ਦੀ ਜੋਤਿ ਸ੍ਰੀ ਗੁਰੂ ਗ੍ਰੰਥ ਸਾਹਿਬ ਜੀ ਦੇ
ਪਾਠ ਦੀਦਾਰ ਦਾ ਧਿਆਨ ਧਰ ਕੇ ਬੋਲੋ ਜੀ ਵਾਹਿਗੁਰੂ!

Transliteration :

Pritham Bhagautī simari kai Gur Nānak laiṅ dhiāi.
Phir Aṁgad Gur te Amardāsu Rāmdāsai hoiṅ sahāi.
Arjan Harigobiṁd no simarau Srī Harirāi.
Srī Harikrishan dhiāīai jis ḍiṭhe sabhi dukh jāi.
Teg Bahādar simariai ghar nau nidhi āvai dhāi.
Sabh thāiṅ hoi sahāi.
Dasweṅ Pātshāh Srī Gurū Gobiṁd Singh Sāhib jī!

Sabh thāīṅ hoi sahāi.

Dasāṅ Pātishāhīāṅ dī joti Srī Gurū Gramth Sāhib jī de pāṭh dīdār dā dhiān dhar ke bolo jī Wāhigurū !

Glossary :

ਪ੍ਰਿਥਮ—at first ; ਭਗੌਤੀ- God ; ਸਿਮਰਿ—remember ; ਧਿਆਇ—meditated, worshipped; ਫਿਰ—then ; ਹੋਈਂ ਸਹਾਇ—became helpful ; ਜਿਸ—whom ; ਡਿਠੇ—seeing ; ਦੁਖ ਜਾਇ—suffering ceases ; ਘਰ—home ; ਨਉ ਨਿਧਿ—nine treasures ; ਆਵੈ—comes ; ਧਾਇ—running ; ਸਭ ਥਾਈਂ—at all places ; ਦਸਵੇਂ ਪਾਤਸ਼ਾਹ—Tenth King (Guru) ; ਜੋਤ—light ; ਪਾਠ—recitation ; ਦੀਦਾਰ—sight ; ਧਿਆਨ ਧਰ ਕੇ—contemplating ; ਬੋਲੋ ਜੀ—utter ; ਵਾਹਿਗੁਰੂ—The Name of the Lord.

Translation :

At first, remember Bhagauti (Primal Power, whose symbol is the sword) and then Guru Nanak. Then (I remember) Gurus : Angad, Amardas and Ramdas, who are helpful to me. Then after remembring Gurus Arjan and Hargobind, I remember (Guru) Har Rai. Then I contemplate on (Guru) Har Krishan, on seeing whom all the afflictions cease. Then by remembring (Guru) Tegh Bahadur, all the nine treasures come running to my home. And (these Gurus) are helpful to me at all places. The Tenth King (Guru) Gobind Singh Sahib ji is helpful to me at all places. Contemplating on the recitation and sight of Sri Guru Gramth Sahib Ji, The *Light* of the ten Kings (Gurus), utter WAHIGURU.

Text :

ਪੰਜਾਂ ਪਿਆਰਿਆਂ, ਚੌਹਾਂ ਸਾਹਿਬਜ਼ਾਦਿਆਂ, ਚਾਲ੍ਹੀਆਂ ਮੁਕਤਿਆਂ,
ਹਠੀਆਂ, ਜਪੀਆਂ, ਤਪੀਆਂ, ਜਿਨ੍ਹਾਂ ਨਾਮ ਜਪਿਆ, ਵੰਡ ਛਕਿਆ,
ਦੇਗ ਚਲਾਈ, ਤੇਗ ਵਾਹੀ, ਦੇਖ ਕੇ ਅਣਡਿੱਠ ਕੀਤਾ,
ਤਿਨ੍ਹਾਂ ਪਿਆਰਿਆਂ ਸਚਿਆਰਿਆਂ ਦੀ ਕਮਾਈ ਦਾ ਧਿਆਨ ਧਰ ਕੇ,
ਖ਼ਾਲਸਾ ਜੀ ! ਬੋਲੋ ਜੀ ਵਾਹਿਗੁਰੂ !

Transliteration :

Paṁjāṅ piāriāṅ, chauhāṅ Sahibzādiāṅ, cālīāṅ muktiāṅ
haṭhīāṅ, japīāṅ, tapīāṅ jinhāṅ nām japiā, waṁḍ chakiā,
deg calāī, teg wāhī, dekh ke aṇḍiṭh kītā.
Tinahāṅ piāriāṅ saciāriāṅ dī kamāī dā dhiān dhar ke,
Khālsā jī, bolo jī Wāhigurū !

Glossary :

ਪੰਜਾਂ ਪਿਆਰਿਆਂ—Five Beloved ones ; ਚੌਹਾਂ ਸਾਹਿਬਜ਼ਾਦਿਆਂ—Four sons of the Tenth Guru ; ਚਾਲ੍ਹੀਆਂ ਮੁਕਤਿਆਂ—fourty saved ones ; ਹਠੀਆਂ—determined ones ; ਜਪੀਆਂ—those who murmur prayers ; ਤਪੀਆਂ—worshippers ; ਜਿਨ੍ਹਾਂ—who ; ਨਾਮ ਜਪਿਆ—repeated the Name of the Lord ; ਵੰਡ ਛਕਿਆ—ate after sharing with others ; ਦੇਗ ਚਲਾਈ—arranged free kitchen ; ਤੇਗ ਵਾਹੀ—used the sword justifiably ; ਦੇਖ ਕੇ ਅਣਡਿੱਠ ਕੀਤਾ—seeing evil action kept it confidential ; ਤਿਨ੍ਹਾਂ—of them ; ਪਿਆਰਿਆਂ—dear ones ; ਸਚਿਆਰਿਆਂ—True ones ; ਕਮਾਈ—performance ; ਧਿਆਨ ਧਰ ਕੇ—contemplating ; ਖਾਲਸਾ ਜੀ—O Khalsa !

Translation :

Contemplating on the performance of the dear and truthful five beloved ones, four princes (sons of Guru Gobind Singh), Forty saved ones, determined ones, prayer-murmuring seekers, worshippers, who repeated the Name of the Lord, who ate after sharing with others, who arranged free kitchen, who used the sword justifiably, who seeing evil action of others kept it confidential, Khalsa ji utter Wahiguru.

Text :

ਜਿਨ੍ਹਾਂ ਸਿੰਘਾਂ ਸਿੰਘਣੀਆਂ ਨੇ ਧਰਮ ਹੇਤ ਸੀਸ ਦਿੱਤੇ, ਬੰਦ ਬੰਦ ਕਟਾਏ, ਖੋਪਰੀਆਂ ਲੁਹਾਈਆਂ, ਚਰਖੜੀਆਂ ਤੇ ਚੜ੍ਹੇ, ਆਰਿਆਂ ਨਾਲ ਚਰਾਏ ਗਏ, ਗੁਰਦੁਆਰਿਆਂ ਦੀ ਸੇਵਾ ਲਈ ਕੁਰਬਾਨੀਆਂ ਕੀਤੀਆਂ, ਧਰਮ ਨਹੀਂ ਹਾਰਿਆ, ਸਿੱਖੀ ਕੇਸਾਂ ਸੁਆਸਾਂ ਨਾਲ ਨਿਬਾਹੀ, ਤਿਨ੍ਹਾਂ ਦੀ ਕਮਾਈ ਦਾ ਧਿਆਨ ਧਰ ਕੇ, ਖ਼ਾਲਸਾ ਜੀ ! ਬੋਲੋ ਜੀ ਵਾਹਿਗੁਰੂ ! ਪੰਜਾਂ ਤਖ਼ਤਾਂ, ਸਰਬੱਤ ਗੁਰਦੁਆਰਿਆਂ ਦਾ ਧਿਆਨ ਧਰ ਕੇ ਬੋਲੋ ਜੀ ਵਾਹਿਗੁਰੂ !

Transliteration :

Jinhāṅ siṁghāṅ siṁghaṇīāṅ ne dharam het sīs ditte, baṁd baṁd kaṭāe, khoparīāṅ luhāīāṅ, carkhaṛīāṅ te caṛhe, āriāṅ nāl carāe gae, gurduāriāṅ dī sewā laī kurbānīāṅ kītīāṅ, dharam nahīṅ hāriā, Sikkhī kesāṅ suāsāṅ nāl nibāhī, tinhāṅ dī kamāī dā dhiān dhar ke, Khālsā jī bolo jī Wāhigurū. Paṁjāṅ takhtāṅ, sarbat gurduāriāṅ dā dhiān dhar ke bolo jī Wāhigurū.

Glossary :

ਜਿਨ੍ਹਾਂ—those ; ਸਿੰਘਾਂ—the Sikh males ; ਸਿੰਘਣੀਆਂ—the Sikh females ; ਧਰਮ—religion ; ਹੇਤ—for ; ਸੀਸ ਦਿੱਤੇ—gave their heads ; ਬੰਦ

ਬੰਦ ਕਟਾਏ—caused the body to be cut bit by bit ; ਖੋਪਰੀਆਂ ਲੁਹਾਈਆਂ—caused to cut off the skulls ; ਚਰਖੜੀਆਂ ਤੇ ਚੜ੍ਹੇ—mounted on the wheels ; ਆਰਿਆਂ ਨਾਲ ਚਰਾਏ ਗਏ—sawed with saws ; ਸੇਵਾ—service ; ਕੁਰਬਾਨੀਆਂ ਕੀਤੀਆਂ—offered sacrifices ; ਧਰਮ ਨਹੀਂ ਹਾਰਿਆ—did not waver on principles ; ਸਿੱਖੀ ਕੇਸਾਂ ਸੁਆਸਾਂ ਨਾਲ ਨਿਬਾਹੀ—guarded their discipline with unshorn hair and with every breath ; ਤਿਨ੍ਹਾਂ—for them ; ਪੰਜਾਂ ਤਖਤਾਂ—Five Thrones ; ਸਰਬੱਤ—all.

Translation :

Those male and female Sikhs who sacrificed their heads for Dharma (righteousness, whose body was cut bit by bit, who caused their skulls to be cut off, who mounted on the wheels, who were sawed alive, who made sacrifices in the service of the Gurdwaras, who did not waver on principles, who guarded their discipline with unshorn hair and with every breath contemplating on their performance, Khalsa ji, utter Wahiguru, contemplating on the five thrones and all Gurdwaras, utter Wahiguru.

Text :

ਪ੍ਰਿਥਮੇ ਸਰਬੱਤ ਖ਼ਾਲਸਾ ਜੀ ਕੀ ਅਰਦਾਸ ਹੈ ਜੀ, ਸਰਬੱਤ ਖ਼ਾਲਸਾ ਜੀ ਕੋ ਵਾਹਿਗੁਰੂ, ਵਾਹਿਗੁਰੂ, ਵਾਹਿਗੁਰੂ ਚਿੱਤ ਆਵੇ, ਚਿੱਤ ਆਵਨ ਕਾ ਸਦਕਾ ਸਰਬ ਸੁਖ ਹੋਵੇ। ਜਹਾਂ ਜਹਾਂ ਖ਼ਾਲਸਾ ਜੀ ਸਾਹਿਬ, ਤਹਾਂ ਤਹਾਂ ਰੱਛਿਆ ਰਿਆਇਤ, ਦੇਗ ਤੇਗ ਫ਼ਤਹ, ਬਿਰਦ ਕੀ ਪੈਜ, ਪੰਥ ਕੀ ਜੀਤ, ਸ੍ਰੀ ਸਾਹਿਬ ਜੀ ਸਹਾਇ, ਖ਼ਾਲਸੇ ਜੀ ਕੇ ਬੋਲ ਬਾਲੇ, ਬੋਲੋ ਜੀ ਵਾਹਿਗੁਰੂ!

Transliteration :

Prithame sarbatt Khālsā jī kī ardās hai jī. Sarbatt Khālsā jī ko Wahigurū, Wahigurū, Wahigurū citt āve, citt āvan kā sadkā sarab sukh hove. Jahāṅ jahāṅ Khālsā jī Sāhib, tahāṅ tahāṅ racchiā riāit, deg teg fateh, birad kī paij, Paṁth kī jīt, Srī Sāhib jī sahāi, Khālse jī ke bol bāle, bolo jī Wāhigurū.

Glossary :

ਪ੍ਰਿਥਮੇ—at first ; ਅਰਦਾਸ—prayer ; ਚਿੱਤ ਆਵੇ—be remembered ; ਕਾ ਸਦਕਾ—for that, in pursuance of that ; ਜਹਾਂ ਜਹਾਂ—wherever ; ਤਹਾਂ ਤਹਾਂ—there ; ਰੱਛਿਆ—protection ; ਰਿਆਇਤ—forgiveness ; ਦੇਗ ਤੇਗ ਫ਼ਤਹ—victory regarding free kitchen and sword ; ਬਿਰਦ ਕੀ ਪੈਜ—guard the honour because of His Greatness and Kind Nature ; ਪੰਥ ਕੀ ਜੀਤ—victory of the Paṁth (faith) ; ਸ੍ਰੀ ਸਾਹਿਬ ਜੀ ਸਹਾਇ—the sword be of help ; ਬੋਲ ਬਾਲੇ—prosperity, superiority.

Translation :

At first, there is the prayer for all Khalsa, let all Khalsa remember Wahiguru, Wahiguru, Wahiguru and for remembring it, it may attain all comforts, wherever the Khalsa abides, let there be protection and forgiveness, there be the victory of the free kitchen and sword, let the Lord guard the honour because of His Greatness and Kind Nature, let there be the victory of the Paṁth (Faith), let the sword be of help, let the Khalsa always prosper—utter Wahiguru.

Text :

ਸਿੱਖਾਂ ਨੂੰ ਸਿੱਖੀ ਦਾਨ, ਕੇਸ ਦਾਨ, ਰਹਿਤ ਦਾਨ, ਬਿਬੇਕ ਦਾਨ, ਵਿਸਾਹ ਦਾਨ, ਭਰੋਸਾ ਦਾਨ, ਦਾਨਾਂ ਸਿਰ ਦਾਨ, ਨਾਮ ਦਾਨ, ਸ੍ਰੀ ਅੰਮ੍ਰਿਤਸਰ ਜੀ ਦੇ ਇਸ਼ਨਾਨ, ਚੌਂਕੀਆਂ, ਝੰਡੇ, ਬੁੰਗੇ, ਜੁਗੋ ਜੁਗ ਅਟੱਲ, ਧਰਮ ਕਾ ਜੈਕਾਰ, ਬੋਲੋ ਜੀ ਵਾਹਿਗੁਰੂ !

ਸਿੱਖਾਂ ਦਾ ਮਨ ਨੀਵਾਂ, ਮਤ ਉੱਚੀ, ਮਤ ਦਾ ਰਾਖਾ ਆਪ ਵਾਹਿਗੁਰੂ !

Transliteration :

Sikhāṅ nūṁ Sikkhī dān, Kes dān, Rahit dān, Bibek dān, Visāh dān, Bharosā dān, dānāṅ sir dān, Nām dān, Srī Amritsar jī de ishnān, chaukīāṅ, jhaṅḍe, buṅge, jugo jug aṭṭal, dharam kā jaikār, bolo jī Wahigurū. Sikhāṅ dā man nīvāṅ, mat uccī, mat dā rākhā āp Wāhigurū.

Glossary :

ਸਿੱਖਾਂ ਨੂੰ ਸਿੱਖੀ ਦਾਨ—Gift of Faith to Sikhs ; ਕੇਸ ਦਾਨ—gift of long hair ; ਰਹਿਤ ਦਾਨ—gift of discipline ; ਬਿਬੇਕ ਦਾਨ—gift of knowledge ; ਵਿਸਾਹ ਦਾਨ—gift of Trust ; ਭਰੋਸਾ ਦਾਨ—gift of reliance ; ਦਾਨਾਂ ਸਿਰ ਦਾਨ—the greater gift ; ਨਾਮ ਦਾਨ—the gift of the Name of the Lord ; ਸ੍ਰੀ ਅੰਮ੍ਰਿਤਸਰ ਜੀ ਦੇ ਇਸ਼ਨਾਨ—the bath in the holy tank at Amritsar ; ਚੌਂਕੀਆਂ—gatherings of Sikhs performing Kirtan ; ਝੰਡੇ—banners ; ਬੁੰਗੇ—the costly buildings erected by the Sardars around the Golden Temple at Amritsar ; ਜੁਗੋ ਜੁਗ ਅਟੱਲ—may last throughout the ages ; ਧਰਮ ਕਾ ਜੈਕਾਰ—victory be of the Faith ; ਮਨ ਨੀਵਾਂ—mind be humble ; ਮਤ ਉੱਚੀ—the intellect be superior ; ਮਤ ਦਾ ਰਾਖਾ—the protector of the intellect.

Translation :

Let there be the gift of Faith to the Sikhs, gift of long hair, gift of discipline, gift of knowledge, gift of trust, gift of reliance and the greatest gift of the Name of the Lord, the bath in the holy tank of Amritsar, let the gatherings of the Sikhs performing Kirtan, banners and costly buildings erected around the Golden Temple may last throughout the ages, let the victory be of the Faith, utter Wahiguru.

Let the mind of the Sikhs be humble, their intellect be superior and the protector of the intellects be the Lord (Wahiguru) Himself.

Text :

ਹੇ ਅਕਾਲ ਪੁਰਖ ਆਪਣੇ ਪੰਥ ਦੇ ਸਦਾ ਸਹਾਈ ਦਾਤਾਰ ਜੀਓ ! ਸ੍ਰੀ ਨਨਕਾਣਾ ਸਾਹਿਬ ਤੇ ਹੋਰ ਗੁਰਦੁਆਰਿਆਂ ਗੁਰਧਾਮਾਂ ਦੇ, ਜਿਨ੍ਹਾਂ ਤੋਂ ਪੰਥ ਨੂੰ ਵਿਛੋੜਿਆ ਗਿਆ ਹੈ, ਖੁੱਲ੍ਹੇ ਦਰਸ਼ਨ ਦੀਦਾਰ ਤੇ ਸੇਵਾ ਸੰਭਾਲ ਦਾ ਦਾਨ ਖ਼ਾਲਸਾ ਜੀ ਨੂੰ ਬਖ਼ਸ਼ੋ । ਹੇ ਨਿਮਾਣਿਆਂ ਦੇ ਮਾਣ, ਨਿਤਾਣਿਆਂ ਦੇ ਤਾਣ, ਨਿਓਟਿਆਂ ਦੀ ਓਟ, ਸੱਚੇ ਪਿਤਾ ਵਾਹਿਗੁਰੂ ! ਆਪ ਦੇ ਹਜ਼ੂਰ ਪੜ੍ਹੀ ਗਈ ਬਾਣੀ ਦੀ ਅਰਦਾਸ ਹੈ ਜੀ ।

Transliteration :

He Akāl Purakh āpaṇe Paṁth de sadā sahāī dātār jīo, Srī Nankāṇā Sāhib te hor gurduāriāṅ gurdhāmāṅ de, jinhāṅ toṅ Paṁth nūṁ vichoṛiā giā hai, khulhe darshan dīdār te sewā saṁbhāl dā dān Khālsā jī nūṁ bakhasho.

He nimāṇiāṅ de māṇ, nitāṇiāṅ de tāṇ, nioṭiāṅ dī oṭ, Sacce Pitā Wāhigurū, āp de hazūr *paṛhī gaī bāṇī* dī ardās hai jī.

Glossary :

ਅਕਾਲ ਪੁਰਖ—Non-temporal Purusha i.e. God ; ਆਪਣੇ—your own ; ਦਾਤਾਰ—Munificent Lord ; ਗੁਰਧਾਮਾਂ—Places related to Gurus ; ਵਿਛੋੜਿਆ ਗਿਆ ਹੈ—separated ; ਖੁੱਲ੍ਹੇ ਦਰਸ਼ਨ ਦੀਦਾਰ—unrestricted visit ; ਸੇਵਾ ਸੰਭਾਲ ਦਾ ਦਾਨ—gift of service and preservation ; ਬਖ਼ਸ਼ੋ— grant ; ਨਿਮਾਣਿਆਂ ਦੇ ਮਾਣ—pride of the lowly ; ਨਿਤਾਣਿਆਂ ਦੇ ਤਾਣ—power of the weak ; ਨਿਓਟਿਆਂ ਦੀ ਓਟ—support of the destitutes ; ਸੱਚੇ ਪਿਤਾ— True father ; ਹਜ਼ੂਰ—in presence.

Translation :

O my Lord-God, the Lord ever munificent and helpful to the Paṁth. Sri Nankana Sahib and other Gurdwaras from which the Paṁth has been separated, O Lord, give the gift of their unrestricted visit and service and preservation to Khalsa ji.

O Lord, the pride of the lowly, the power of the weak, the support of the destitutes, O True father Wahiguru, this is the prayer regarding the hymns recited in Thy presence.

Text :

ਅੱਖਰ ਵਾਧਾ ਘਾਟਾ ਭੁੱਲ ਚੁੱਕ ਮਾਫ਼ ਕਰਨੀ। ਸਰਬੱਤ ਦੇ ਕਾਰਜ ਰਾਸ ਕਰਨੇ।
ਸੇਈ ਪਿਆਰੇ ਮੇਲ, ਜਿਨ੍ਹਾਂ ਮਿਲਿਆਂ ਤੇਰਾ ਨਾਮ ਚਿੱਤ ਆਵੇ।
ਨਾਨਕ ਨਾਮ ਚੜ੍ਹਦੀ ਕਲਾ,
ਤੇਰੇ ਭਾਣੇ ਸਰਬੱਤ ਦਾ ਭਲਾ।

Transliteration :

Akkhar wādhā ghāṭā bhull cukk māf karnī, sarbatt de kāraj rās karane. Seī piāre mel, jinhāṅ miliāṅ terā nām citt āvai, Nānak nām caṛhadī kalā, tere bhāṇe sarbatt dā bhalā.

Glossary :

ਅੱਖਰ—syllable, letter ; ਵਾਧਾ—increase ; ਘਾਟਾ—decrease ; ਭੁੱਲ ਚੁੱਕ—any error or omission ; ਮਾਫ਼ ਕਰਨੀ—forgive ; ਕਾਰਜ—affairs ; ਰਾਸ ਕਰਨੇ—set right ; ਸੇਈ—those ; ਪਿਆਰੇ—loved ones ; ਮੇਲ—cause to meet ; ਜਿਨ੍ਹਾਂ ਮਿਲਿਆਂ—meeting whom ; ਚਿੱਤ ਆਵੇ—remembered ; ਚੜ੍ਹਦੀ ਕਲਾ—high spirits ; ਤੇਰੇ ਭਾਣੇ—under Thy Will ; ਸਰਬੱਤ ਦਾ ਭਲਾ—welfare of all.

Translation :

Forgive any error or omission of syllables, increased or decreased. Set right the affairs of all. Cause to meet such persons on meeting whom Thy Name is remembered. Nanak says : Thy Name brings high spirits and under Thy Will there is welfare of all.

KĪRTAN SOHILĀ

THE BED-TIME PRAYER

ਸੋਹਿਲਾ

SOHILĀ (EULOGY)

ਰਾਗੁ ਗਉੜੀ ਦੀਪਕੀ ਮਹਲਾ ੧॥

Rāgu Gauṛī Dīpakī Mahlā 1.

ੴ ਸਤਿਗੁਰਪ੍ਰਸਾਦਿ॥

IK AUMKĀR SATIGURPRASĀDI

(Mūl Mantra in brief)

Text :

ਜੈ ਘਰਿ ਕੀਰਤਿ ਆਖੀਐ ਕਰਤੇ ਕਾ ਹੋਇ ਬੀਚਾਰੋ॥
ਤਿਤੁ ਘਰਿ ਗਾਵਹੁ ਸੋਹਿਲਾ ਸਿਵਰਿਹੁ ਸਿਰਜਣਹਾਰੋ॥੧॥
ਤੁਮ ਗਾਵਹੁ ਮੇਰੇ ਨਿਰਭਉ ਕਾ ਸੋਹਿਲਾ॥
ਹਉ ਵਾਰੀ ਜਿਤੁ ਸੋਹਿਲੈ ਸਦਾ ਸੁਖੁ ਹੋਇ॥੧॥ਰਹਾਉ॥
ਨਿਤ ਨਿਤ ਜੀਅੜੇ ਸਮਾਲੀਅਨਿ ਦੇਖੈਗਾ ਦੇਵਣਹਾਰੁ॥
ਤੇਰੇ ਦਾਨੈ ਕੀਮਤਿ ਨਾ ਪਵੈ ਤਿਸੁ ਦਾਤੇ ਕਵਣੁ ਸੁਮਾਰੁ॥੨॥
ਸੰਬਤਿ ਸਾਹਾ ਲਿਖਿਆ ਮਿਲਿ ਕਰਿ ਪਾਵਹੁ ਤੇਲੁ॥
ਦੇਹੁ ਸਜਣ ਅਸੀਸੜੀਆ ਜਿਉ ਹੋਵੈ ਸਾਹਿਬ ਸਿਉ ਮੇਲੁ॥੩॥
ਘਰਿ ਘਰਿ ਏਹੋ ਪਾਹੁਚਾ ਸਦੜੇ ਨਿਤ ਪਵੰਨਿ॥
ਸਦਣਹਾਰਾ ਸਿਮਰੀਐ ਨਾਨਕ ਸੇ ਦਿਹ ਆਵੰਨਿ॥੪॥੧॥

Transliteration :

Jai ghari kīrati ākhīai karate kā hoi bīcāro.
Titu ghari gāvahu Sohilā sivarihu Sirjaṇhāro.1.
Tum gāvahu mere nirbhau kā Sohilā.
Hau vārī jitu sohilai sadā sukhu hoi.1.*Rahāu.*
Nit nit jīaṛe samālīani dekhaigā devanhāru.

Tere dānai kīmati nā pavai tisu dāte kavaṇu sumāru.2.
Saṁbati sāhā likhiā mili kari pāvahu telu.
Dehu sajaṇ asīsaṛīā jiu hovai sahib sīu melu.3.
Ghari ghari eho pāhucā sadaṛe nit pavaṁni.
Sadaṇhārā simarīai Nānak se dih āvaṁni.4.1.

Glossary :

ਜੈ (ਜਹ)—in which ; ਘਰਿ—house ; ਕੀਰਤਿ—praise ; ਆਖੀਐ—uttered ; ਕਰਤੇ ਕਾ—of the creator ; ਹੋਇ ਬੀਚਾਰੋ—meditated upon ; ਤਿਤੁ—in that ; ਗਾਵਹੁ—sing ; ਸੋਹਿਲਾ—praise ; ਸਿਵਰਿਹੁ—remember; ਸਿਰਜਣਹਾਰੋ—the creator ; ਤੁਮ—you ; ਮੇਰੇ—my ; ਨਿਰਭਉ—Fearless Lord; ਹਉ—I ; ਵਾਰੀ—a sacrifice ; ਜਿਤੁ—by which ; ਸਦਾ—ever; ਸੁਖੁ ਹੋਇ—peace is attained ; ਨਿਤ—always ; ਜੀਅੜੇ—jivas ; ਸਮਾਲੀਅਨਿ—look after ; ਦੇਖੈਗਾ—will behold ; ਦੇਵਣਹਾਰੁ—giver ; ਤੇਰੇ—Thy ; ਦਾਨੈ—gift; ਕੀਮਤਿ ਨਾ ਪਵੈ—cannot be evaluated ; ਤਿਸੁ—that ; ਦਾਤੇ—giver ; ਕਵਣੁ—how ; ਸੁਮਾਰੁ—reckoned, estimated ; ਸੰਬਤਿ—year ; ਸਾਹਾ—the fixed day of wedding ; ਲਿਖਿਆ—written ; ਮਿਲਿ ਕਰਿ—meet ; ਪਾਵਹੁ ਤੇਲੁ—pour oil ; ਦੇਹੁ—give ; ਸਜਣ—friend ; ਅਸੀਸੜੀਆ—blessings ; ਜਿਉ ਹੋਵੈ—that (I) may attain ; ਸਾਹਿਬ—Lord ; ਸਿਉ—with ; ਮੇਲੁ—union ; ਘਰਿ ਘਰਿ—in every home ; ਏਹੋ—this ; ਪਾਹੁਚਾ— summons, wedding invitation ; ਸਦੜੇ—call ; ਨਿਤ ਪਵੰਨਿ—received always ; ਸਦਣਹਾਰਾ—the caller, summoner ; ਸਿਮਰੀਐ—remembered, meditated ; ਸੇ—that ; ਦਿਹ—day ; ਆਵੰਨਿ—coming, approaching.

Translation :

The house in which the Praises of the Lord are uttered and the creator is meditated upon, in that house sing His *Sohila* (Praises) and remember Him. Sing ye the Praises of my Fearless Lord. I am a sacrifice to such Praises which bring peace for ever. The jivas are always looked after, The Donor (Lord) will scan Himself. O' Lord, Thy gifts cannot be evaluated. How that Donor can be reckoned ? The year and the fixed day of the wedding are written, meet (O friends) and pour oil. O friends, give me the blessings, so that the union with the Lord is attained. In every home there is this wedding invitation and the calls are ever received. That day is approaching, therefore the caller-Lord be meditated.

Comments :

In this hymn, Guru Nanak Dev, has cautioned every jiva (being) to think of the fast approaching day when we have to leave this home (world) and go to meet the Lord who is sending us His gifts always and whose calls are also being received. In order to prove ourselves worthy of the impending meeting, we must always remember the bounties of the Gracious Lord and sing His Praises.

ਰਾਗੁ ਆਸਾ ਮਹਲਾ ੧

Ragū Āsā Mahlā 1

Text :

ਛਿਅ ਘਰ ਛਿਅ ਗੁਰ ਛਿਅ ਉਪਦੇਸ ॥
ਗੁਰੁ ਗੁਰੁ ਏਕੋ ਵੇਸ ਅਨੇਕ ॥੧॥
ਬਾਬਾ ਜੈ ਘਰਿ ਕਰਤੇ ਕੀਰਤਿ ਹੋਇ ॥
ਸੋ ਘਰੁ ਰਾਖੁ ਵਡਾਈ ਤੋਇ ॥੧॥ਰਹਾਉ॥
ਵਿਸੁਏ ਚਸਿਆ ਘੜੀਆ ਪਹਰਾ ਥਿਤੀ ਵਾਰੀ ਮਾਹੁ ਹੋਆ ॥
ਸੂਰਜੁ ਏਕੋ ਰੁਤਿ ਅਨੇਕ ॥
ਨਾਨਕ ਕਰਤੇ ਕੇ ਕੇਤੇ ਵੇਸ ॥੨॥੨॥

Transliteration :

Chia ghar chia gur chia updes.
Guru guru eko ves anek.1.
Bābā jai ghari karte kīrati hoi.
So gharu rākhu vaḍāī toi.1.*Rahau.*
Visue casiā ghaṛīā pahrā thitī vārī māhu hoā.
Sūraju eko ruti anek.
Nānak karte ke kete ves.2.2.

Glossary :

ਛਿਅ—six ; ਘਰਿ—house, systems of philosophy ; ਗੁਰ—Guru, Teacher ; ਉਪਦੇਸ—instructions, doctrines ; ਗੁਰੁ ਗੁਰੁ ਏਕੋ—The Teacher of Teachers is One ; ਵੇਸ—vesture ; ਅਨੇਕ—many ; ਬਾਬਾ—father ; ਜੈ—in which ; ਘਰਿ—house ; ਕਰਤੇ—creator ; ਕੀਰਤਿ ਹੋਇ—praised ; ਸੋ—that ; ਰਾਖੁ—keep, preserve ; ਵਡਾਈ—merit, greatness ; ਤੋਇ—Thy ; ਵਿਸੁਏ—very small unit of time ; ਚਸਿਆ—about a minute ; ਘੜੀਆ—a ਘੜੀ is a period of 24 minutes ; ਪਹਰਾ—of eight gharis, watch ; ਥਿਤੀ—lunar day ; ਵਾਰੀ—week days ; ਮਾਹੁ—month ; ਹੋਆ—become ; ਸੂਰਜੁ—sun ; ਏਕੋ—one ; ਰੁਤਿ—seasons ; ਅਨੇਕ—several, many ; ਕਰਤੇ—creator ; ਕੇ—of ; ਕੇਤੇ—many ; ਵੇਸ—garbs, guises.

Translation :

There are six houses (systems of philosophy) six teachers and six doctrines. The teacher of teachers is one, but there are many vestures. O father! the house in which the creator is praised, preserve that house, that will bring you merit. The units of time (like second, minute, hour, watch, lunar day, week days, month and seasons) are formed by one sun, there are many vestures of the creator.

Comments :

In this hymn, Guru Nanak Dev, giving the instance of the units of time created by one sun, makes a mention of six systems of philosophy (Saṁkhya, Yoga, Vaisheshika, Nyaya, Purva Mimansa and Uttara Mimansa) giving six types of instructions by six teachers (Kapila, Patanjali, Kannada, Gautama, Jaimini and Vyasa). But the teacher of teachers is the Lord Himself like the sun. Only that doctrine be followed, which consists of the Praises of this teacher of teachers. That will lead towards the spiritual greatness.

ਰਾਗੁ ਧਨਾਸਰੀ ਮਹਲਾ ੧

Rāgu Dhanāsarī Mahlā 1

Text :

ਗਗਨ ਮੈ ਥਾਲੁ ਰਵਿ ਚੰਦੁ ਦੀਪਕ ਬਨੇ ਤਾਰਿਕਾ ਮੰਡਲ ਜਨਕ ਮੋਤੀ ॥
ਧੂਪੁ ਮਲਆਨਲੋ ਪਵਣੁ ਚਵਰੋ ਕਰੇ ਸਗਲ ਬਨਰਾਇ ਫੂਲੰਤ ਜੋਤੀ ॥੧॥
ਕੈਸੀ ਆਰਤੀ ਹੋਇ ॥ ਭਵਖੰਡਨਾ ਤੇਰੀ ਆਰਤੀ ॥
ਅਨਹਤਾ ਸਬਦ ਵਾਜੰਤ ਭੇਰੀ ॥੧॥ਰਹਾਉ॥
ਸਹਸ ਤਵ ਨੈਨ ਨਨ ਨੈਨ ਹਹਿ ਤੋਹਿ ਕਉ ਸਹਸ ਮੂਰਤਿ ਨਨਾ ਏਕ ਤੋੁਹੀ ॥
ਸਹਸ ਪਦ ਬਿਮਲ ਨਨ ਏਕ ਪਦ ਗੰਧ ਬਿਨੁ ਸਹਸ ਤਵ ਗੰਧ ਇਵ ਚਲਤ ਮੋਹੀ ॥੨॥
ਸਭ ਮਹਿ ਜੋਤਿ ਜੋਤਿ ਹੈ ਸੋਇ ॥
ਤਿਸ ਦੈ ਚਾਨਣਿ ਸਭ ਮਹਿ ਚਾਨਣੁ ਹੋਇ ॥
ਗੁਰ ਸਾਖੀ ਜੋਤਿ ਪਰਗਟੁ ਹੋਇ ॥
ਜੋ ਤਿਸੁ ਭਾਵੈ ਸੁ ਆਰਤੀ ਹੋਇ ॥੩॥
ਹਰਿ ਚਰਣ ਕਵਲ ਮਕਰੰਦ ਲੋਭਿਤ ਮਨੋ ਅਨਦਿਨੋੁ ਮੋਹਿ ਆਹੀ ਪਿਆਸਾ ॥
ਕ੍ਰਿਪਾ ਜਲੁ ਦੇਹਿ ਨਾਨਕ ਸਾਰਿੰਗ ਕਉ ਹੋਇ ਜਾ ਤੇ ਤੇਰੈ ਨਾਇ ਵਾਸਾ ॥੪॥੩॥

Transliteration :

Gagan mai thālu ravi caṁdu dīpak bane
tārikā maṁḍal janak motī.

Dhūpu malānalo pavaṇu cavro kare sagal
banrāi phūlaṁt jotī.1.
Kaisī ārtī hoe. Bhavkhaṁḍanā terī ārtī.
Anahatā sabad vājaṁt bherī.1.*Rahāu*.
Sahas tav nain nan nain hahi tohi
kau sahas mūrati nanā ek tohī.
Sahas pad bimal nan ek pad gaṁdh binu
sahas tav gaṁdh iv calat mohī.2.
Sabh mahi joti joti hai soi.
Tis dai cānaṇi sabh mahi cānaṇu hoi.
Gur sākhī joti pargaṭu hoi.
Jo tisu bhāvai su āratī hoi.3.
Hari caraṇ kaval makraṁd lobhit
mano andino mohi āhī piāsā.
Kripa jalu dehi Nānak sāriṁg kau hoi jā te terai nāi vāsā.4.3.

Glossary :

ਗਗਨ—sky ; ਮੈ—in the form of ; ਥਾਲੁ—salver ; ਰਵਿ—sun ; ਚੰਦੁ—moon ; ਦੀਪਕ—lamp ; ਬਨੇ—made ; ਤਾਰਿਕਾ—stars ; ਮੰਡਲ—spheres, orbs ; ਜਨਕ—like ; ਮੋਤੀ—pearls ; ਧੂਪੁ—incense ; ਮਲਆਨਲੋ—wind carrying the scent of sandal from the western ghats ; ਪਵਣੁ—wind ; ਚਵਰੋ—fly-whisk ; ਕਰੇ—moves ; ਸਗਲ—the whole ; ਬਨਰਾਇ—vegetation ; ਫੂਲੰਤ—blossom ; ਜੋਤੀ—divine light ; ਕੈਸੀ—what ; ਆਰਤੀ—ceremony of circumambulating the image ; ਹੋਇ—is performed ; ਭਵਖੰਡਨਾ—destroyer of fear ; ਅਨਹਤਾ ਸਬਦ—the celestial strain, the immortal sound ; ਵਾਜੰਤ—sounding of ; ਭੇਰੀ—kettledrum ; ਸਹਸ—a thousand ; ਤਵ— Thine ; ਨੈਨ—eyes ; ਨਨਾ—not any ; ਹੈ—is ; ਤੋਹਿ ਕਉ—Thine ; ਮੂਰਤਿ—forms ; ਪਦ—feet ; ਬਿਮਲ—pure ; ਨਨ—not ; ਗੰਧ—fragrance ; ਬਿਨੁ—without ; ਇਵ—in this way ; ਚਲਤ—play ; ਮੋਹੀ—bewitches ; ਸਭ—all ; ਮਹਿ—in ; ਜੋਤਿ—light ; ਸੋਇ—that; ਤਿਸ ਦੈ—whom ; ਚਾਨਣਿ—light ; ਗੁਰ ਸਾਖੀ—Guru's teaching ; ਪਰਗਟੁ ਹੋਇ—becomes manifest ; ਜੋ—whatever ; ਤਿਸੁ—Him ; ਭਾਵੈ—pleases ; ਹਰਿ—Hari, Lord ; ਚਰਣ—feet ; ਕਵਲ—lotus ; ਮਕਰੰਦ—honey ; ਲੋਭਿਤ—attracted ; ਮਨੋ—mind ; ਅਨਦਿਨੋ—night and day, always ; ਮੋਹਿ—I ; ਆਹੀ—have ; ਪਿਆਸਾ—thirst ; ਕ੍ਰਿਪਾ—grace ; ਜਲੁ—water ; ਦੇਹਿ—give ; ਸਾਰਿੰਗ—pied cuckoo ; ਕਉ—to ; ਹੋਇ ਜਾ ਤੇ—so that I may have ; ਤੇਰੈ—Thy ; ਨਾਇ—Name ; ਵਾਸਾ—abode.

Translation :

In the salver of the sky, the sun and moon are made the lamps, the spheres of stars are like pearls with incense from the mountains growing sandalwood and the fly-whisk of the wind with the whole vegetation giving the lively flowers—what type of *aarti* (circumambulation) that will be, O destroyer of fear, your *aarti*, when there is celestial strain of the sounding of kettledrum. Thou hast a thousand eyes but Thou art without eyes. Thou hast a thousand forms, but Thou hast no form. Thou hast a thousand pure feet, but thou hast no feet. Thou hast no fragrance, but Thou hast a thousand fragrances. Such a play of Thine bewitches me. That light is within all. Because of that light everything is lighted. That light becomes manifest because of Guru's teaching. Whatever pleases Him, the same is His *aarti*. The lotus-feet of the Lord are like honey, my mind is attracted towards them, I am always thirsty for them. O Lord, give to this pied cuckoo the water of Thy Grace, so that it may have abode in Thy Name.

Comments :

Through this hymn, Guru Nanak Dev has decried the practice of performing *aarti* around the image in a temple. He was against image-worship. In the Temple of Jagannath Puri, he did not join the *aarti*, but instead sang his own *aarti* through this hymn. While performing the *aarti*, the priest alongwith devotees, circumambulates the image, holding a salver with lighted earthen lamps and showering the flowers over the image. For Guru Nanak the deity was not confined in the temple image. He is omnipresent and the whole world joins with the Guru for His *aarti* in which the sun, moon, stars, fragrance-bearing winds and the flowers of the whole vegetation take part. Like the Purusa Sukta of Rig Veda, the Immanent aspect of the Lord has been portrayed as having a thousand eyes, a thousand feet and a thousand forms, but at the same time the Transcendental aspect has been depicted who is the Formless One. All the lights emanate from God's Light. The Guru at the end of the hymn exhibits his love for the Lord and begs for His Name.

ਰਾਗੁ ਗਉੜੀ ਪੂਰਬੀ ਮਹਲਾ ੪

Rāgu Gauṛī Pūrabī Mahlā 4

Text :

ਕਾਮਿ ਕਰੋਧਿ ਨਗਰੁ ਬਹੁ ਭਰਿਆ ਮਿਲਿ ਸਾਧੂ ਖੰਡਲ ਖੰਡਾ ਹੇ ॥
ਪੂਰਬਿ ਲਿਖਤ ਲਿਖੇ ਗੁਰੁ ਪਾਇਆ ਮਨਿ ਹਰਿ ਲਿਵ ਮੰਡਲ ਮੰਡਾ ਹੇ ॥੧॥
ਕਰਿ ਸਾਧੂ ਅੰਜੁਲੀ ਪੁਨੁ ਵਡਾ ਹੇ ॥

ਕਰਿ ਡੰਡਉਤ ਪੁਨੁ ਵਡਾ ਹੇ ॥੧॥ਰਹਾਉ॥
ਸਾਕਤ ਹਰਿ ਰਸ ਸਾਦੁ ਨ ਜਾਣਿਆ ਤਿਨ ਅੰਤਰਿ ਹਉਮੈ ਕੰਡਾ ਹੇ ॥
ਜਿਉ ਜਿਉ ਚਲਹਿ ਚੁਭੈ ਦੁਖੁ ਪਾਵਹਿ ਜਮਕਾਲੁ ਸਹਹਿ ਸਿਰਿ ਡੰਡਾ ਹੇ ॥੨॥
ਹਰਿ ਜਨ ਹਰਿ ਹਰਿ ਨਾਮਿ ਸਮਾਣੇ ਦੁਖੁ ਜਨਮ ਮਰਣ ਭਵ ਖੰਡਾ ਹੇ ॥
ਅਬਿਨਾਸੀ ਪੁਰਖੁ ਪਾਇਆ ਪਰਮੇਸਰੁ ਬਹੁ ਸੋਭ ਖੰਡ ਬ੍ਰਹਮੰਡਾ ਹੇ ॥੩॥
ਹਮ ਗਰੀਬ ਮਸਕੀਨ ਪ੍ਰਭ ਤੇਰੇ ਹਰਿ ਰਾਖੁ ਰਾਖੁ ਵਡ ਵਡਾ ਹੇ ॥
ਜਨ ਨਾਨਕ ਨਾਮੁ ਅਧਾਰੁ ਟੇਕ ਹੈ ਹਰਿ ਨਾਮੇ ਹੀ ਸੁਖੁ ਮੰਡਾ ਹੇ ॥੪॥੪॥

Transliteration :

Kāmi karodhi nagaru bahu bhariā mili sādhū khaṁḍal khaṁḍā he.
Pūrabi likhat likhe guru pāiā mani Hari liv maṁḍal maṁḍā he.1.
Kari sādhū aṁjulī punu vaḍā he.
Kari ḍaṁḍaut punu vaḍā he.1.*Rahāu*.
Sākat Hari ras sādu na jāṇiā tin aṁtari haumai kaṁḍā he.
Jiu jiu calahi cubhai dukhu pāvahi jamkālu sahahi siri ḍaṁḍā he.2.
Hari jan hari hari nāmi samāṇe dukhu janam maraṇ bhav khaṁḍā he.
Abināsī purakhu pāiā Paramesaru bahu sobh khaṁḍ brahamaṁḍā he.3.
Ham garīb maskīn prabh tere Hari rākhu rākhu vaḍ vaḍā he.
Jan Nānak nāmu adhāru ṭek hai Hari nāme hī sukhu maṁḍā he.4.4.

Glossary :

ਕਾਮਿ—lust ; ਕਰੋਧਿ—anger ; ਨਗਰੁ—town ; ਬਹੁ—very ; ਭਰਿਆ—full ; ਮਿਲਿ—meet ; ਸਾਧੂ—saint ; ਖੰਡਲ ਖੰਡਾ ਹੇ—broken into bits ; ਪੂਰਬਿ—preordained ; ਲਿਖਤ—writ ; ਲਿਖੇ—written ; ਗੁਰੁ—Guru ; ਪਾਇਆ—obtained ; ਮਨਿ—mind ; ਹਰਿ—Lord ; ਲਿਵ—love ; ਮੰਡਲ ਮੰਡਾ ਹੇ—entered the sphere ; ਕਰਿ—make; ਅੰਜੁਲੀ—obeisance with folded hands ; ਪੁਨੁ—meritorious act ; ਵਡਾ—great ; ਡੰਡਉਤ—a prostrate salutation ; ਸਾਕਤ—a Shakta, a mammon-worshipper ; ਹਰਿ ਰਸ—elixir of God ; ਸਾਦੁ—relish ; ਨ—not ; ਜਾਣਿਆ—known ; ਤਿਨਿ ਅੰਤਰਿ—in him ; ਹਉਮੈ—ego ; ਕੰਡਾ—thorn ; ਜਿਉ ਜਿਉ—as, the more ; ਚਲਹਿ—move; ਚੁਭੈ—pricks ; ਦੁਖੁ ਪਾਵਹਿ—suffer the pain ; ਜਮਕਾਲੁ—death's messenger; ਸਹਹਿ—bear ; ਸਿਰਿ—head ; ਡੰਡਾ—staff ; ਹਰਿ ਜਨ—men of God ; ਸਮਾਣੇ—absorbed ; ਦੁਖ ਜਨਮ ਮਰਣ—pain of birth and death ; ਭਵ—fear ; ਖੰਡਾ—break away ; ਅਬਿਨਾਸੀ—immortal ; ਪੁਰਖੁ—Purusha, Lord ; ਪਾਇਆ—obtained ; ਪਰਮੇਸਰੁ—The Supreme Lord ; ਬਹੁ—much ; ਸੋਭ—honour ; ਖੰਡ—region ; ਬ੍ਰਹਮੰਡਾ—universe ; ਹਮ—I, we ; ਗਰੀਬ—poor ; ਮਸਕੀਨ—humble ; ਪ੍ਰਭ—Lord ; ਰਾਖੁ—protect, save ; ਵਡ ਵਡਾ—greatest ; ਜਨ—person ; ਨਾਮੁ—Name of the Lord ; ਅਧਾਰੁ—sustenance ; ਟੇਕ—support ; ਸੁਖੁ ਮੰਡਾ ਹੇ—enjoys peace.

Translation :

The town of the world is very much full of lust and anger which can be broken into bits on meeting the saint. As pre-ordained in the writ, I obtained the Guru through whom the mind entered the sphere of the love of the Lord. Make obeisance to the saint, it is a meritorious act. Prostrate before him, it is a meritorious act. A mammon-worshipper does not know the relish of the elixir of God, the thorn of ego is within him. As they move more and more, it pricks them and they suffer the pain, they bear the staff of the death's messenger on their heads. The men of God are absorbed in the Name of the Lord, their pain of birth and death and the fear breaks away. They realise the Supreme Ishvara and Immortal Purusha, they receive much honour in the regions and universes. We are Thy poor and humble people, O Lord, O the Greatest Hari, protect us. The Name is the only sustenance and support of this person Nanak who enjoys peace because of the Lord's Name.

Comments :

In this hymn, Guru Ramdas, the fourth Guru, in great humility and utmost reverence, talks about the Guru, the real saint, who inculcates the Lord's love in the mind of the devotee and gives him the Name of the Lord. It is a meritorious act to bow before such a saint. The world is full of lust and anger and other vices like maya and ego. The worshippers of maya indulge in ego which causes suffering for them. They undergo transmigration. It is only the gracious Lord who protects the humble devotees from such sufferings, by leading them to the Guru and giving them the remedy of the Name (of the Lord).

ਰਾਗੁ ਗਉੜੀ ਪੂਰਬੀ ਮਹਲਾ ੫
Rāgu Gauṛī Pūrabī Mahlā 5

Text :

ਕਰਉ ਬੇਨੰਤੀ ਸੁਣਹੁ ਮੇਰੇ ਮੀਤਾ ਸੰਤ ਟਹਲ ਕੀ ਬੇਲਾ ॥
ਈਹਾ ਖਾਟਿ ਚਲਹੁ ਹਰਿ ਲਾਹਾ ਆਗੈ ਬਸਨੁ ਸੁਹੇਲਾ ॥੧॥

ਅਉਧ ਘਟੈ ਦਿਨਸੁ ਰੈਣਾਰੇ ॥
ਮਨ ਗੁਰ ਮਿਲਿ ਕਾਜ ਸਵਾਰੇ ॥੧॥ਰਹਾਉ॥
ਇਹੁ ਸੰਸਾਰੁ ਬਿਕਾਰੁ ਸੰਸੇ ਮਹਿ ਤਰਿਓ ਬ੍ਰਹਮ ਗਿਆਨੀ ॥
ਜਿਸਹਿ ਜਗਾਇ ਪੀਆਵੈ ਇਹੁ ਰਸੁ ਅਕਥ ਕਥਾ ਤਿਨਿ ਜਾਨੀ ॥੨॥
ਜਾ ਕਉ ਆਏ ਸੋਈ ਬਿਹਾਝਹੁ ਹਰਿ ਗੁਰ ਤੇ ਮਨਹਿ ਬਸੇਰਾ ॥
ਨਿਜ ਘਰਿ ਮਹਲੁ ਪਾਵਹੁ ਸੁਖ ਸਹਜੇ ਬਹੁਰਿ ਨ ਹੋਇਗੋ ਫੇਰਾ ॥੩॥
ਅੰਤਰਜਾਮੀ ਪੁਰਖ ਬਿਧਾਤੇ ਸਰਧਾ ਮਨ ਕੀ ਪੂਰੇ ॥
ਨਾਨਕ ਦਾਸੁ ਇਹੈ ਸੁਖੁ ਮਾਗੈ ਮੋ ਕਉ ਕਰਿ ਸੰਤਨ ਕੀ ਧੂਰੇ ॥੪॥੫॥

Transliteration :

Karau benamtī suṇahu mere mītā saṁt ṭahal kī belā.
Īhā khāṭi calhu Hari lāhā āgai basanu suhelā.1.
Audh ghaṭai dinasu raiṇāre.
Man gur mili kāj savāre.1.*Rahāu*.
Ihu saṁsār bikāru saṁse mahi tario braham giānī.
Jisahi jagāi pīāvai ihu rasu akath kathā tini jānī.2.
Jā kau āe soī bihājhahu Hari gur te manahi baserā.
Nij ghari mahalu pāvahu sukh sahaje
bahuri na hoigo pherā.3.
Aṁtarjāmī Purakh Bidhāte saradhā man kī pūre.
Nānak dāsu ihai sukhu māgai mo kau kari saṁtan kī dhūre.4.5.

Glossary :

ਕਰਉ—make ; ਬੇਨੰਤੀ—request, supplication ; ਸੁਣਹੁ—listen ; ਮੇਰੇ—my ; ਮੀਤਾ—friend ; ਸੰਤ—saint ; ਟਹਲ—service ; ਕੀ—of ; ਬੇਲਾ—time ; ਈਹਾ—here ; ਖਾਟਿ ਚਲਹੁ—earn ; ਹਰਿ—Lord ; ਲਾਹਾ—profit ; ਆਗੈ—hereafter ; ਬਸਨੁ—abode ; ਸੁਹੇਲਾ—peaceful ; ਅਉਧ—age ; ਘਟੈ—decrease ; ਦਿਨਸੁ ਰੈਣਾਰੇ—by day and night ; ਮਨ—mind ; ਗੁਰ—Guru ; ਮਿਲਿ—meet ; ਕਾਜ—work, effort ; ਸਵਾਰੇ—set right ; ਇਹੁ—this ; ਸੰਸਾਰੁ—world ; ਬਿਕਾਰੁ—vice ; ਸੰਸੇ—suspicion, illusion ; ਮਹਿ—in ; ਤਰਿਓ—crosses ; ਬ੍ਰਹਮ ਗਿਆਨੀ—knower of Brahma ; ਜਿਸਹਿ—whom ; ਜਗਾਇ—awakens ; ਪੀਆਵੈ—causes to drink ; ਇਹੁ—this ; ਰਸੁ—elixir ; ਅਕਥ ਕਥਾ—inexpressible discourse ; ਤਿਨਿ—he ; ਜਾਨੀ—knows ; ਜਾ ਕਉ—for which; ਆਏ—have come ; ਸੋਈ— that ; ਬਿਹਾਝਹੁ—purchase ; ਮਨਹਿ—in the mind ; ਬਸੇਰਾ—abode ; ਨਿਜ—own ; ਘਰਿ—homes ; ਮਹਲੁ—Lord's presence, palace ; ਸਹਜੇ— with ease ; ਬਹੁਰਿ—again ; ਨ ਹੋਇਗੋ—will not be ; ਫੇਰਾ—re-birth ; ਅੰਤਰਜਾਮੀ—inner-controller ; ਪੁਰਖ ਬਿਧਾਤੇ—Purusa, the makers of destiny ; ਸਰਧਾ—faith, yearning ;

ਪੂਰੇ—fulfil ; ਦਾਸੁ—servant ; ਇਹੈ—this ; ਮਾਗੈ—begs ; ਮੋ ਕਉ—me ; ਕਰਿ—make ; ਸੰਤਨ—saints ; ਕੀ—of ; ਧੂਰੇ—dust.

Translation :

Listen, my friend, I make (this) request : this is time for the service of the saint, earn the profit of (meeting) the Lord here and a peaceful abode hereafter. The age decreases by (the passing away of) day and night. O mind, meet the Guru and set right your affair. This world is in vice and illusion, only the knower of Brahman crosses it. He whomsoever Thou causest to awaken and drink this elixir, he knows the inexpressible discourse, (the purpose) for which you have come, purchase that from the Lord and Guru and make its abode in the mind. Get the presence of the Lord in your own home and attain peace with ease, so that you will not be born again. O inner controller Lord (Purusha) and the maker of destiny, fulfil the yearning of the mind. Thy servant Nanak begs for this peace, make me the dust of the saints.

Comments :

In this hymn, Guru Arjan Dev lays emphasis on the company of the saints who themselves have gained access to the Lord and are in a position to help the devotees to gain access to the Lord. They obtained the Name of the Lord from the Guru and this is the only commodity worth purchasing. Through this Name one becomes the knower of Brahman (Lord). In this world of vice and illusion, this knower of Brahman can help the devotee who attains peace and ends transmigration. Thus the man of God must give full veneration to the saints and for the achievement of perpetual peace one must pray to the Lord to grant the company of the saintly persons.

APPENDIX

A Critical Study of Japuji

Japuji is considered as the epitome of the *Adi Granth* and the crux of Sikh Thought. It is said to have been composed by Guru Nanak in the later years of his life, when he settled down at Kartarpur after his long journeys. People from far and near used to gather around him and listen to his discourses. He composed this longer poem for their recitation, guidance and spiritual advancement. It was meant to be recited by the disciples in the early hours of the morning. Though Guru Nanak did not consider mere recitation as a sufficient dose for the spiritual progress, he wanted his disciples to comprehend the basic tenets through regular study and practice.

Besides the *Mul Mantra* (the original sacred formula), the prologue and the epilogue, there are thirty-eight stanzas of varying metre and length in this poem. The *Mul Mantra* gives us an insight into the nature of ultimate reality. The sacred formula is followed by a *Shloka,* which forms the prologue of the poem. The subject is introduced to us in this *Shloka*. This subject is *Truth*. In the next thirty-eight stanzas, the poet has dealt with this subject, laying emphasis on those medias through which the wall of falsehood can be completely demolished. The last *Shloka* or the epilogue presents before us the conclusive remarks of the poet.

Like Gita and the Upanishads, *Japuji* is poem of perennial importance, because it deals with the perennial philosophy. It talks of time and space in relation to the Timeless and the non-spatial entity. We live in the world of Name and Form, but our ideal is the attainment of the Formless and Attributeless Lord. For the realisation of this ideal several hints have been given in *Japuji*. Since this poem is a compendium of Sikh Thought, we shall try to touch upon all the main points contained in it.

The main subject : As has been said above, the main subject of this poem is *Truth*. A question has been posed in the very beginning : "How can we become true and how the wall of falsehood can be demolished ?" The poet himself has given the answer to this question in the next verse : "To work under the Divine Will Nanak hath written it with (the above question)." This clearly shows that Guru Nanak believed that *Truth* can only be realised in concurrence with the Divine Will. But the question arises as to the nature of this *Truth*. The answer to this question is found in the prologue of the poem :

Truth was in the beginning,
Truth was in the beginning of the ages,
Truth is prevalent in the present,
Truth will be prevalent in future also.

Only Brahman or God pervades all the three divisions of Time i.e. past, present and future, therefore only God is the Truth referred to in the Prologue. Thus the attainment of *Truth* is the realisation of the ultimate reality.

In the *Mul Mantra,* the poet has given the name of God as *Truth*, the ever-existent ONE. Truth is indivisible and imperishable. The world of Form, Action and Name perishes, but the Lord of this world abides for ever alongwith the finite selves. The soul or the finite self, which is a part and parcel of the Higher Soul enters the world of form, action and name and undergoes births and deaths. But this cycle ceases, whenever the *Truth* dawns upon the finite self. The entry into the plane of *Truth* can only be achieved through the Grace of the Lord which puts us on the right track and brings an equilibrium of action, devotion and knowledge.

Since God is *Truth,* the *Truthfulness* in practical life is, therefore, godliness. All the attributes of God, whenever practised, take us nearer God.

Time and Space : The eternal and non-spatial Lord has created this world of time and space, which may be called *Qudrat* (Nature) or māyā. Hinduism talks of several ages and periods in the process of creation. Science also gives its estimate of different ages in the evolution of the world. In different countries and different schools of thought, different times of the origin and the periods of the evolution of the world have been imagined. Some scriptures have even given the number of years that have passed since the creation of the world by God. But Guru Nanak does not agree with all such thinking, pondering and rumination. He holds that only God Himself knows the time of the origin of the creation. This question in *Japuji* is significant :

Which is that time, lunar date or the day,
Which is that season or month when the material world came into being ?

The Guru himself has replied :

Only the Creator, who hath created the world, knows it.

Thus none knows or can know the exact time of the birh of the universe. The natural corollary of this fact will come to this that all the divisions of time are the result of mere human imagination. The apparent division of time i.e. Past, Present and Future is only for the human body and the soul suffers because of this limitation of the body attached to it. When it knows itself and the Lord, time-element vanishes. The body experiences birth, childhood, youth, old age and death, but the soul always remains the same.

The concept of time works in the created space. According to Guru Nanak the creation of the Infinite Lord cannot be delimited. He talks of an immeasurable expanse in the sense of 'Neti, Neti' :

There is no limit of the created material world,
There is no limit and no end.
Several people wander for the knowledge of His limits,
None can know this limit,
The more we think of it, the more it goes farther.

Some cosmological systems extend the limits of the universe created by God to seven skies and seven nether-worlds, but Guru Nanak talks of lakhs of skies and lakhs of nether-worlds :

There are lakhs of nether-worlds and skies,
The ends were explored, the Vedas declare, but in vain.
The source is only one, the Hindu and Muslim scriptures say,
He is unaccountable. Whosoever takes account, perishes.
Only He *THE SUPREME* knows Himself, saith Nanak.

Thus time and space have value only in relation to *jiva* i.e. the embodied soul and no significance in relation to God.

Jiva : Time and space are an imprisonment for the soul. The jiva acts under the will of Brahman and enters the arena of his Sport, which is called *Jagat* or *Samsara* in Indian Philosophy. The *Samsara* is a *Karma-Bhoomi* (field of action) bound by the Laws of God. In this field of action the *jiva* undergoes a very hard test, because it is surrounded on all sides by such forces which keep him away from the Lord. The worldly pleasures attract him, but he gets no satisfaction out of them. At times he is subjected to lust, anger, greed, worldly affection and ego. At times he is hungry and thirsty. At times he is jealous of others. He is subjected to several ills and finds his release very difficult. He approaches the Perfect enlightener by the grace of God and addresses him thus :

O Guru ! Give me the knowledge of ONE
Who is the only sustainer of all the *Jivas*.
I may never forget Him.

Karma and Grace : Because of our *karmas* (actions), we are enchained to the world of duality and ego and thus face misery and grief in this world. We are known by our actions only which are judged in the court of the Lord. The plane on which we live is the plane of action, therefore we have to be very much cautious about our actions. By our actions we become lowly, by our actions we rise in esteem. We rise and fall because of our actions. There are certain actions which we are enjoined by Shastras to perform for our spiritual remuneration, but Guru Nanak has strongly rejected such actions. He says :

The birth is due to our actions,
The final liberation is due to Grace.

Great emphasis is, thus, laid on the *grace* of the Lord. *Karma* and *grace*, the two opposing factors, have been reconciled. Both are necessary for the spiritual development. Through the grace of the Lord, we are put on the right track and the necessary effects and precautions are performed on this path through the *grace* of the Lord.

Hukm : The surrender to the Judgement or Will of the Lord is the beginning of the grace of the Lord. The Arabic equivalent to the Judgement of the Lord is known as *Hukm*. It is also interpreted as the laws of God (or Nature). These laws are universal. Among these laws are the physical law of causation, the moral law of causation (known as the *doctrine of Karma*) and the spiritual law of love. The whole world moves and works under the Laws of God. The Guru has said :

The world of matter is created by His *Hukm*,
The *Hukm* of the Lord is inexplicable;
The *Jivas* are created by His *Hukm*,
The esteem is gained by His *Hukm*;
One rises higher or falls lower according to His *Hukm*,
The comforts and sorrows are written and obtained by His *Hukm*,
Some attain grace according to His *Hukm*,
And some are led astray by His *Hukm*;
Everything is within His *Hukm*, none is outside of it;
If one comprehends His Hukm, he loses his ego.

Shravan, Mannan and Niddhyasan : But the understanding of *Hukm* or TRUTH is brought about by the *Shravan* (Hearing), *Mannan* (thinking constantly) and *Niddhyasan* (meditation). Four stanzas of *Japuji* are devoted to *Shravan* and four to *Mannan*. No stanza is devoted to *Niddhyasan*. The first stage *Shravan* signifies the hearing of the scriptures in order to get an insight into the transitoriness of the body and the immortality of the soul. *Mannan* leads us further to staunch faith and constant thought about the soul. It will bring peace and control of the mind which will be suitable state for beginning *Niddhyasan* (meditation). After constant meditation, the seeker achieves the end i.e. *Darshan* or realization. In the four stanzas *of Shravan,* the Guru tells us clearly that on hearing the Name of the Lord through sacred scriptures and divine personalities, the seeker attains the state of bliss and all his sins and sorrows are washed away. He gains the knowledge of the method of *Yoga* and the secrets of the body. He imbibes the qualities of truth and contentment. He gets knowledge of higher spheres. The state of *Mannan* is indescribable. At this stage, the mind and intellect are refined. The seeker thinks of piety and concentrates only on the Name of the Lord. He cannot be led astray and moves on the right path. At one place in the poem the Guru has said :

> Having heard, thought constantly and loved whole-heartedly,
> We take full bath at the innermost holy sanctuary.

The above verses pointedly refer to the state of *Niddhyasan* which is a state of meditation through love and devotion and which leads us to the realization of the Lord.

Devotion and Virtues : But there can be no devotion without a practical virtuous life. The Guru says :

> All virtues are Thine, I have none.

The Lord is a treasury of virtues, therefore in order to be virtuous, we have to adopt the qualities of the Lord in our lives. Truth, Fearlessness, friendliness, sweetness etc. are godly qualities and, therefore, they are the required virtues of a saintly life. These virtues are received by us by the *Grace* of the Lord :

> He gives virtues to the virtue-less and bestows more virtues to the virtuous.
>
> There seems to be none who can give a virtue to Him.

In the concluding stanza of *Japuji* preceding the epilogue, Guru Nanak has made it clear that the Name of the Lord resides only in a virtuous heart. The Name abides where continence, patience, knowledge, fear, fortitude and love abide.

Name and Guru : By an analogy, the Guru has emphasised the significance of the Name. When the hands, feet and body are smeared with dust, they are cleaned with water. When the clothes are polluted with urine, they are washed with soap. In a similar manner the sins are washed away by the Name of the Lord. The *Name* is the *Word* of the Guru, which leads us to the knowledge of ONE. The *Shravan* and *Mannan* of the Name are the forward steps in the spiritual domain. By the Grace of the God, we meet the Guru and by the grace of the Guru we get the Name through which we meet the Lord. The functions of the Guru are two-fold :

> There is WORD with the Guru,
> There is KNOWLEDGE with the Guru.

The Guru, thus, gives both the Word and the Knowledge. Those who remember the Word of the Guru or the Name, not only obtain final emancipation for themselves, but others also, who adopt their line :

> Those who have remembered the Name have laboured well.
> They are revered in the Court of the Lord and get release of others.

Panchas or Liberated Ones : Such persons are known as *Panchas* or the liberated ones. These perfect beings not only get high positions in the Court of Lord, but they are also recipients of best regards in this world. They are the disciples of the True Guru and are invaluable traders of the invaluable Name. By dint of their efforts, grim determination and the Grace of the Lord, they enter the 'tenth door' into the presence of the Lord. *'That door'* has been depicted in one of the stanzas of *Japuji*. All the gods, goddesses and other forces, while awaiting there the orders of the Almighty, sing His praises. There are countless singers and countless musical instruments being played.

Shastric Injunctions and Formalism : The religion of *Panchas* is love and devotion. They have no faith in Shastric injunctions or religious practices. For them all *Karma Kand* is of no avail for spiritual development. The pilgrimage to holy places is useful only if the Lord approves it. All formalism is absurd. A true *Yogi* wears the ear-rings of contentment and the staff of faith. The inner qualities are essential and not the outer garb. The love of the Lord should be for love's sake and not for any material gain. A yogi who attains miraculous powers through concentration and meditation should neglect these powers because they will drag him down from spiritual heights.

Higher Planes : The plane, where we are born, is the plane of piety *(Dharma Khand)*. It is a plane of actions. In this world of time and space, of days and nights, of lunar dates and seasons, of air, water and fire, there are *Jivas* of diverse types, colours and names. These *Jivas* reap the fruit of their actions. Only *Panchas* are received with respect in the Court of the Lord because of their actions. Thus the plane of piety is the initial state of actions requiring us to adopt the real virtues in life by discriminating between good or bad actions.

Having imbibed the virtues in our practical life and having acted or moved on the right path, we enter the next plane i.e. the plane of knowledge *(Gyan Khand)*. In this plane the seeker observes the vastness of the Universe. He comes to know of various winds, waters, fires, Vishnus, Shivas, Brahmas, *Karma Bhumis* (fields of action), pole stars, Indras, moons, suns, spheres, countries, Siddhas, Buddhas, Nathas, goddesses, gods, demons, sages, gems, seas, *Khanis* (divisions of creation), *Vanis* (modes of speech), kings, scriptures and their believers. There is no end to all these created forces. This plane gives an idea to the seeker of his position in this huge set-up. It gives him an impetus to recognise his own potentialities and try to rise on higher planes. He feels elated.

After leaving the plane of knowledge, the seeker enters the plane of effort *(Saram Khand)* wherein he washes away all the dust of passions, vices and ego. He is purified and beautified. The intellect and mind become pure and beautiful. The seeker becomes a *Sidha* and godlike.

But the real power and strength comes when the seeker enters the next plane i.e. the plane of grace *(Karam Khand)*. The Lord is All-Powerful. His powers manifest themselves in a seeker through His Grace. With full health and vigour, beautiful thing looks many times more beautiful. Thus the state of full bloom is attained in this plane. The saint-soldier reaches this plane and resides here in full ecstasy and glory.

The state achieved in the fourth plane leads the seeker to his goal i.e. the plane of Truth *(Sach Khand)*. This plane is the abode of the Formless, who is Infinite and Creator and Master of the infinite creation. He controls the whole universe and directs it according to His Will. He is a conscious Power and sees and enjoys the sport of his Creation conscientiously.

Triple Interpretation of the Five Planes : The above-mentioned five planes can be explained physically, morally and spiritually. The physical interpretation takes the whole of the creation under its purview. Our earth is the *plane of piety*. When we rise above the earth, we pass through different planets and spheres in the *plane of knowledge*. When we rise above the *plane of effort* the creation becomes subtle and beautiful. In the *plane of grace*, there are abodes of saints who are always absorbed in whole-hearted devotion to the Lord. The final *plane of Truth* exhibits the Infinite creation of Infinite Lord. From the first to the fifth plane we are conscious of physical dimensions both finite and infinite, which shows that all these planes exist physically.

The moral and the spiritual interpretations of the planes remind us of the journey and goal of the seeker. In order to rise from the *plane of piety* to the *plane of Truth* the seeker has to seek knowledge and make efforts to obtain the Grace of the Lord. Truth can only be achieved by becoming pious, seeking knowledge of the path from the Guru, by following that path by the *Graces* of the Guru and God both. Truth can be realised by a balanced combination of *Karma* (efforts for piety), *Bhakti* (devotion by grace) and *Gyan* (knowledge).

Truth is God. In order to realize God, the spirit has to travel incessantly through the spiritual planes inwardly. Macrocosm is present in the Microcosm. Whatever is inward is also outward and whatever is outward is also inward. The planes are the spiritual planes through which the spirit rises during its ascent. As the soul ascends, body becomes subtle gradually and vanishes when it reaches the plane of Truth, where the Formless soul merges in Formless God.